T0215536

Network Programming with Go Language

Essential Skills for Programming, Using and Securing Networks with Open Source Google Golang

Second Edition

Dr. Jan Newmarch
Ronald Petty

Apress®

Network Programming with Go Language: Essential Skills for Programming, Using and Securing Networks with Open Source Google Golang

Dr. Jan Newmarch
Oakleigh, VIC, Australia

Ronald Petty
San Francisco, CA, USA

ISBN-13 (pbk): 978-1-4842-8094-2
https://doi.org/10.1007/978-1-4842-8095-9

ISBN-13 (electronic): 978-1-4842-8095-9

Managing Director, Apress Media LLC: Welmoed Spahr
Acquisitions Editor: Steve Anglin
Development Editor: James Markham
Coordinating Editor: Mark Powers

Cover designed by eStudioCalamar

Cover image by Pat Kay on Unsplash (www.unsplash.com)

Distributed to the book trade worldwide by Apress Media, LLC, 1 New York Plaza, New York, NY 10004, U.S.A. Phone 1-800-SPRINGER, fax (201) 348-4505, e-mail orders-ny@springer-sbm.com, or visit www.springeronline.com. Apress Media, LLC is a California LLC and the sole member (owner) is Springer Science + Business Media Finance Inc (SSBM Finance Inc). SSBM Finance Inc is a Delaware corporation.

For information on translations, please e-mail booktranslations@springernature.com; for reprint, paperback, or audio rights, please e-mail bookpermissions@springernature.com.

Apress titles may be purchased in bulk for academic, corporate, or promotional use. eBook versions and licenses are also available for most titles. For more information, reference our Print and eBook Bulk Sales web page at http://www.apress.com/bulk-sales.

Any source code or other supplementary material referenced by the author in this book is available to readers on GitHub. For more detailed information, please visit https://github.com/Apress/network-prog-with-go-2e.

Printed on acid-free paper

I dedicate this to my family.

Table of Contents

About the Authors

Dr. Jan Newmarch was head of ICT (higher education) at Box Hill Institute before retiring, and still is adjunct professor at Canberra University, and adjunct lecturer in the School of Information Technology, Computing and Mathematics at Charles Sturt University. He is interested in more aspects of computing than he has time to pursue, but the major thrust over the last few years has developed from user interfaces under UNIX into Java, the Web, and then into general distributed systems. Jan developed a number of publicly available software systems in these areas. For the last few years, he had been looking at sound for Linux systems and programming the Raspberry Pi's GPU. He is now exploring aspects of the IoT and Cyber Security. He lives in Melbourne, Australia, and enjoys the food and culture there, but is not so impressed by the weather.

Ronald Petty, M.B.A., M.S., is a principal consultant at RX-M and founder of Minimum Distance LLC. He is interested in many aspects of computing including distributed systems and machine learning. Kubernetes and Go have occupied much of his time in recent years, including presenting at KubeCon. He hopes his own experiences help the next generation of developers.

About the Technical Reviewer

Eldon Alameda is a web developer who currently resides in the harsh climates of Kansas. He works as a regional webmaster for the US National Weather Service. Prior to this, he did development for a variety of companies including local startups, advertising firms, Sprint PCS, and IBM. During the 1990s, he also acquired a nice stack of worthless stock options from working for dot-com companies.

Acknowledgments

I want to share my appreciation for Jan Newmarch for collaborating on this book. This project has offered me a tremendous sense of achievement and allowed me to cross a much-anticipated item off my bucket list. I would also like to thank Eldon Alameda for his thoughtful approach at letting me know when I am off the mark and for providing me with solid advice.

Additionally, I owe gratitude to my partners at Apress, both Steve Anglin for the opportunity and Mark Powers for the guidance to help see this through. Thank you to my colleagues at RX-M, including Randy Abernethy, Christopher Hanson, Andrew Bassett, and Anita Wu. Our work over the years has allowed for my participation in a project such as this book.

Finally, I want to thank my wife Julie and daughter Charlotte. Julie's capacity to manage the world while I hide out on a computer is unmatched and most appreciated. Charlotte's energy, abilities, and creativity inspire me to become better every day.

—Ronald Petty

Preface to the Second Edition

While an age has passed in Internet years, Go remains a primary destination for programmers. Go conquered the container technology space. It continues to find affection in Cloud Native development. Go strives to remain true to itself, backward compatible, yet adding new language features like Generics. Tooling improvements such as Fuzzing allow for more secure application development.

Go has changed, and so has this book. The first edition used Go 1.8; we are now on Go 1.18. The code has been updated to reflect this new reality. The examples have been largely developed to show a particular feature of Go networking without forcing complexity like managing several projects or packages scattered across the book; the associated repository can be found here `https://github.com/Apress/network-prog-with-go-2e`.

The first version of this book assumed familiarity with Go, and that remains in this edition. We expand slightly what we are willing to discuss in this book with the inclusion of more third-party modules, tools, and techniques. Jan was correct to keep the focus on Go and not to be distracted with the ecosystem at large.

If you desire to learn about implementing networking concepts with Go, I hope this book serves you well.

As a point of comparison, what follows is Jan's original preface, reflecting Go in 2017.

Preface to the First Edition

It's always fun to learn a new programming language, especially when it turns out to be a major one. Prior to the release of Go in 2009, I was teaching a Master's level subject in network programming at Monash University. It's good to have a goal when learning a new language, but this time, instead of building yet another wine cellar program, I decided to orient my lecture notes around Go instead of my (then) standard delivery vehicle of Java.

The experiment worked well: apart from the richness of the Java libraries that Go was yet to match, all the programming examples transferred remarkably well, and in many cases were more elegant than the original Java programs.

This book is the result. I have updated it as Go has evolved and as new technologies such as HTTP/2 have arisen. But if it reads like a textbook, well, that is because it is one. There is a large body of theoretical and practical concepts involved in network programming and this book covers some of these as well as the practicalities of building systems in Go.

In terms of language popularity, Go is clearly rising. It has climbed to 16th in the TIOBE index, is 18th in the PYPL (Popularity of Programming Language), and is 15th in the RedMonk Programming Language rankings. It is generally rated as one of the fastest growing languages.

There is a growing community of developers both of the core language and libraries and of the independent projects. I have tried to limit the scope of this book to the standard libraries only and to the "sub-repositories" of the Go tree. While this eliminates many excellent projects that no doubt make many programming tasks easier, restricting the book to the official Go libraries provides a clear bound.

This book assumes a basic knowledge of Go. The focus is on using Go to build network applications, not on the basics of the language. Network applications are different than command-line applications, are different than applications with a graphical user interface, and so on. So the first chapter discusses architectural aspects of network programs. The second chapter is an overview of the features of Go that we use in this book. The third chapter on sockets covers the Go version of the basics underlying all TCP/IP systems. Chapters 4, 5, and 6 are more unusual in network programming books. They cover the topics of what representations of data will be used, how a network interaction will proceed, and for text, which language formats are used. Then in Chapter 7, we look at the increasingly important topic of security. In Chapter 8, we look at one of the most common application layer protocols in use, HTTP. The next four chapters are about topics related to HTTP and common data formats carried above HTTP – HTML and XML. In Chapter 13, we look at an alternative approach to network programming, remote procedure calls. Chapters 14 and 15 consider further aspects of network programming using HTTP.

## CHAPTER 1

Architectural Layers

This chapter covers the major architectural features of distributed systems. A distributed system is a collection of components interacting over a network. You can't build a system without some idea of what you want to build. And you can't build it if you don't know the environment in which it will work. GUI programs are different than batch processing programs; games programs are different than business programs; and distributed programs are different than stand-alone programs. They each have their approaches, their common patterns, the problems that typically arise, and the solutions that are often used.

This chapter covers the high-level architectural aspects of distributed systems. There are many ways of looking at such systems, and many of these are dealt with. We begin with a layering model to help us understand component boundaries, discuss network implementation details, and consider how our components message each other, wrapping up with error conditions and how to think about them.

Protocol Layers

Distributed systems are *hard*. There are multiple computers involved, which have to be connected in some way. Programs have to be written to run on each computer in the system, and they all have to cooperate to get a distributed task done.

The common way to deal with complexity is to break it down into smaller and simpler parts. These parts have their own structure, but they also have defined means of communicating with other related parts. In distributed systems, the parts are called *protocol layers,* and they have clearly defined functions. They form a stack, with each layer communicating with the layer above and the layer below. The communication between layers is defined by protocols.

Network communications require protocols to cover high-level application communication all the way down to wire communication and the complexity handled by encapsulation in protocol layers.

ISO OSI Protocol

Although it was never properly implemented, the OSI (Open Systems Interconnect) protocols have been a major influence in ways of talking about and influencing distributed systems design. It is commonly given as shown in Figure 1-1.

© Jan Newmarch and Ronald Petty 2022
J. Newmarch and R. Petty, *Network Programming with Go Language*,
https://doi.org/10.1007/978-1-4842-8095-9_1

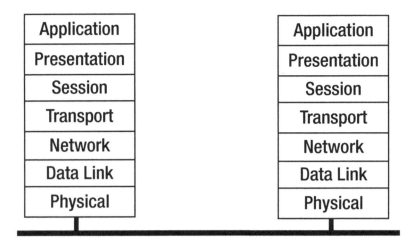

Figure 1-1. *The Open Systems Interconnect protocol*

OSI Layers

The function of each layer from bottom to top is as follows:

- The Physical layer conveys the bit stream using electrical, optical, or radio technologies.

- The Data Link layer puts the information packets into network frames for transmission across the Physical layer and back into information packets.

- The Network layer provides switching and routing technologies.

- The Transport layer provides transparent transfer of data between end systems and is responsible for end-to-end error recovery and flow control.

- The Session layer establishes, manages, and terminates connections between applications.

- The Presentation layer provides independence from differences in data representation (e.g., encryption).

- The Application layer supports application and end-user processes.

A layer in the OSI model often maps to a modern protocol; for example, the IP from TCP/IP maps to the Network layer, also known as layer 3 (Physical is layer 1). The Application layer, layer 7, maps to HTTP. Some protocols like HTTPS seem to blend layers, 5 (Session) and 6 (Presentation). No model is perfect; alternatives exist to the OSI model that maps closer to a given reality, such as the TCP/IP protocol model.

TCP/IP Protocol

While the OSI model was being argued, debated, partly implemented, and fought over, the DARPA Internet research project was busy building the TCP/IP protocols. These have been immensely successful and have led to *The Internet* (with capitals). This is a much simpler stack, as shown in Figure 1-2.

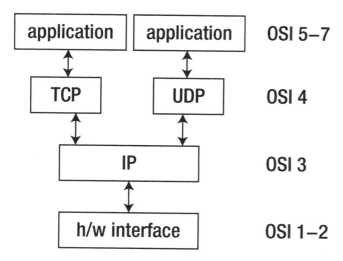

Figure 1-2. *The TCP/IP protocols*

Some Alternative Protocols

Although it almost seems like it, the TCP/IP protocols are not the only ones in existence and in the long run may not even be the most successful. Wikipedia's list of network protocols (see https://en.wikipedia.org/wiki/List_of_network_protocols_(OSI_model)) has a huge number more, at each of the OSI ISO layers. Many of these are obsolete or of little use, but due to advances in technology in all sorts of areas – such as the Internet in Space and the Internet of Things – there will always be room for new protocols.

The primary focus in this book is on OSI layers 3 and 4 (TCP/IP, including UDP), but you should be aware that there are other ones.

Networking

A *network* is a communications system for connecting end systems called hosts. The mechanisms of connection might be copper wire, Ethernet, fiber optic, or wireless, but that won't concern us here. A local area network (LAN) connects computers that are close together, typically belonging to a home, small organization, or part of a larger organization.

A wide area network (WAN) connects computers across a larger physical area, such as between cities. There are other types as well, such as MANs (metropolitan area networks), PANs (personal area networks), and even BANs (body area networks).

An internet is a connection of two or more distinct networks, typically LANs or WANs. An intranet is an Internet with all networks belonging to a single organization.

There are significant differences between an internet and an intranet. Typically, an intranet will be under a single administrative control, which will impose a single set of coherent policies. An internet, on the other hand, will not be under the control of a single body, and the controls exercised over different parts may not even be compatible.

A trivial example of such differences is that an intranet will often be restricted to computers by a small number of vendors running a standardized version of a particular operating system. On the other hand, an internet will often have a smorgasbord of different computers and operating systems.

The techniques of this book are applicable to internets. They are also valid with intranets, but there you will also find specialized, nonportable systems.

And then there is the "mother" of all internets: The Internet. This is just a very, very large internet that connects us to Google, my computer to your computer, and so on.

Gateways

A *gateway* is a generic term for an entity used to connect two or more networks. A repeater operates at the Physical level and copies information from one subnet to another. A bridge operates at the Data Link layer level and copies frames between networks. A router operates at the Network level and not only moves information between networks but also decides on the route.

Host-Level Networking

On a single host, we have additional concerns when designing, debugging, or deploying network-based software. Some of these items include the following:

- DNS (domain name system, i.e., human-friendly naming)

- Firewalls (e.g., blocking inbound or outbound traffic)

- Routing (e.g., figuring out which network to place a packet)

- Host Identity management (e.g., IP address)

- Performance controls (e.g., traffic shaping or retries)

- Connection issues (e.g., missing network adapter, intramachine process communication)

Through examples, we will see how a host misconfiguration might manifest in our software.

Packet Encapsulation

The communication between layers in either the OSI or the TCP/IP stacks is done by sending packets of data from one layer to the next and then eventually across the network. Each layer has administrative information that it has to keep about its own layer. It does this by adding header information to the packet it receives from the layer above, as the packet passes down. On the receiving side, these headers are removed as the packet moves up.

For example, the TFTP (Trivial File Transfer Protocol) moves files from one computer to another. It uses the UDP protocol on top of the IP protocol, which may be sent over ethernet. This looks like the diagram shown in Figure 1-3.

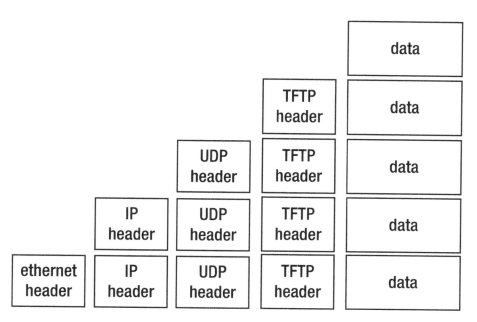

Figure 1-3. *The TFTP (Trivial File Transfer Protocol)*

Connection Models

In order for two computers to communicate, they must set up a path whereby they can send at least one message in a session. There are two major models for this:

- Connection oriented
- Connectionless

Connection Oriented

A single connection is established for the session. Two-way communications flow along the connection. When the session is over, the connection is broken. The analogy is to a phone conversation. An example is TCP.

Connectionless

In a connectionless system, messages are sent independent of each other. Ordinary mail is the analogy. Connectionless messages may arrive out of order. Messages do not have an impact on each other. An example is the IP protocol. UDP is a connectionless protocol above IP and is often used as an alternative to TCP, as it is much lighter weight. Connectionless is also known as unconnected or stateless.

Connection-oriented transports may be established on top of connectionless ones – TCP over IP. Connectionless transports may be established on top of connection-oriented ones – HTTP over TCP. Messages over a connection-oriented transport protocol have some kind of relation, for example, a sequence number used to keep order. Having state allows for functionality and optimizations; it also has an associated cost of storage and computing.

There can be variations on these. For example, a session might enforce messages arriving but might not guarantee that they arrive in the order sent. However, these two are the most common.

Connection models are not the only way a protocol can vary. One often desired feature is reliability; this is where the protocol has logic to fix some types of errors; for example, TCP resends a missing packet. It's pretty common to assume connection-oriented protocols are reliable; this is not always the case (e.g., MPLS). Additional features of a network protocol could include message boundary management, delivery ordering, error checking, flow control, etc. These features can exist in one protocol layer and not another, partly why there are so many network protocol stacks.

Sometimes, these features are reworked throughout the protocol stack. An example of this kind of feature rework is with HTTP/3. In HTTP/2, reliability is provided using TCP at layer 4. In HTTP/3, TCP is being replaced with UDP, which is not reliable. Instead, reliability will be provided with another protocol known as QUIC. While QUIC is considered a Transport layer, like TCP or UDP, it works on top of UDP. As you can see, the layer model is not an exact science.

Communications Models

In a distributed system, there will be many components (i.e., processes) running that have to communicate with each other. There are two primary models for this, message passing and remote procedure calls. In the context of networking, these models allow interprocess (and/or thread) communication with intent to invoke behavior on the remote process.

Message Passing

Some languages are built on the principle of *message passing*. Concurrent languages (and tools) often use such a mechanism, and the most well-known example is probably the UNIX pipeline. The UNIX pipeline is a pipeline of bytes, but this is not an inherent limitation: Microsoft's PowerShell can send objects along its pipelines, and concurrent languages such as Parlog can send arbitrary logic data structures in messages between concurrent processes. Recent languages such as Go have mechanisms for message passing (between threads).

Message passing is a primitive mechanism for distributed systems. Set up a connection and pump some data down it. At the other end, figure out what the message was and respond to it, possibly sending messages back. This is illustrated in Figure 1-4.

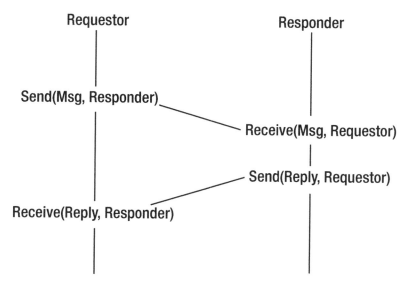

Figure 1-4. *The message passing communications model*

Event-driven systems act in a similar manner. At a low level, the programming language node.js runs an event loop waiting for I/O events, dispatching handlers for these events and responding. At a higher level, most user interface systems use an event loop waiting for user input, while in the networking world, Ajax uses the XMLHttpRequest to send and receive requests.

Remote Procedure Call

In any system, there is a transfer of information and flow control from one part of the system to another. In procedural languages, this may consist of the procedure call, where information is placed on a call stack and then control flow is transferred to another part of the program.

Even with procedure calls, there are variations. The code may be statically linked so that control transfers from one part of the program's executable code to another part. Due to the increasing use of library routines, it has become commonplace to have such code in shared objects (.so) or dynamic link libraries (.dll), where control transfers to an independent piece of code.

Libraries run in the same machine as the calling code. it is a simple (conceptual) step to transfer control to a procedure running in a different machine (i.e., remote library). The mechanics of this are not so simple! However, this model of control has given rise to the remote procedure call (RPC), which is discussed in much detail in a later chapter. This is illustrated in Figure 1-5.

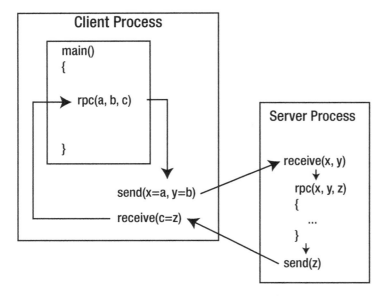

Figure 1-5. *The remote procedure call communications model*

There are many examples of this: some based on particular programming languages such as the Go rpc package (discussed in Chapter 13) or RPC systems covering multiple languages such as SOAP and Google's gRPC.

It may not be clear how message passing and RPC differ. At one level, they both are involved with invoking behavior "somewhere else." Generally speaking, RPC tends to be less abstract (i.e., looks and feels like regular procedure calls) compared to message passing where we could be calling remote queueing system. Under the hood though, RPC will be passing messages.

Distributed Computing Models

At the highest level, we could consider the equivalence or the nonequivalence of components of a distributed system. The most common occurrence is an asymmetric one: a client sends requests to a server, and the server responds. This is a *client-server* system.

If both components are equivalent, both able to initiate and to respond to messages, then we have a *peer-to-peer* system. Note that this is a logical classification: one peer may be a 16,000-core supercomputer; the other might be a mobile phone. But if both can act similarly, then they are peers.

These are illustrated in Figure 1-6.

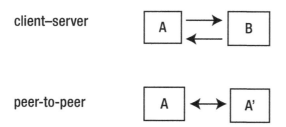

Figure 1-6. *Client-server vs. peer-to-peer systems*

An example of a client-server is a browser talking to a web server. An example of a peer-to-peer system could be database system where data is replicated and available on both peers.

Combinations of these systems result in what is known as multitier architectures, where three-tier architecture is one of the most common (i.e., presentation -> application -> data or browser -> web server -> database).

Client-Server System

Another view of a client-server system is shown in Figure 1-7.

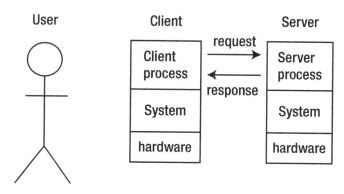

Figure 1-7. *The client-server system*

This view may be held by a developer who needs to know the components of a system. It is also the view that may be held by a user: a user of a browser knows it is running on their system but is communicating with servers elsewhere.

The prior diagram looks similar to the OSI model we discussed earlier. Layers in Figure 1-7 are also optional; for example, we can have both the client and server process on a single piece of hardware. Being located on the same machine means we can potentially remove some layers of the OSI model including layer 1 (Physical), layer 2 (Data Link), and layer 3 (Network). We say potentially because these layers still may be desired for various reasons including tooling homogeneity or security.

Client-Server Application

Some applications may be seamlessly distributed, with the user unaware that it is distributed. Users will see their view of the system, as shown in Figure 1-8.

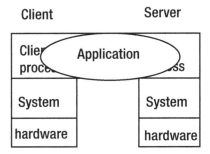

Figure 1-8. *The user's view of the system*

In order to function, both components must be installed, how seamless this complexity will vary by application (and its usage).

Server Distribution

A client-server system need not be simple. The basic model is a single client, single server system, as shown in Figure 1-9.

Figure 1-9. *The single-client, single-server system*

However, you can also have multiple clients, single server, as illustrated in Figure 1-10.

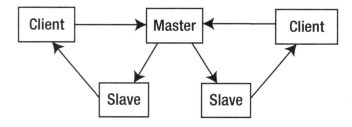

Figure 1-10. *The multiple-clients, single-server system*

In this system, the master receives requests, and instead of handling them one at a time itself, it passes them to other servers to handle. This is a common model when concurrent clients are possible.

There are also single client, multiple servers, as shown in Figure 1-11.

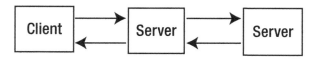

Figure 1-11. *The single-client, multiple-servers system*

This type of system occurs frequently when a server needs to act as a client to other servers, such as a business logic server getting information from a database server. And of course, there could be multiple clients with multiple servers.

Again, these components may or may not be on the same physical hardware.

Communication Flows

The previous diagrams have shown the connection views between high-level components of a system. Data will flow between these components, and it can do so in multiple ways, discussed in the following sections.

Synchronous Communication

In a synchronous communication, one party will send a message and block, waiting for a reply. This is often the simplest model to implement and just relies on blocking I/O. However, there may need to be a timeout mechanism in case some error means that no reply will ever be sent.

Asynchronous Communication

In asynchronous communication, one party sends a message and, instead of waiting for a reply, carries on with other work. When a reply eventually comes, it is handled. This may be in another thread or by interrupting the current thread. Such applications are harder to build but are much more flexible to use.

When thinking of these protocol layers and related implementations, it's not always obvious how you describe communication flow. For example, TCP, is it synchronous or asynchronous? When designing network applications, communication flow is used to describe the applications logic (Are you waiting for a response or are you not waiting for a response?). When we provide the Transport layer (TCP) data, we don't wait for it to send and respond, our application keeps moving. In that light, we say TCP is asynchronous.

Streaming Communication

In streaming communication, one party sends a continuous stream of messages. Online video is a good example. The streaming may need to be handled in real time, may or may not tolerate losses, and can be one-way or allow reverse communication as in control messages. This is why TCP is often used over UDP, even if that ordering comes at a cost.

Publish/Subscribe

In pub/sub systems, parties subscribe to topics, and others post to them. This can be on a small or massive scale, as demonstrated by services like Twitter and software like Kafka. Designing a multitier system to include pub/sub allows producer and consumers to be decoupled. Decoupling allows us to become more fault tolerant and generally improves the ability to grow the system (e.g., more producers and consumers). Storage of messages on a third party (i.e., remote queue) provides this ability. How the queue performs and grows is its own area of study and distributed computing (and storage).

Component Distribution

A simple but effective way of decomposing many applications is to consider them as made up of three parts:

- Presentation component

- Application logic

- Data access

The *presentation component* is responsible for interactions with the user, both displaying data and gathering input. It may be a modern GUI interface with buttons, lists, menus, etc., or an older command-line style interface, asking questions and getting answers. It could also encompass wider interaction styles, such as the interaction with physical devices such as a cash register and ATM. It could also cover the interaction with a nonhuman user, as in a machine-to-machine system. The details are not important at this level.

The *application logic* is responsible for interpreting the users' responses, for applying business rules, for preparing queries, and for managing responses from the third component.

The *data access* component is responsible for storing and retrieving data. This will often be through a database, but not necessarily.

Gartner Classification

Based on this threefold decomposition of applications, Gartner considered how the components might be distributed in a client-server system. They came up with five models, shown in Figure 1-12. These models conceptualize various purposes on the client or server. While high level, they still enumerate numerous possibilities regarding placement of functionality.

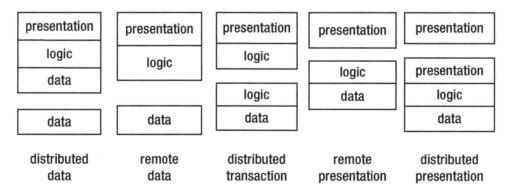

Figure 1-12. *Gartner's five models*

Example: Distributed Database

Gartner model - distributed data (see Figure 1-13)

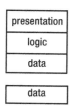

Figure 1-13. *Gartner model – distributed data*

Modern mobile phones make good examples of this. Due to limited memory, they may store a small part of a database locally so that they can usually respond quickly. However, if data is required that is not held locally, then a request may be made to a remote database for that additional data.

Google Maps is another good example. All of the maps reside on Google's servers. When one is requested by a user, the "nearby" maps are also downloaded into a small database in the browser. When the user moves the map a little bit, the extra bits required are already in the local store for quick response.

Example: Network File Service

Gartner model - remote data (see Figure 1-14)

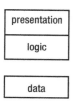

Figure 1-14. *Gartner model – remote data*

This classification allows remote clients access to a shared file system. There are many examples of such systems: NFS, DCE, etc.

Example: Web

Gartner classification - distributed transaction (see Figure 1-15)

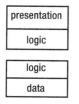

Figure 1-15. *Gartner model – distributed transaction*

13

On the Web the client may have logic in JavaScript (in the past Java Applets or even Adobe Flash) while the server has logic in CGI scripts or similar (Ruby on Rails, etc). This is a distributed hypertext system, with many additional mechanisms.

Example: Terminal Emulation

Gartner classification - remote presentation (see Figure 1-16)

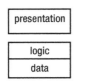

Figure 1-16. *Gartner model – remote presentation*

Terminal emulation allows a remote system to act as a normal terminal on a local system. Telnet is the most common example of this.

Example: Secure Shell

Gartner classification - distributed presentation (see Figure 1-17)

Figure 1-17. *Gartner model – distributed presentation*

The secure shell on UNIX allows you to connect to a remote system, run a command there, and display the presentation locally. The presentation is prepared on the remote machine and displayed locally. Under Windows, remote desktop behaves similarly.

Three-Tier Models

Of course, if you have two tiers, then you can have three, four, or more. Some of the three-tier possibilities are shown in Figure 1-18.

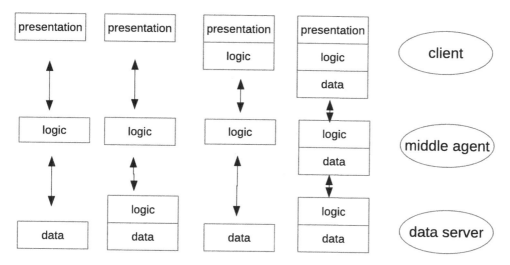

Figure 1-18. *Three-tier models*

The modern Web is a good example of the rightmost of these. The back end is made up of a database, often running stored procedures to hold some of the database logic. The middle tier is an HTTP server such as Apache running PHP scripts (or Ruby on Rails, or JSP pages, Go net/http package, etc.). This will manage some of the logic and will have data such as HTML pages stored locally. The front end is a browser to display the pages, under the control of some JavaScript. In HTML5, the front end may also have a local database.

Fat vs. Thin

A common labeling of components is "fat" or "thin." Fat components take up a lot of memory and do complex processing. Thin components, on the other hand, do little of either. There don't seem to be any "normal" size components, only fat or thin!

Fatness or thinness is a relative concept. Browsers are often labeled as thin because all they do is display web pages. However, Firefox on my Linux box takes nearly half a gigabyte of memory, which I don't regard as small at all!

Middleware Model

Middleware is the "glue" connecting components of a distributed system. These components are things in addition to what the operating system offers. The middleware model is shown in Figure 1-19.

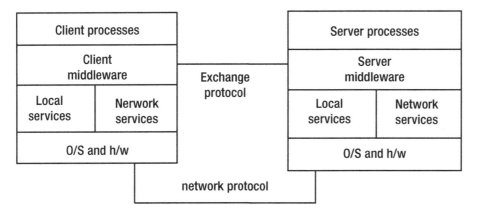

Figure 1-19. *The middleware model*

Components of middleware include the following:

- The middleware layer is an application-independent software using the network services.

- Ability to normalize access and/or actions across differing applications.

- Configuration (e.g., security profiles).

TCP/IP is an example of a service normally provided by the operating system.

Middleware Examples

Examples of middleware include the following:

- Primitive services such as file transfer or email

- Basic services such as RPC (e.g., Apache Thrift or gRPC)

- Object services such as RMI and Jini

- Integrated services such as DCE (Distributed Computing Environment – DNS, time, and more)

- Distributed object services such as CORBA and OLE/ActiveX (i.e., discovery)

- The World Wide Web

- Enterprise Service Buses

We use middleware libraries to minimize the need to develop custom solutions, like any shared library but with a focus on network-based services.

Middleware Functions

The functions of middleware can include these:

- Initiation of processes at different computers

- Session management

- Directory services to allow clients to locate servers

- Remote data access (e.g., encoding/decoding)

- Concurrency control to allow servers to handle multiple clients

- Security and integrity

- Monitoring

- Termination of processes, both local and remote

The term "middleware" is also used when building custom web servers. For example, if you want to log each request and/or response to a local file, you can add functions (known as middleware) into a stack of operations. When your function happens to leverage a network service as we mention before, we simple call it middleware.

Continuum of Processing

The Gartner model is based on a breakdown of an application into the components of presentation, application logic, and data handling. A finer-grained breakdown is illustrated in Figure 1-20.

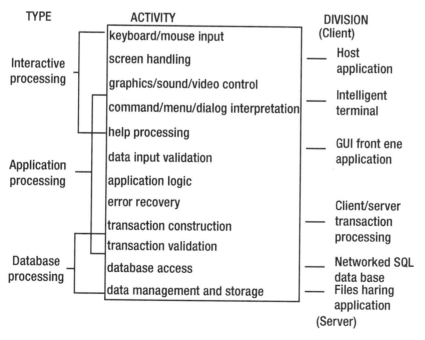

Figure 1-20. *Breakdown of an application into its components of presentation*

Points of Failure

Distributed applications run in a complex environment. This makes them much more prone to failure than stand-alone applications on a single computer. The points of failure include the following:

- Client-side errors
  - The client side of the application could crash (out of memory, divide by zero).
  - The client system may have hardware problems (trip on powercord).
  - The client's network card could fail.
- Network errors
  - Network contention could cause timeouts (server is slow to respond, including routers).
  - There may be network address conflicts (routing to wrong host if one even is found).
  - Network elements such as routers could fail.
  - Transmission errors may lose messages.
  - Misconfigured DNS.
- Client-server errors
  - The client and server versions may be incompatible (API changes – HTTP path, default port configuration, etc.).
- Server errors
  - The server system may have hardware problems (including network card).
  - The server software may crash (out of memory, divide by zero).
  - The server's database may become corrupted (deduplication process fails midway).

Applications have to be designed with these possible failures in mind. Any action performed by one component must be recoverable if failure occurs in some other part of the system. Techniques such as transactions and continuous error checking need to be employed to avoid errors. It should be noted that while a stand-alone application may have a lot of control over the errors that can occur, that is not the case with distributed systems. For example, the server has no control over network or client errors and can only be prepared to handle them. In many cases, the cause of an error may not be available: Did the client crash or did the network go down? Very often, the most complicated development work around has a stable and predictable distributed system.

Acceptance Factors

The acceptance factors of a distributed system are similar to those of a stand-alone system. They include the following:

- Reliability (it doesn't crash or corrupt)
- Performance (how fast an action is performed internally)

- Responsiveness (how fast an action seems to you)

- Scalability (Can we increase capacity with more instances?)

- Capacity (how much can we keep asking of the software)

- Security (operations are authenticated)

Currently, users often tolerate worse behavior than from a stand-alone system. "Oh, the network is slow" seems to be an acceptable excuse. Well, it isn't really, and developers should not get into the mindset of assuming that factors under their control can have ignorable effects.

Another point of comparison, distributed systems are often designed to scale in a more intelligent way vs. simply running a stand-alone program more than once and figuring out how to split the input across them.

Thoughts on Distributed Computing

What follows are considerations when constructing distributed systems, whether its software, hardware, or both.

Transparency

The notion of transparency means the details are hidden from us. Implementing solutions to these concepts is not trivial, still a reasonable design goal. The "holy grails" of distributed systems are to provide the following:

- Access transparency

- Location transparency

- Migration transparency

- Replication transparency

- Concurrency transparency

- Scalability transparency

- Performance transparency

- Failure transparency

Access Transparency

The user should not know (or need to know) if access to all or parts of the system is local or remote.

Location Transparency

The location of a service should not matter.

Migration Transparency

If part of the system moves to another location, it should make no difference to a user.

Replication Transparency

It should not matter if one or multiple copies of the system are running.

Concurrency Transparency

There should be no interference between parts of the system running concurrently. For example, if I am accessing the database, then you should not know about it.

Scalability Transparency

It shouldn't matter if one or a million users are on the system.

Performance Transparency

Performance should not be affected by any of the system or network characteristics.

Failure Transparency

The system should not fail. If parts of it fail, the system should recover without the user knowing the failure occurred.

Most of these transparency factors are observed more in the breach than in the observance. There are notable cases where they are almost met. For example, when you connect to Google, you don't know (or care) where the servers are. Systems using Amazon Web Services are able to scale up or down in response to demand. Netflix has what almost seems cruel testing strategies, regularly and deliberately breaking large sections of its system to ensure that the whole still works.

Eight Fallacies of Distributed Computing

Sun Microsystems was a company that performed much of the early work in distributed systems and even had a mantra: "The network is the computer." Based on their experience over many years, a number of the scientists at Sun came up with the following list of fallacies commonly assumed:

1. The network is reliable.

2. Latency is zero.

3. Bandwidth is infinite.

4. The network is secure.

5. Topology doesn't change.

6. There is one administrator.

7. Transport cost is zero.

8. The network is homogeneous.

Fallacy: The Network Is Reliable

A paper by Bailis and Kingsbury entitled "The Network is Reliable" (see https://queue.acm.org/detail.cfm?id=2655736) examines this fallacy. It finds many instances, such as Microsoft reporting on their data centers giving 5.2 device failures per day and 40.8 link failures per day.

The Chinese government uses "DNS poisoning" as one of its techniques to censor what it considers to be undesirable websites. China also runs one of the DNS root servers. In 2010, this server was misconfigured and poisoned the DNS servers of many other countries. This made many non-Chinese websites inaccessible outside of China as well as inside (see http://www.pcworld.com/article/192658/article.html).

There are many other possible cases, such as DDoS (distributed denial of service) attacks making websites unavailable. At Box Hill Institute, a contractor once put a backhoe through the fiber cable connecting our DHCP server to the rest of the network, and so we went home for the rest of the day.

The network is *not* reliable. The implications are that any networked program must be prepared to deal with failure. This led to the design choices of Java's RMI and most later frameworks, with application design allowing for each network call possibly failing.

Fallacy: Latency Is Zero

Latency is the delay between sending a signal and getting a reply. In a single-process system, latency can depend on the amount of computation performed in a function call before it can return, but on the network, it is usually caused by simply having to traverse transports and be processed by all sorts of nodes such as routers on the way.

The ping command is a good way of showing latency. A ping to Google's Australia server takes about 20 milliseconds from Melbourne. A ping to Baidu's Chinese servers takes about 200 msecs.[1]

By contrast, Williams (see http://www.eetimes.com/document.asp?doc_id=1200916) discusses the latency of the Linux scheduler and comes up with a mean latency of 88 *micro*seconds. The latency of network calls is thousands of times greater. Additional popular paper includes "numbers to know," by P. Norvig, showing where latency happens and how components affect it (see https://norvig.com/21-days.html#answers).

Latency can greatly affect distributed computing design and functionality. An example is computing scheduling decisions; if data is too slow to gather, incorrect decisions can happen.

Fallacy: Bandwidth Is Infinite

Everyone who goes to make a cup of tea or coffee while a download takes place knows this is a fallacy. I run my own web server and on ADSL2 get an upload speed of 800 Kbps. I am unfortunate enough to have HFC to my home, and the disastrous Australian National Broadband Network will upgrade this to 1000 Kbps perhaps – in three years' time, by 2020.

In the meantime, I use a local wireless connection to give me 75 Mbps up and down, and it still isn't fast enough!

In the revised edition, in 2021, Ron is getting 400 Mbps down and 12 Mbps up via a cable modem in San Francisco. In the future, we will update with Starlink (or the dominant satellite provider); as of 2022, it is supposedly providing 200 Mbps down and 20 Mbps up.

---

[1] From my Melbourne, Australia, location, I see the ping time by

$ ping www.google.com.au

PING google.com.au (216.58.203.99) 56(84) bytes of data.

64 bytes from syd09s15-in-f3.1e100.net (216.58.203.99): icmp_seq=1 ttl=50 time=27.1 ms

64 bytes from syd09s15-in-f3.1e100.net (216.58.203.99): icmp_seq=2 ttl=50 time=19.7 ms

Fallacy: The Network Is Secure

There is a strong push by technology companies for strong crypto to be used for all network communications and an equally strong push by governments all over the world for weaker systems or for backdoors "only for particular governments." This seems to apply equally well to *demoncratic* (my accidental misspelling may be accurate!) as well as totalitarian governments.

In addition, of course, there are the general "baddies," stealing and selling credit card numbers and passwords by the millions.

Fallacy: Topology Doesn't Change

Well it does. Generally, this may affect latency and bandwidth. But the more hard-coding of routes or of IP addresses, the more prone to failure network applications will become. Not uncommon today, moving to the cloud or even cloud native is causing many changes in how network applications integrate.

Fallacy: There Is One Administrator

So what? No problem when everything is working fine. It's when it goes wrong that problems start – who to blame, who to fix it?

A major research topic for years was *grid computing*, which distributed computing tasks across typically many university and research organizations to solve huge scientific problems. This had to resolve many complex issues due to not only multiple administrators but also different access and security problems, different maintenance schedules, and so on. The advent of cloud computing has *solved* many of these issues, reducing the number of administrators and systems, so cloud computing is more resilient than many grid systems.

Fallacy: Transport Cost Is Zero

Once I've bought my PC, the transport cost from CPU to monitor is zero (well, minor electricity!). But we all pay our IP providers money each month because they have to build server rooms, lay cables, and so on. It's just a cost that has to be factored in (e.g., paying monthly or forced to watch advertisements).

Fallacy: The Network Is Homogeneous

The network isn't homogenous, and neither are the endpoints – for example, your and my PCs, iPads, Android devices, and mobile phones – let alone with the IoT bringing a myriad of connected devices into the picture. There are continual attempts by vendors for product lockin and continually restrictive work environments trying to simplify their control systems, which succeed to some extent. But when they fail, systems dependent on homogeneity fail too.

As we build our applications and learn the techniques, it pays to remember the layering models we discussed earlier. It will help us categorize purposes and activities. Clients and servers may not be the same hardware or software, but we can model them, which helps us understand and make sense of it all.

Conclusion

This chapter has tried to emphasize that distributed computing has its own unique features compared to other styles of computing. Ignoring these features can only lead to failure of the resultant systems. There are continual attempts to simplify the architectural model, with the latest being "microservices" and "serverless" computing, but in the end, the complexities still remain.

These have to be addressed using any programming language, and subsequent chapters consider how Go manages them.

CHAPTER 2

▨ ▨ ▨

Overview of the Go Language

There is a continual stream of programming languages being invented. Some are highly specialized; others are quite generic, while a third group is designed to fill broad but to some extent niche areas. Go was created in 2007 and released publicly in 2009. It was intended to be a systems programming language, augmenting (or replacing) C++ and other statically compiled languages for production network and multiprocessing systems.

Go joins a group of modern languages including Rust, Swift, Julia, and several others. Go's particular features are a simple syntax, fast compilation of multiple program units based on "structural" typing, and of course the benefit of lessons learned from large-scale programs in C, C++, and Java.

The language popularity listings in Q1 2022 such as TIOBE (see http://www.tiobe.com/tiobe-index/) rank Go as currently the 13th most popular language. PYPL (see http://pypl.github.io/PYPL.html) places it also at number 13. This is alongside the 20+-year-old languages of Java, Python, C, C++, JavaScript, and more.

This book assumes you are an experienced programmer with some or extensive knowledge of Go at some level. This could be by an introductory text such as *Introducing Go* by Caleb Doxsey (O'Reilly) or *The Little Go Book* by Karl Seguin or by reading the more formal documentation such as The Go Programming Language Specification at https://go.dev/ref/spec.

If you are an experienced programmer, you can skip this chapter. If not, this chapter points out the bits of Go that are used in this book, but you should go elsewhere to get the necessary background. There are several tutorials on the Go website at https://go.dev such as the following:

- Getting started – https://go.dev/learn/

- A tutorial for the Go programming language – https://go.dev/doc/tutorial/getting-started

- Online and interactive tutorial – https://go.dev/tour/list

- Effective Go – https://go.dev/doc/effective_go

Installing Go is best done from the Go programing language website. Examples in this book will run using Go 1.18. The first edition of this book used 1.8. The core language and libraries have largely remained the same. The package management and tooling though continues to improve. The primary goal of this book is to implement networking concepts in your program and less about "perfect" Go. We will desire to keep up with the time and make sure you have the knowledge to not only create but also inspect other code.

You don't actually need to install Go to test the programs. Go has a "playground" accessible from the main page that can be used to run code (https://go.dev/play/). There are also several REPL (Read–Eval–Print Loop) environments, but these are third party. However, you will not be able to run network-related code typically. This is for safety reasons; the playground limits what you can do. It still is valuable for learning nonnetwork code and better still sharing code.

© Jan Newmarch and Ronald Petty 2022
J. Newmarch and R. Petty, *Network Programming with Go Language*,
https://doi.org/10.1007/978-1-4842-8095-9_2

The book predominantly uses libraries and packages from the Go Standard Library (`https://pkg.go.dev/std`). The Go team also built a further set of packages as "subrepositories," which often do not have the same support as the Standard Library. These are occasionally used. They will need to be installed using the `go get` command. These have package names including an "x," such as `golang.org/x/net/ipv4`.

In this revised edition, we will expand upon the related network ecosystem where Go is heavily used; examples include common Go networking middleware and microservice tooling (e.g., gRPC).

Types

There are predefined types of Boolean, numeric, and string types. The numeric types include `uint32`, `int32`, `float32`, and other sized numbers, as well as bytes (`uint8`) and runes. Runes (alias for int32) and strings are dealt with extensively in Chapter 6, as issues of internationalization can be significant in distributed programs.

There are more complex types, discussed next.

Slices and Arrays

Arrays are sequences of elements of a single type. Slices are segments of an underlying array. Slices are often more convenient to deal with in Go. Slices allow a developer to create many views of an array in theory saving memory.

An array can be created statically:

```
var x [128]int
```

or dynamically as a pointer:

```
xp := new([128]int)
```

A slice may be created along with its underlying array:

```
x := make([]int, 50, 100)
```

or

```
x := new([100]int)[0:50]
```

These last two are both of type `[]int` (as shown by `reflect.TypeOf(x)`), capacity of 100, length of 50. Elements of an array or slice are accessed by their index:

```
x[1]
```

The indices are from 0 to `len(x)-1`.

A slice may be taken of an array or slice by using the lower (inclusive) and upper (exclusive) indices of the array or slice:

```
a := [5]int{-1, -2, -3, -4, -5}
s := a[1:4]  // s is now [-2, -3, -4]
```

```
Slices are struct like object that has three key pieces of information contained in them.
```

- Reference to the underlying array

- Length of your slices view into the array

- Capacity field that controls how much more we can see of the underlying array

In the preceding example, s is a slice, while a is an array. Arrays have fixed type and size, and those aspects cannot change. So a is of type [5]int, and s is []int. While we see the type with slice s, we do not see the length. To retrieve the length or capacity, we have the following built-in functions.

```
$ go doc builtin.len

package builtin // import "builtin"

func len(v Type) int
    The len built-in function returns the length of v, according to its type:

        Array: the number of elements in v.
        Pointer to array: the number of elements in *v (even if v is nil).
        Slice, or map: the number of elements in v; if v is nil, len(v) is zero.
        String: the number of bytes in v.
        Channel: the number of elements queued (unread) in the channel buffer;
                if v is nil, len(v) is zero.

    For some arguments, such as a string literal or a simple array expression,
    the result can be a constant. See the Go language specification's "Length
    and capacity" section for details.

$ go doc builtin.cap

package builtin // import "builtin"

func cap(v Type) int
    The cap built-in function returns the capacity of v, according to its type:

        Array: the number of elements in v (same as len(v)).
        Pointer to array: the number of elements in *v (same as len(v)).
        Slice: the maximum length the slice can reach when resliced;
        if v is nil, cap(v) is zero.
        Channel: the channel buffer capacity, in units of elements;
        if v is nil, cap(v) is zero.

    For some arguments, such as a simple array expression, the result can be a
    constant. See the Go language specification's "Length and capacity" section
    for details.
```

We can now see the length and capacity of each. Other types are mentioned, but we are focusing on array and slice here.

```
fmt.Println(len(a), cap(a)) // 5 5
fmt.Println(len(s), cap(s)) // 3 4
```

A goal of slices is we can have many different views into the same array data. For example, a[2:] creates a slice where the length is 3 and the capacity is also 3. When the length and the capacity are equal, it means the slice cannot grow without modifying the underlying data structure. For example, if we append() to a slice, it inserts to the underlying array in the relative position. If cap() – len() == 0, then the underlying array would need to be increased in size. This increase does happen in such a case but can be unexpected. There is more to learn about this process and how slices share the array (or not if append is too large). More details about the relation of slices/arrays including memory details can be found here: `https://go.dev/blog/slices-intro`.

Maps

A *map* is an unordered group of elements of one type, indexed by a key of another type. We do not use maps much in this book, although one place is in Chapter 10, where the values of fields of an HTTP request may be accessed through a map using the field name as key.

```
myval := 10
x := map[string]int{"mykey": myval}
```

The preceding assignment has a few items worth discussing.

- map[string]int is declaring our maps type.
- {"mykey": myval} is using literal syntax to initialize our typed map.
- Ultimately assigning to x.

Per the prior section, we can retrieve the number of keys via the len built-in function.

```
len(x) // 1
```

Looping over a map (e.g., print out keys and values) in key sorted order is possible since 1.12. Deleting a map key can be accomplished via another built-in function called delete.

```
delete(x, "mykey")
```

A map of length 0 is not the same thing as a nil map.

Pointers

Pointers behave similarly to pointers in other languages. The * operator dereferences a pointer, while the & operator takes the address of a variable. Go simplifies the use of pointers so that most of the time you don't have to worry about them. The most we do in this book is check if a pointer value is nil, which will usually signify an error, or conversely, if a possible error value is not nil, as described in the next section.

```
// returns new pointer to an address that holds an int zero value
x := new(int)

// sets integer value at pointed address location
*x = 10
```

```
// pointing to, address of the pointer, value where we are pointing to
fmt.Println(x, &x, *x)
// 0xc000094010 0xc000096018 10

//every variable has an address, the value
y := 12
fmt.Println(&y, y)
// 0xc000094018 12
```

Something to note, when declaring function parameters, pointers and arrays are not the same thing. If you intend to pass an array, normally, you want to pass the address; this is because Go is pass by value.

Functions

Functions are defined using a notation unique to Go. Why the familiar C syntax (or any other for that matter) is not used is explained in the Go's Declaration Syntax blog (see https://go.dev/blog/declaration-syntax). We leave it to the textbooks to explain the details of the syntax.

Every Go program must have a main function declared as follows:

```
func main() { ... }
```

We will frequently use a function checkError defined as follows:

```
func checkError(err error) {
        if err != nil {
                fmt.Fprintf(os.Stderr, "Fatal error: %s", err.Error())
                os.Exit(1)
        }
}
```

It takes one parameter and has no return value. It starts with a lowercase letter, so it is local to the package in which it is declared.

Functions that return values will often return an error status as well as a substantive value, as in this function from Chapter 3:

```
func readFully(conn net.Conn) ([]byte, error) { ... }
```

It takes net.Conn as a parameter and returns an array of bytes and an error status (nil if no error occurred).

In this book, no more complex definitions than this are used.

Structures

Structures are similar to those in other languages. In Chapter 4, we consider serialization of data and use the example of the following structs:

```
type Name struct {
        Family   string
        Personal string
}
```

```go
type Email struct {
        Kind     string
        Address string
}
type Person struct {
        Name   Name
        Email []Email
}
```

A compound struct can be declared as follows:

```go
person := Person{
        Name: Name{Family: "Newmarch", Personal: "Jan"},
        Email: []Email{Email{Kind: "home", Address: "jan@newmarch.name"},
                        Email{Kind: "work", Address: "j.newmarch@boxhill.edu.au"}}}
```

Methods

Go does not have classes in the sense that languages like Java do. However, *types* can have *methods* associated with them, and these act similar to methods of more standard O/O languages.

We will make heavy use of the methods defined for the various networking types. This will happen from the very first programs of the next chapter. For example, the type IPMask is defined as an array of bytes:

```go
type IPMask []byte
```

A number of functions are defined on this type, such as

```go
func (m IPMask) Size() (ones, bits int)
```

A variable of type IPMask can have the method Size() applied, as follows:

```go
var m IPMask
...
ones, bits := m.Size()
```

Learning how to use the methods of the network-related types is the principal aim of this book.

We won't be defining our own methods much in this book. That's because to illustrate the Go libraries, we don't need many of our own complex types. A typical use will be pretty-printing a type like the Person type defined previously:

```go
func (p Person) String() string {
        s := p.Name.Personal + " " + p.Name.Family
        for _, v := range p.Email {
                s += "\n" + v.Kind + ": " + v.Address
        }
        return s
}
```

More specifically, triggering the preceding method would look as follows:

```
p := Person{}
details := p.String() // String is a method
len(details) // len is a function
```

There is more extensive use in Chapter 10, where a number of types and methods on these types are used. This is because we *do* need our own types when we are building more realistic systems.

Go also supports first class and higher-order functions. First class functions imply we can store a reference to a function (or method) in a variable. Higher-order functions imply that function (or method) can accept or return a function. Here is an example of first-class functions.

```
m := p.String
m() // triggers the p.String() method
```

Here is an example of a higher-order function.

```
package main

import (
        "fmt"
)

func f1(f func(string) int, data string) {
        fmt.Println(f(data))
}

func main() {
        f1(func(s string) int { return len(s) }, "testing")
}

$ go run prog.go
7
```

Multithreading

Go has a simple mechanism for starting additional threads using the go command. In this book, that is all we will need. Complex tasks such as synchronizing multiple threads are not needed here.

Packages

Go programs are built from linked packages. The packages used by any block of code have to be imported by an import statement at the head of the code file. Our own programs are declared to be in package main.

Apart from Chapter 10 again, nearly all of the programs in this book are in the main package.

Most packages are imported from the Standard Library. Some are imported from the subrepositories such as golang.org/x/net/ipv4.

The *visibility* of a structure's fields is controlled by the case of the first character of the field's name. If it is uppercase, it is visible outside of the package it is declared in; if it is lowercase, it is not. In the previous example, all the fields of all the structures are visible.

Modules

Go modules track packages and their versions. Modules allow the tracking of direct and indirect dependencies.

While modules are the proper way to group and share code (packages) in Go, users still often use a package-only approach.

We will use modules when a singular package will not do. Even were modules are used, the intent is to keep the examples focused on the networking code. In this example, a file called "go.mod" is generated, which is used by Go tooling to manage our dependencies.

```
//example
$ mkdir myapp; cd myapp
$ go mod init example.com
$ // create program
$ go mod tidy
$ go run prog.go
```

You can learn more about modules here: https://go.dev/blog/using-go-modules.

In Go 1.18, a new feature is included to help manage local development across modules; this feature is called workspace. We do not leverage this feature in this book, but you can find out more about it here: https://go.dev/doc/tutorial/workspaces.

Type Conversion

The first one we need to worry about in this book is conversion of strings to byte arrays and vice versa. To convert a string to a byte array, you do

```
var b []byte
b = []byte("string")
```

To convert the whole of an array/slice to a string, use this:

```
var s string
s = string(b[:])
```

The second casting we need to note is called a function adapter, most often in the following form:

```
...
http.Handle("/", http.HandlerFunc(func (w ResponseWriter, r *Request) {fmt.
Fprintf(w,"hi")}))
...

$ go doc --src http.HandlerFunc

package http // import "net/http"

// The HandlerFunc type is an adapter to allow the use of
// ordinary functions as HTTP handlers. If f is a function
// with the appropriate signature, HandlerFunc(f) is a
```

```
// Handler that calls f.
type HandlerFunc func(ResponseWriter, *Request)

func (f HandlerFunc) ServeHTTP(w ResponseWriter, r *Request)
```

By using this type, a call to HandlerFunc.ServeHTTP will now trigger our passed-in function.

Statements

A function or method will be composed of a set of statements. These include assignments, if and switch statements, for and while loops, and several others.

Apart from syntax, these have essentially the same meaning as in other programming languages. Nearly all of the statements types will be used in later chapters.

GOPATH

There are two ways of organizing workspaces for projects: put every project in a shared workspace or have a separate workspace for each project.

Either way is supported in the go tool by the environment variable GOPATH. This can be set to a list of directories (a ' : ' separated list in Linux/UNIX a ' ; ' separated list on Windows, and a list on Plan9). It defaults to the directory go in the user's home directory if it's unset.

For each directory in GOPATH, there will be three subdirectories – src, pkg, and bin. The directory src will typically contain one directory per package name and under that will be the source files for that package. For example, in Chapter 10, we have a complete web server that uses packages we define of dictionary and flashcards. The src/flashcards directory contains the file FlashCards.go.

GOPATH is used as the central location for downloading dependencies, even when using modules. There are reasons to set GOPATH to alternative locations, but much of those reasons were prior to Modules and Workspaces existing.

Running Go Programs

A Go program must have a file defining the package main. Most of the programs in this book are defined in a single file, such as the program IP.go in Chapter 3. The simplest way to run it is from the directory containing the file:

```
go run IP.go <IP address>
```

Alternatively, you can build an executable and then run it:

```
go build IP.go
./IP <IP address>
```

Standard Libraries

Go has an extensive set of Standard Libraries. Not as large as C, Java, or C++, for example, but those languages have been around for a *long* time. The Go packages are documented at https://pkg.go.dev/std. We will use these extensively in this book, particularly the net, crypto, and encoding packages.

In addition, there is a subrepositories group of packages available from the same page. These are less stable but sometimes have useful packages, which we will use occasionally.

In addition to these, there is a large set of user-contributed packages. They will not be used in the body of this book, which deals with principles, but in practice, you may find many of them very useful. Some are discussed in the concluding chapter.

Error Values

We discussed in the last chapter that a major difference between distributed and local programming is the greatly increased likelihood of errors occurring during execution. A local function call may fail because of simple programming errors such as divide by zero; more subtle errors may occur such as out-of-memory errors, but their possible occurrences are generally predictable.

On the other hand, almost any function that utilizes the network can fail for reasons beyond the application's control. Networking programs are consequently riddled with error checks. This is tedious, but necessary. Just like operating system kernel code is always error checking – errors need to be managed.

In this book, we generally exit a program with errors with appropriate messages on the client side, and for servers, attempt to recover by dropping the offending connection and carrying on.

Languages like C generally signal errors by returning "illegal" values such as negative integers and null pointers or by raising a signal. Languages like Java raise exceptions, which can lead to messy code and are often slow. The standard Go functions give an error in an extra parameter return from a function call.

For example, in the next chapter, we discuss the function in the net package:

```
func ResolveIPAddr(net, addr string) (*IPAddr, error)
```

The typical code to manage this is

```
addr, err := net.ResolveIPAddr("ip", name)
if err != nil {
        ...
}
```

Conclusion

This book assumes a knowledge of the Go programming language. This chapter just highlighted those parts that will be needed for later chapters.

CHAPTER 3

■ ■ ■

Socket-Level Programming

A socket is an abstract representation of a network endpoint. Depending on the operating system, we can construct sockets based on the following features: domain, type, and protocol. A "domain" typically represents either a remote network connection (e.g., via IPv4 or IPv6) or a local connection (e.g., via filesystem). Various optimizations can be acquired when we don't have to concern ourselves crossing many networks. A "type" selects a connection-oriented or connectionless pairing of sockets. Sockets provide the necessary abstraction to set up point-to-point communication.

There are many kinds of networks in the world. These range from the very old networks, such as serial links, to wide area networks made from copper and fiber, to wireless networks of various kinds, both for computers and for telecommunications devices such as phones. These networks obviously differ at the physical link layer, but in many cases, they also differ at higher layers of the OSI stack.

Over the years, there has been a convergence to the "Internet stack" of IP and TCP/UDP. For example, Bluetooth defines physical layers and protocol layers, but on top of that, it has an IP stack, so the same Internet programming techniques can be employed on many Bluetooth devices. Similarly, developing Internet of Things (IoT) wireless technologies such as LoRaWAN and 6LoWPAN includes an IP stack.

While IP provides the networking layer 3 of the OSI stack, TCP and UDP deal with layer 4. These are not the final word, even in the Internet world: SCTP (Stream Control Transmission Protocol) has come from the telecommunications world to challenge both TCP and UDP, while to provide Internet services in interplanetary space requires new, under-development protocols such as DTN (Delay-Tolerant Networking). Nevertheless, IP, TCP, and UDP hold sway as principal networking technologies now and at least for a considerable time into the future. Go has full support for this style of programming.

This chapter shows how to do TCP and UDP programming using Go and how to use a raw socket for other protocols.

The TCP/IP Stack

The OSI model (ISO/IEC 7498) was devised using a committee process wherein the standard was set up and then implemented. Some parts of the OSI standard are obscure, some parts cannot easily be implemented, and some parts have not been implemented.

The TCP/IP protocol was devised through a long-running DARPA project. This worked by implementation followed by RFCs (Request for Comments). TCP/IP is the principal UNIX networking protocol. TCP/IP stands for Transmission Control Protocol/Internet Protocol (RFC 793/RFC 791).

© Jan Newmarch and Ronald Petty 2022
J. Newmarch and R. Petty, *Network Programming with Go Language*,
https://doi.org/10.1007/978-1-4842-8095-9_3

The TCP/IP stack is shorter than the OSI one, as shown in Figure 3-1.

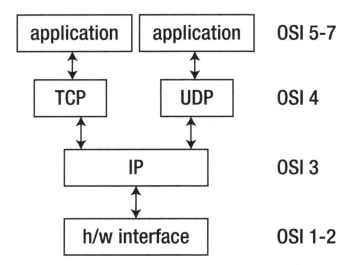

Figure 3-1. *TCP/IP stack vs. the OSI*

TCP is a connection-oriented protocol, whereas UDP (User Datagram Protocol) is a connectionless protocol.

We next discuss the layers above the point-to-point communication (Physical/Data Link) layers.

IP Datagrams

The IP layer provides a connectionless and unreliable delivery system. It considers each datagram independently of the others. Any association between datagrams must be supplied by the higher layers. The datagram itself is a well-defined format; at a high level, it includes a header and a payload. Fields of importance include address information and higher layer protocol choice.

The IP layer supplies a checksum of its own header. The IP protocol defaults any error correction to other layers. The header includes the source and destination addresses. The IP layer handles routing through an Internet. It is also responsible for breaking up large datagrams into smaller ones for transmission and reassembling them at the other end. Combining the prior statements, each router verifies IP packet correctness via its checksum. Additionally, a router will modify the IP packet header (e.g., modified TTL) triggering it to recalculate and replace the header.

Above the networking layer, we have the following transport layer options.

UDP

UDP is also connectionless and unreliable. What it adds to IP is a checksum for the contents of the datagram and *port numbers*. These are used to give a client-server model, which you'll see later. Think of ports as apartment numbers, and an IP address is an apartment street number.

TCP

TCP supplies logic to give a reliable connection-oriented protocol above IP. It provides a *virtual circuit* that two processes can use to communicate. It also uses port numbers to identify services on a host. With TCP, the two sockets used in the client-server connection over TCP represent a virtual circuit. While it feels like a dedicated physical connection, many virtual circuits can run over the same physical connection(s).

We briefly touched the networking (IP) and transport (UDP/TCP) layers, there is much more to learn. For example, IP fragmentation and TCP segmentation allow each layer to control the size of each packet it passes to the next layer. It may sound similar, but in this example, TCP segments include sequence information to keep packets in order (reliability), and IP fragmentation is focused on optimizing passing data to the layers below it (which have their own maximum size).

It is the IP address that is key for the usage of sockets.

Internet Addresses

In order to use a service, you must be able to find it. The Internet uses an address scheme for devices such as computers so that they can be located. This addressing scheme was originally devised when there were only a handful of connected computers and very generously allowed up to 2^32 addresses using a 32-bit unsigned integer. These are the so-called IPv4 addresses. In recent years, the number of connected (or at least directly addressable) devices has threatened to exceed this number, and there is a progressive transition to IPv6. The transition is patchy and shown, for example, in the graph by Google (https://www.google.com/intl/en/ipv6/statistics.html – ~37% as of January 2022). Sadly – from Jan's viewpoint – few of the Australian IP providers support IPv6 (~30% as of 2022). In the United States (for Ron), it's a little higher at ~50%. These numbers are based on observed incoming traffic and related records.

IPv4 Addresses

The address is a 32-bit integer that gives the IP address. This addresses down to a network interface card on a single device. The address is usually written as four bytes in decimal with a dot between them, as in 127.0.0.1 or 66.102.11.104. This dotted-decimal format captures multiple pieces of information in a human-friendly way.

The IP address of any device is generally composed of two parts: the address of the network in which the device resides and the address of the device within that network. Once upon a time, the split between network address and internal address was simple and was based on the bytes (between dots) used in the IP address.

- In a class A network, the first byte identifies the network, while the last three identify the device. There are only 128 class A networks, owned by the very early players in the Internet space such as IBM, General Electric Company, and MIT.[1] Example: 3.x.y.z.

- Class B networks use the first two bytes to identify the network and the last two to identify devices within the subnet. This allows up to 2^16 (65,536) devices on a subnet. Example: 142.90.y.z.

- Class C networks use the first three bytes to identify the network and the last one to identify devices within that network. This allows up to 2^8 (actually 254, not 256, as the bottom and top addresses are reserved) devices. Example: 192.168.123.z.

---

[1] Recently, MIT have returned their class A network to the pool. http://www.iana.org/assignments/ipv4-address-space/ipv4-address-space.xml. Amazon purchased 3.0.0.0/8 from General Electric Company in 2018.

There are classes defined beyond class C (D and E). We stop here as it becomes more of historical study than useful knowledge when discussing networking today.

This scheme doesn't work well if you want, say, 400 computers on a network. 254 is too small (class C), while 65,536 (-2) is too large (class B). In binary arithmetic terms, you want about 512 (-2). This can be achieved by using a 23-bit network address and 9 bits for the device addresses. Similarly, if you want up to 1024 (-2) devices, you use a 22-bit network address and a 10-bit device address. A newer scheme was created to replace class-based addressing, known as Classless Inter-Domain Routing (a.k.a. CIDR), allowing for the scenario we are describing.

Given an IP address of a device and knowing how many bits N are used for the network address gives a relatively straightforward process for extracting the network address and the device address within that network. Form a "network mask" (also called a subnet mask), which is a 32-bit binary number with all ones in the first N places and all zeroes in the remaining ones. For example, if 16 bits are used for the network address, the mask is 11111111111111110000000000000000. It's a little inconvenient using binary, so decimal bytes are usually used. The netmask for 16-bit network addresses is 255.255.0.0; for 24-bit network addresses, it is 255.255.255.0; for 23-bit addresses, it would be 255.255.254.0; and for 22-bit addresses, it would be 255.255.252.0. This network mask is a generalization for the class-based addressing. Shorthand for a 24-bit network is /24; for a 22-bit address, it is /22.

So to find the network address of a device, bit-wise AND its IP address with the network mask, while the device address within the subnet is found with bit-wise AND of the one's complement of the mask with the IP address. For example, the binary value of the IP address 192.168.1.3 is 11000000101010000000000100000011 (using the IP Address Subnet Mask Calculator). If a 16-bit netmask is used, the network is 1100000010101000 0000000000000000 (or 192.168.0.0), while the device address is 0000000000000000 0000000100000011 (or 0.0.1.3).

A network mask is provided when a network provider gives you a network. For example, a local ISP provides your office a w.x.y.z/29 (six host addresses). An ISP gets a block (large number of hosts) from a RIR (Regional Internet Registry)/IANA (Internet Assigned Numbers Authority). In general, each reduction of the network subnet number results in doubling the number of hosts (power of 2).

IPv6 Addresses

The Internet has grown vastly beyond original expectations. The initially generous 32-bit addressing scheme is on the verge of running out. There are unpleasant workarounds such as NAT (Network Address Translation) addressing, but eventually we will have to switch to a wider address space. IPv6 uses 128-bit addresses. Even bytes become cumbersome to express such addresses, so hexadecimal digits are used, grouped into four digits and separated by a colon. A typical address might be FE80:CD00:0000:0CDE:1257 :0000:211E:729C.

These addresses are not easy to remember! DNS will become even more important. There are tricks to reducing some addresses, such as leading zeroes and repeated digits. For example, "localhost" is 0:0:0:0:0:0:0:1, which can be shortened to ::1.

Each address is divided into three components. The first is the network address used for Internet routing and is the first 64 bits of the address. The next part is 16 bits for the netmask. This is used to divide the network into subnets. It can give anything from one subnet only (all zeroes) to 65,535 subnets (all 1s). The last part is the device component, of 48 bits. The preceding address would be FE80:CD00:0000:0CDE for the network, 1257 for the subnet, and 0000:211E:729C for the device.

Some points of comparison between IPv6 and IPv4:

- IPv6 has no checksum header (it assumes other layers perform verification).

- Many fields in header are optional in IPv6.

- While larger in general, overall packet header structure is quicker to parse (simplifying router processing).

- IPv6 reduces fragmentation compared to IPv4 due to larger datagram sizing and reduced router reconstructing (moving to edge nodes).

IP Address Type

Finally, we can start using some of the Go language network packages. The package net defines many types, functions, and methods of use in Go network programming. The type IP is defined as an array of bytes:

```
type IP []byte
```

There are several functions to manipulate a variable of type IP, but you are likely to use only some of them in practice. For example, the function ParseIP(String) will take a dotted IPv4 address or a colon IPv6 address, while the IP method String() will return a string. Note that you may not get back what you started with: the string form of 0:0:0:0:0:0:0:1 is ::1.

A program that illustrates this process is ip.go:

```
$ mkdir ch3
$ cd ch3
ch3$ vi ip.go

/* IP
 */
package main

import (
        "fmt"
        "log"
        "net"
        "os"
)

func main() {
        if len(os.Args) != 2 {
                log.Fatalln("Usage: %s ip-addr\n", os.Args[0])
        }
        name := os.Args[1]
        addr := net.ParseIP(name)
        if addr == nil {
                fmt.Println("Invalid address")
        } else {
                fmt.Println("The address is ", addr.String())
        }
}
```

This can be run, for example, as follows:

```
ch3$ go run ip.go 127.0.0.1
```

Here is the response:

```
The address is 127.0.0.1
```

Or it could be run as

```
ch3$ go run IP.go 0:0:0:0:0:0:0:1
```

with this response:

```
The address is ::1
```

If you are unfamiliar, the colon addresses are IPv6, including the ::1, which is the IPv6 version of 127.0.0.1 (in IPv4).

The backing store for the IP type is a byte array. As hinted in the preceding example, we can store both IPv4 and IPv6 addresses in the same type. Some purposes for ParseIP (and ultimate storage into IP) are for serialization purposes, ease of access of related octets (e.g., class A would be myip[0] – first byte), and general normalization of various input forms (e.g., 127.000.000.001 -> 127.0.0.1).

Of potential interest, ParseIP doesn't necessarily normalize all forms; these nonstandard forms are called "Rare IP Address Formats." As example of a rare ip, some tools expand 127.1 to 127.0.0.1; net.ParseIP does not. Like all programming environments, it's hard to capture all the planned or unplanned standards or de facto standards. We can see an ongoing discussion about this very issue on the Golang project tracker ("net: should expand IP address 1.1 to 1.0.0.1 #36822", https://github.com/golang/go/issues/36822).

Using Available Documentation and Examples

As you proceed with the examples in this book, you use the built-in examples and documentation to dig deeper into the standard library. For example, show the alias type known as IP in the net package along with functions and methods that use it.

```
ch3$ go doc net.IP

package net // import "net"

type IP []byte
    An IP is a single IP address, a slice of bytes. Functions in this package
    accept either 4-byte (IPv4) or 16-byte (IPv6) slices as input.

    Note that in this documentation, referring to an IP address as an IPv4
    address or an IPv6 address is a semantic property of the address, not just
    the length of the byte slice: a 16-byte slice can still be an IPv4 address.

func IPv4(a, b, c, d byte) IP
func ParseIP(s string) IP
func (ip IP) DefaultMask() IPMask
func (ip IP) Equal(x IP) bool
```

```
func (ip IP) IsGlobalUnicast() bool
func (ip IP) IsInterfaceLocalMulticast() bool
func (ip IP) IsLinkLocalMulticast() bool
func (ip IP) IsLinkLocalUnicast() bool
func (ip IP) IsLoopback() bool
func (ip IP) IsMulticast() bool
func (ip IP) IsUnspecified() bool
func (ip IP) MarshalText() ([]byte, error)
func (ip IP) Mask(mask IPMask) IP
func (ip IP) String() string
func (ip IP) To16() IP
func (ip IP) To4() IP
func (ip *IP) UnmarshalText(text []byte) error
```

Notice some functions return IP; others are methods that use it. Most of the methods appear to be property checks; for example, is the IP the loopback IP?

Next, let's drill down into net.ParseIP.

```
ch3$ go doc net.ParseIP

package net // import "net"

func ParseIP(s string) IP
    ParseIP parses s as an IP address, returning the result. The string s can be
    in IPv4 dotted decimal ("192.0.2.1"), IPv6 ("2001:db8::68"), or IPv4-mapped
    IPv6 ("::ffff:192.0.2.1") form. If s is not a valid textual representation
    of an IP address, ParseIP returns nil.
```

Eventually, you will want to find examples of usage of given function or type. Your Go distribution will normally include examples, either via a test function or internal usage. We can find tests related to ParseIP (in a Unix-based system) as follows:

```
ch3$ go test -list ".*ParseIP.*" $(go env GOROOT)/src/net

TestParseIP
BenchmarkParseIP
ExampleParseIP
ok          net         0.106s
```

Here is an example of running the related test and benchmark from before, focused on net.ParseIP.

```
ch3$ go test -run ParseIP -bench ParseIP -count=1 $(go env GOROOT)/src/net

goos: darwin
goarch: amd64
pkg: net
cpu: Intel(R) Core(TM) i7-9750H CPU @ 2.60GHz
BenchmarkParseIP-12                 934454                 1309 ns/op
PASS
ok          net         2.295s
```

There are a couple of items to note regarding these prior commands. "go env GOROOT" will produce where the Go standard library is installed; the $( ) is for UNIX subshell execution (on Windows, you can just run go env GOROOT and copy/paste). Assuming standard package layout, we know the net package would be located in "$(go env GOROOT)/src/net". The remaining commands are standard Go test commands:

- -list *regex* // finds test/bench/example that matches *regex*.

- -run *regex* // runs Test*regex*.

- -bench *regex* // runs Bench*regex*.

- -count=1 // prevents tests from caching results.

Running a test example is a start; reviewing the code will provide more in-depth knowledge. In the case of ParseIP, once we locate the test source, we can review it (your output may differ):

```
ch3$ grep -l TestParseIP -nr $(go env GOROOT)/src/net

/usr/local/go/src/net/ip_test.go
/usr/local/go/src/net/netip/netip_pkg_test.go (netip package has a 'smaller' ip type)
```

If you review the related test and its input inside ip_test.go, we can get a feel for the types of input ParseIP expects and its related output.

```
...
var parseIPTests = []struct {
        in   string
        out  IP
}{
        {"127.0.1.2", IPv4(127, 0, 1, 2)},
        {"127.0.0.1", IPv4(127, 0, 0, 1)},
        {"127.001.002.003", IPv4(127, 1, 2, 3)},
        {"::ffff:127.1.2.3", IPv4(127, 1, 2, 3)},
        {"::ffff:127.001.002.003", IPv4(127, 1, 2, 3)},
        {"::ffff:7f01:0203", IPv4(127, 1, 2, 3)},
        {"0:0:0:0:0000:ffff:127.1.2.3", IPv4(127, 1, 2, 3)},
        {"0:0:0:0:000000:ffff:127.1.2.3", IPv4(127, 1, 2, 3)},
        {"0:0:0:0::ffff:127.1.2.3", IPv4(127, 1, 2, 3)},

        {"2001:4860:0:2001::68", IP{0x20, 0x01, 0x48, 0x60, 0, 0, 0x20, 0x01, 0, 0, 0, 0, 0,
        0, 0x00, 0x68}},
        {"2001:4860:0000:2001:0000:0000:0000:0068", IP{0x20, 0x01, 0x48, 0x60, 0, 0, 0x20,
        0x01, 0, 0, 0, 0, 0, 0, 0x00, 0x68}},

        {"-0.0.0.0", nil},
        {"0.-1.0.0", nil},
        {"0.0.-2.0", nil},
        {"0.0.0.-3", nil},
        {"127.0.0.256", nil},
        {"abc", nil},
        {"123:", nil},
        {"fe80::1%lo0", nil},
        {"fe80::1%911", nil},
        {"", nil},
```

```
            {"a1:a2:a3:a4::b1:b2:b3:b4", nil}, // Issue 6628
}

func TestParseIP(t *testing.T) {
        for _, tt := range parseIPTests {
                if out := ParseIP(tt.in); !reflect.DeepEqual(out, tt.out) {
                        t.Errorf("ParseIP(%q) = %v, want %v", tt.in, out, tt.out)
                }
                if tt.in == "" {
                        // Tested in TestMarshalEmptyIP below.
                        continue
                }
                var out IP
                if err := out.UnmarshalText([]byte(tt.in)); !reflect.DeepEqual(out, tt.out)
                || (tt.out == nil) != (err != nil) {
                        t.Errorf("IP.UnmarshalText(%q) = %v, %v, want %v", tt.in, out,
                        err, tt.out)
                }
        }
}
...
```

Hopefully, this convinces you to review the available documentation and examples. Maybe it will convince you to also create good documentation and examples for your own code. We shouldn't just stop at the examples or tests. One often overlooked feature of Go is Go is written in Go. This means it's pretty easy to follow. Since the test is located in test_ip.go, it's safe to assume the actual code to ParseIP (and in this case, IP) is in ip.go.

Beyond this section, we assume you are finding and reviewing related examples in the standard library.

The IPMask Type

An IP address is typically divided into the components of a network address, a subnet, and a device portion. The network address and subnet form a *prefix* to the device portion. The mask is an IP address of all binary ones to match the prefix length, followed by all zeroes.

In order to handle masking operations, you use this type:

```
type IPMask []byte
```

The simplest function to create a netmask uses the CIDR notation of ones followed by zeroes up to the number of bits:

```
func CIDRMask(ones, bits int) IPMask
```

A mask can then be used by a method of an IP address to find the network for that IP address:

```
func (ip IP) Mask(mask IPMask) IP
```

An example of the use of this is the following program called mask.go:

```
ch3$ vi mask.go

/* Mask
 */
package main

import (
        "fmt"
        "log"
        "net"
        "os"
        "strconv"
)

func main() {
        if len(os.Args) != 4 {
                log.Fatalln("Usage: %s dotted-ip-addr ones bits\n", os.Args[0])
        }
        dotAddr := os.Args[1]
        ones, _ := strconv.Atoi(os.Args[2])
        bits, _ := strconv.Atoi(os.Args[3])
        addr := net.ParseIP(dotAddr)
        if addr == nil {
                log.Fatalln("nil Invalid address")
        }
        mask := net.CIDRMask(ones, bits)
        computedOnes, computedBits := mask.Size()
        network := addr.Mask(mask)
        fmt.Println("Address is ", addr.String(),
                "\nMask length is ", computedBits,
                "\nLeading ones count is ", computedOnes,
                "\nMask is (hex) ", mask.String(),
                "\nNetwork is ", network.String())
}
```

This can be compiled (go build mask.go) to mask and run as follows:

```
ch3$ mask <ip-address> <ones> <zeroes>
```

Or it can be run directly as follows:

```
ch3$ go run mask.go <ip-address> <ones> <zeroes>
```

For an IPv4 address of 103.232.159.187 on a /24 network, we get the following:

```
ch3$ go run mask.go 103.232.159.187 24 32

Address is  103.232.159.187
Mask length is  32
```

```
Leading ones count is  24
Mask is (hex)  ffffff00
Network is  103.232.159.0
```

For an IPv6 address fda3:97c:1eb:fff0:5444:903a:33f0:3a6b where the network component is fda3:97c:1eb, the subnet is fff0, and the device part is 5444:903a:33f0:3a6b, we get the following:

```
ch3$ go run mask.go fda3:97c:1eb:fff0:5444:903a:33f0:3a6b 52 128

Address is  fda3:97c:1eb:fff0:5444:903a:33f0:3a6b
Mask length is  128
Leading ones count is  52
Mask is (hex)  fffffffffffff0000000000000000000
Network is  fda3:97c:1eb:f000::
```

When you review the documentation of a function, take note of the result and related error checks. In the prior example, if we pass in a "bits" value that doesn't match the width of IPv4 or IPv6 addresses, it will cause CIDRMask to return nil. The nil mask value passed into addr.Mask will then in turn return nil. We can debate if the preceding example is too simple to handle errors (probably); it's also simply good to note what the library is returning (even if it doesn't explain why, e.g., why nil and not an error string).

```
ch3$ go run mask.go 103.232.159.187 24 44 # 44 != 32 nor 128

Address is  103.232.159.187
Mask length is  0
Leading ones count is  0
Mask is (hex)  <nil>
Network is  <nil>
```

IPv4 netmasks are often given in the 4-byte dotted notation such as 255.255.255.0 for a /24 network. There is a function to create a mask from such a 4-byte IPv4 address:

```
func IPv4Mask(a, b, c, d byte) IPMask
```

Also, there is a method of IP that returns the default mask for IPv4 (only):

```
func (ip IP) DefaultMask() IPMask
```

Note that the string form of a mask is a hex number, such as ffffff00 for a /24 mask.
The following program called ipv4mask.go illustrates these:

```
ch3$ vi ipv4mask.go

/* IPv4Mask
 */
package main

import (
        "fmt"
        "log"
        "net"
        "os"
)
```

```go
func main() {
        if len(os.Args) != 2 {
                log.Fatalln("Usage: %s dotted-ip-addr\n", os.Args[0])
        }
        dotAddr := os.Args[1]
        addr := net.ParseIP(dotAddr)
        if addr == nil {
                log.Fatalln("nil Invalid address")
        }
        mask := addr.DefaultMask()
        network := addr.Mask(mask)
        ones, bits := mask.Size()
        fmt.Println("Address is ", addr.String(),
                "\nDefault mask length is ", bits,
                "\nLeading ones count is ", ones,
                "\nMask is (hex) ", mask.String(),
                "\nNetwork is ", network.String())
        derivedMask := net.IPv4Mask(255, 255, 0, 0) // working on mask
        fmt.Printf("Network using %s: %s\n", derivedMask, addr.Mask(derivedMask))
}
```

For example, running this

```
ch3$ go run ipv4mask.go 192.168.1.3
```

in my home network gives the following result:

```
Address is   192.168.1.3
Default mask length is   32
Leading ones count is   24
Mask is (hex)   ffffff00
Network is   192.168.1.0
Network using ffff0000: 192.168.0.0
```

Basic Routing

Now that we see how you can take an IP address and add (binary) to a subnet mask to reveal the network IP, what do we use it for? The primary purpose is in routing, where a router needs to figure out the next hop (where to send this packet). Since computers are usually more than one hop away, we use a series of routers to move traffic around. Each router has a lookup table and decides where to forward traffic. It would be very ineffective to map every destination IP to a specific next hop, so instead, we route many IPs to a specific next hop. In other words, a subnet goes to a specific next hop. Here is an example for routing packets to particular destinations.

```
ch3$ vi ipv4router.go

/* IPv4Router
 */
package main

import (
```

```go
        "fmt"
        "net"
)

func main() {
        routingTable := []struct {
                subnetmask net.IP
                network    net.IP
                nextHop    net.IP
        }{
                {net.IP{255, 255, 255, 240}, net.IP{192, 17, 7, 208}, net.IP{192, 12,
                7, 15}},
                {net.IP{255, 255, 255, 240}, net.IP{192, 17, 7, 144}, net.IP{192, 12,
                7, 67}},
                {net.IP{255, 255, 255, 0}, net.IP{192, 17, 7, 0}, net.IP{192, 12, 7, 251}},
                {net.IP{0, 0, 0, 0}, net.IP{0, 0, 0, 0}, net.IP{10, 10, 10, 10}},
        }
        incomingPacketsToRoute := []struct {
                sourceAddr      net.IP
                destinationAddr net.IP
                data            string
        }{
                {net.IP{1, 2, 3, 4}, net.IP{2, 3, 4, 5}, "who knows, send to 0.0.0.0"},
                {net.IP{1, 2, 3, 4}, net.IP{192, 17, 7, 20}, "better be 192.17.7.251"},
        }
        for _, packetToRoute := range incomingPacketsToRoute {
                for _, routingEntry := range routingTable {
                        r := packetToRoute.destinationAddr.Mask(net.IPMask(routingEntry.
                        subnetmask))
                        if r.Equal(routingEntry.network) {
                                fmt.Printf("For destination %s nexthop is %s\n",
                                packetToRoute.destinationAddr, routingEntry.nextHop)
                                break //check remaining ips
                        }
                }
        }
}
```

```
ch3$ go run IPv4Router.go

For destination 2.3.4.5 nexthop is 10.10.10.10
For destination 192.17.7.20 nexthop is 192.12.7.251
```

As we see in the prior output, the first packet had a destination of 2.3.4.5, and our routing table didn't find a match. The last entry in routing tends to be the catch-all route. Our table defaults to the next hop of 10.10.10.10. The second packet destination for 192.17.7.20 matched the network IP of 192.17.7.0, which has the next hop of 192.12.7.251.

The IPAddr Type

Many of the other functions and methods in the net package return a pointer to an IPAddr. This is simply a structure containing an IP (and a zone which may be needed for IPv6 addresses). The zone may be needed for ambiguous IPv6 addresses with multiple network interfaces. You can learn about zones (IPv6 scoped addresses) here: https://datatracker.ietf.org/doc/html/rfc4007.

```
type IPAddr {
    IP IP
    Zone string
}
```

The primary use of this type is to perform DNS lookups on IP hostnames.

```
func ResolveIPAddr(net, addr string) (*IPAddr, error)
```

where net is one of ip, ip4, or ip6. This is shown in the program called resolveip.go:

```
ch3$ vi resolveip.go
```

```go
/* ResolveIP
 */
package main

import (
        "fmt"
        "log"
        "net"
        "os"
)

func main() {
        if len(os.Args) != 2 {
                log.Fatalln("Usage: %s hostname\n", os.Args[0])
        }
        name := os.Args[1]
        addr, err := net.ResolveIPAddr("ip", name)
        if err != nil {
                log.Fatalln("Resolution error", err.Error())
        }
        fmt.Println("Resolved address is ", addr.String())
}
```

Running this

```
ch3$ go run resolveip.go www.google.com
```

returns the following:

```
Resolved address is 142.250.64.22
```

If the first parameter to ResolveIPAddr() for the net type is given as ip6 instead of ip, I get this result:

```
Resolved address is  2404:6800:4006:801::2004
```

You may get different results, depending on where Google appears to live from your address's perspective.

Per the documentation of ResolveIPAddr, arguments are documented under Dial (go doc net.Dial). The *network* parameter must belong to the IP family, either "ip", "ip4", or "ip6". Optionally appended to the *network* parameter is a protocol such as "icmp" or its protocol number, "1".

```
        addr, err := net.ResolveIPAddr("ip4:icmp", name)
```

The usage of the *network* parameter and optional *protocol* allows us to verify that the *name* can be used for that given purpose. For example, if we use an IPv6 address with "ip4:icmp", it will fail. A starting point to learn more is following the internal documentation, go doc -u net.protocols. "-u" is needed because the "var protocols" are not exported.

The preceding code uses the variable called *name*. The official documentation calls the parameter *address*. We use *name* to show it's not just an IP address that can be passed in. In general, you should not use ResolveIPAddr if your IP end point (*name/address*) can resolve to more than one IP address. The following functions will be more helpful when there is more than a single result.

Host Canonical Name and Addresses Lookup

The ResolveIPAddr function will perform a DNS lookup on a hostname and return a single IP address. How it does this depends on the operating system and its configuration. For example, a Linux/UNIX system may use /etc/resolv.conf or /etc/hosts with the order of the search set in /etc/nsswitch.conf.

Many hosts can have more than one name (e.g., www.myserver.com -> myserver.com); these CNAME records (canonical name) eventual resolve to an A record (e.g., myserver.com -> IP). If you want to find the canonical name, use LookupCNAME:

```
func LookupCNAME(name string) (cname string, err error).
```

Some hosts may have multiple IP addresses, usually from multiple network interface cards. They may also have multiple hostnames, acting as aliases. The LookupHost function will return a slice of addresses.

```
func LookupHost(name string) (cname string, addrs []string, err error)
```

Both are shown in the following program called lookuphost.go:

```
ch3$ vi lookuphost.go

/* LookupHost
 */
package main

import (
        "fmt"
        "log"
        "net"
        "os"
)
```

```go
func main() {
        if len(os.Args) != 2 {
                log.Fatalln("Usage: %s hostname\n", os.Args[0])
        }
        name := os.Args[1]
        cname, _ := net.LookupCNAME(name)
        fmt.Println(cname)
        addrs, err := net.LookupHost(cname)
        if err != nil {
                log.Fatalln("Error: ", err.Error())
        }
        for _, addr := range addrs {
                fmt.Println(addr)
        }
}
```

We first normalize the hostname by looking for the canonical name. Then we see if that resulting name has one or more IPs. Note that this function returns strings, not IP address values. When you run the preceding program:

```
ch3$ go run lookuphost.go go.dev
```

it prints something similar to this:

```
2001:4860:4802:32::15
2001:4860:4802:36::15
2001:4860:4802:38::15
2001:4860:4802:34::15
216.239.32.21
216.239.36.21
216.239.38.21
216.239.34.21
```

If you are on a UNIX platform, you can compare these results via the dig command.

```
ch3$ ch3 % dig go.dev A go.dev AAAA +short
216.239.34.21
216.239.38.21
216.239.32.21
216.239.36.21
2001:4860:4802:38::15
2001:4860:4802:34::15
2001:4860:4802:36::15
2001:4860:4802:32::15
```

There are many additional Lookup functions to learn.

```
go doc net | grep Lookup
```

```
like Dial or directly with functions like LookupHost and LookupAddr, varies
func LookupAddr(addr string) (names []string, err error)
```

```
func LookupCNAME(host string) (cname string, err error)
func LookupHost(host string) (addrs []string, err error)
func LookupIP(host string) ([]IP, error)
func LookupMX(name string) ([]*MX, error)
func LookupNS(name string) ([]*NS, error)
func LookupPort(network, service string) (port int, err error)
func LookupSRV(service, proto, name string) (cname string, addrs []*SRV, err error)
func LookupTXT(name string) ([]string, error)
```

Some are related to email, including MX and TXT, others for general resource identification such as CNAME, Host, and NS.

Services

Services run on host machines. They are typically long lived and are designed to wait for requests and respond to them. There are many types of services, and there are many ways in which they can offer their services to clients. The Internet world bases many of these services on two methods of communication – TCP and UDP – although there are other communication protocols such as SCTP waiting in the wings to take over. Many other types of service, such as peer to peer, remote procedure calls, communicating agents, and many others, are built on top of TCP and UDP.

Ports

Services live on host machines. We can locate a host using an IP address. But on each computer, there may be many services, and a simple way is needed to distinguish between them. The method used by TCP, UDP, SCTP, and others is to use a *port number*. This is an unsigned integer between 1 and 65,535, and each service will associate itself with one or more of these port numbers.

There are many "standard" ports. Telnet typically uses port 23 with the TCP protocol. DNS uses port 53, either with TCP or with UDP. FTP uses ports 21 and 20, one for commands and the other for data transfer. HTTP usually uses port 80, but it often uses ports 8000, 8080, and 8088, all with TCP. The X Window System often takes ports 6000–6007, both on TCP and UDP.

On a UNIX system, the commonly used ports are listed in the file /etc/services. Go has a function to look up ports on all systems:

```
func LookupPort(network, service string) (port int, err error)
```

The network argument is a string such as "tcp" or "udp", while the service is a string such as "telnet" or "domain" (for DNS).

A program using this is lookupport.go:

```
ch3$ vi lookupport.go

/* LookupPort
 */
package main

import (
        "fmt"
        "log"
```

```
        "net"
        "os"
)

func main() {
        if len(os.Args) != 3 {
                log.Fatalln("Usage: %s network-type service\n", os.Args[0])
        }
        networkType := os.Args[1]
        service := os.Args[2]
        port, err := net.LookupPort(networkType, service)
        if err != nil {
                log.Fatalln("Error: ", err.Error())
        }
        fmt.Println("Service port ", port)
}
```

For example:

```
ch3$ go run lookupport.go tcp telnet

Service port  23

ch3$ go run lookupport.go udp quake

Service port  26000
```

There is more to port management than using a default service mapping (e.g., SSH to 22). One idea is called ephemeral ports; these ports range typically from 32768 to 60999 (they can vary by OS). Ephemeral ports are used by services to move per-client traffic to a temporary (i.e., ephemeral) port; at the communication session conclusion, the port is released. As an additional concern, various software platforms also use ranges of ports for predefined purposes; for example, Kubernetes uses the range 32000 to 32768 by default for exposing services on its internal network. There is no central management for port usage, and collisions can occur. Verification and recovery logic is the best practice when dealing with ports.

The TCPAddr Type

The TCPAddr type is a structure containing an IP, a port, and a zone. The zone is required to distinguish between possible ambiguous IPv6 link-local and site-local addresses, as different network interface cards (NICs) may have the same IPv6 address.

```
type TCPAddr struct {
    IP    IP
    Port int
    Zone string
}
```

The function to create a TCPAddr is ResolveTCPAddr:

```
func ResolveTCPAddr(net, addr string) (*TCPAddr, error)
```

where net is one of tcp, tcp4, or tcp6 and the addr is a string composed of a hostname or IP address, followed by the port number after a :, such as www.google.com:80 or 127.0.0.1:ssh. If the address is an IPv6 address, which already has colons in it, then the host part must be enclosed in square brackets, such as [::1]:23. Another special case is often used for servers, where the host address is zero, so the TCP address is really just the port name, as in :80 for an HTTP server.

Similar to IPAddr, resolving to TCPAddr (or UDPAddr – will see later) allows us to verify and normalize our network end points.

TCP Sockets

When you know how to reach a service via its network and port IDs, what then? If you are a client, you need an API that will allow you to connect to a service and then to send messages to that service and read replies back from the service.

If you are a server, you need to be able to bind to a port and listen at it. When a message comes in, you need to be able to read it and write back to the client.

The net.TCPConn is the Go type that allows full duplex communication between the client and the server. Two major methods of interest are as follows:

```
func (c *TCPConn) Write(b []byte) (n int, err error)
func (c *TCPConn) Read(b []byte) (n int, err error)
```

A TCPConn is used by both a client and a server to read and write messages.

Note that a TCPConn implements the io.Reader and io.Writer interfaces so that any method using a reader or writer can be applied to a TCPConn.

TCP Client

Once a client has established a TCP address for a service, it "dials" the service. If successful, the dial returns a TCPConn for communication. The client and the server exchange messages on this. Typically, a client writes a request to the server using the TCPConn and reads a response from the TCPConn. This continues until either (or both) side closes the connection. A TCP connection is established by the client using this function:

```
func DialTCP(net string, laddr, raddr *TCPAddr) (*TCPConn, error)
```

where laddr is the local address (client side), which is usually set to nil, and raddr is the remote address of the service (server side). The net string is one of "tcp4", "tcp6", or "tcp", depending on whether you want a TCPv4 connection or a TCPv6 connection or don't care.

A simple example can be provided by a client to a web (HTTP) server. We will deal in substantially more detail with HTTP clients and servers in a later chapter, so for now, we will keep it simple.

One of the possible messages that a client can send is the HEAD message. This queries a server for information about the server and a document on that server. The server returns information but does not return the document itself. The request sent to query an HTTP server could be as follows:

```
"HEAD / HTTP/1.0\r\n\r\n"
```

This asks for information about the root document and the server. A typical response might be

```
HTTP/1.0 200 OK
Content-Type: text/html; charset=ISO-8859-1
P3P: CP="This is not a P3P policy! See g.co/p3phelp for more info."
Date: Mon, 02 Aug 2021 21:56:38 GMT
Server: gws
X-XSS-Protection: 0
X-Frame-Options: SAMEORIGIN
Expires: Mon, 02 Aug 2021 21:56:38 GMT
Cache-Control: private
Set-Cookie: 1P_JAR=2021-08-02-21; expires=Wed, 01-Sep-2021 21:56:38 GMT; path=/; domain=.
google.com; Secure
Set-Cookie: NID=220=U9k4rAwVrhFaS2OKHOOFfoEQv6ZxzK_3zgVTlf3uBLPl6G1PZ_040Kz
6SpQvCba7aA9bZo3bKbKadUCN9EQNNPMUJh11QLUsnYeMoS1iOC7QZa-eKDCheZcywo_nMt__
KcKHLIUIc6BUFEIAayyEala5qb4d7YanhTrKPQsEqaA; expires=Tue, 01-Feb-2022 21:56:38 GMT; path=/;
domain=.google.com; HttpOnly
```

We first give the program (getheadinfo.go) to establish the connection for a TCP address, send the request string, and then read and print the response. The program is getheadinfo.go:

```
ch3$ vi getheadinfo.go

/* GetHeadInfo
 */
package main

import (
        "fmt"
        "io/ioutil"
        "log"
        "net"
        "os"
)

func main() {
        if len(os.Args) != 2 {
                log.Fatalln("Usage: %s host:port ", os.Args[0])
        }
        service := os.Args[1]
        tcpAddr, err := net.ResolveTCPAddr("tcp4", service)
        checkError(err)
        conn, err := net.DialTCP("tcp", nil, tcpAddr)
        checkError(err)
        _, err = conn.Write([]byte("HEAD / HTTP/1.0\r\n\r\n"))
        checkError(err)
        result, err := ioutil.ReadAll(conn)
        checkError(err)
        fmt.Println(string(result))
}
```

```
func checkError(err error) {
        if err != nil {
                log.Fatalln("Fatal error: %s", err.Error())
        }
}
```

```
ch3$ go run getheadinfo.go golang.org:80
```

```
HTTP/1.0 200 OK
Content-Type: text/html; charset=ISO-8859-1
P3P: CP="This is not a P3P policy! See g.co/p3phelp for more info."
Date: Mon, 03 Jan 2022 23:37:35 GMT
Server: gws
X-XSS-Protection: 0
X-Frame-Options: SAMEORIGIN
Expires: Mon, 03 Jan 2022 23:37:35 GMT
Cache-Control: private
Set-Cookie: 1P_JAR=2022-01-03-23; expires=Wed, 02-Feb-2022 23:37:35 GMT; path=/; domain=.
google.com; Secure
Set-Cookie: NID=511=iZvpsJc9liI44GQwANJFCMUc5Xgko8dCWw9Q2_L4QwwizOtxQ3my4Uk8MFjPs
YbOXCsGEntPRPnyHSJoE3UfPqQ6WH3akir2iks2GzKZYv-58SFCx2qN7hFIXalS2nLT5V7X4EBH9wAkzo
dE-5sEcv6gDvuOfAliFXxnuFAFHdw; expires=Tue, 05-Jul-2022 23:37:35 GMT; path=/; domain=.
google.com; HttpOnly
```

The first point to note is the almost excessive amount of error checking that is going on. This is normal for networking programs (and Golang): the opportunities for failure are substantially greater than for stand-alone programs. Hardware may fail on the client, the server, or on any of the routers and switches in the middle; communication may be blocked by a firewall; timeouts may occur due to network load; the server may crash while the client is talking to it. The following checks are performed:

- There may be syntax errors in the address specified. An example is an unspecified port.

- The attempt to connect to the remote service may fail. For example, the service requested might not be running, or there may be no such host connected to the network. An example is a typo in the hostname.

- Although a connection has been established, writes to the service might fail if the connection has died suddenly, or if the network times out.

- Similarly, the reads might fail as above.

Reading from the server requires a comment. In this case, we read essentially a single response from the server. This will be terminated by end of file on the connection. However, it may consist of several TCP packets, so we need to keep reading until the end of file. The io/ioutil function ReadAll will look after these issues and return the complete response. (Thanks to Roger Peppe on the golang-nuts mailing list.)

There are some language issues involved. First, most of the functions return a dual value, with the possible error as second value. If no error occurs, then this will be nil. In C, the same behavior is gained by special values such as NULL, or -1, or zero being returned – if that is possible. In Java, the same error checking is managed by throwing and catching exceptions, which can make the code look very messy.

A Daytime Server

The simplest service that we can build is the daytime service. This is a standard Internet service, defined by RFC 867, with a default port of 13 on both TCP and UDP. Unfortunately, with the (justified) increase in paranoia over security, hardly any sites run a daytime server anymore. Never mind; we can build our own. (For those interested, if you install inetd/systemd on your system, you usually get a daytime server thrown in.)

A server registers itself on a port and listens on that port. Then it blocks on an "accept" operation, waiting for clients to connect. When a client connects, the accept call returns, with a connection object. The daytime service is very simple and just writes the current time to the client, closes the connection, and resumes waiting for the next client.

The relevant calls are as follows:

```
func ListenTCP(network string, laddr *TCPAddr) (*TCPListener, error)
func (l *TCPListener) Accept() (Conn, error)
```

The argument net can be set to one of the strings: "tcp", "tcp4", or "tcp6". The IP address should be set to zero if you want to listen on all network interfaces, or to the IP address of a single network interface if you only want to listen on that interface. If the port is set to zero, then the O/S will choose a port for you. Otherwise, you can choose your own. Note that on a UNIX system, you cannot listen on a port below 1024 unless you are the system supervisor, root, and ports below 128 are standardized by the IETF. The example program chooses port 1200 for no particular reason. The TCP address is given as :1200 – all interfaces, port 1200. The program is daytimeserver.go:

```
ch3$ vi daytimeserver.go

/* DaytimeServer
 */
package main

import (
        "log"
        "net"
        "time"
)

func main() {
        service := ":1200"
        tcpAddr, err := net.ResolveTCPAddr("tcp", service)
        checkError(err)
        listener, err := net.ListenTCP("tcp", tcpAddr)
        checkError(err)
        for {
                conn, err := listener.Accept()
                if err != nil {
                        continue
                }
                daytime := time.Now().String()
                conn.Write([]byte(daytime)) // don't care about return value
                conn.Close()                // we're finished with this client
        }
}
```

```go
func checkError(err error) {
        if err != nil {
                log.Fatalln("Fatal error: %s", err.Error())
        }
}
```

If you run this server, it will just wait there, not doing much. When a client connects to it, it will respond by sending the daytime string to it and then return to waiting for the next client.

```
ch3$ go run daytimeserver.go
```

Note the changed error handling in the server as compared to a client. The server should run forever so that if any error occurs with a client, the server just ignores that client and carries on. A client could otherwise try to mess up the connection with the server and bring it down!

We haven't built a client. That is easy, just changing the previous client to omit the initial write. Alternatively, just open a telnet connection to that host:

```
ch3$ telnet localhost 1200
```

This will produce output such as the following:

```
Trying ::1...
Connected to localhost.
Escape character is '^]'.
2022-01-03 18:40:16.602125 -0500 EST m=+2.486360923Connection closed by foreign host.
```

where the date is the output from the server.

Multithreaded Server

echo is another simple IETF service. The simpleechoserver.go program just reads what the client types and sends it back:

```
ch3$ vi simpleechoserver.go
```

```go
/* SimpleEchoServer
 */
package main

import (
        "fmt"
        "log"
        "net"
)

func main() {
        service := ":1201"
        tcpAddr, err := net.ResolveTCPAddr("tcp4", service)
        checkError(err)
        listener, err := net.ListenTCP("tcp", tcpAddr)
        checkError(err)
```

```go
        for {
                conn, err := listener.Accept()
                if err != nil {
                        continue
                }
                handleClient(conn)
                conn.Close() // we're finished
        }
}
func handleClient(conn net.Conn) {
        var buf [512]byte
        for {
                n, err := conn.Read(buf[0:])
                checkError(err)
                fmt.Println(string(buf[0:]))
                _, err = conn.Write(buf[0:n])
                checkError(err)
        }
}
func checkError(err error) {
        if err != nil {
                log.Fatalln("Fatal error: %s", err.Error())
        }
}
```

```
ch3$ go run simpleechoserver.go
```

But if you open two more terminals and try to telnet both to the echo service like so, the second will fail:

```
ch3$ telnet localhost 1201 # in one terminal
// type hello

ch3$ telnet localhost 1201 # in second terminal, blocked by the first telnet client
```

While it works, there is a significant issue with this server: it is single threaded (just like our daytime service). While a client has a connection open to it, no other client can fully connect. Other clients are blocked and will probably time out. Fortunately, this is easily fixed by making the client handler a goroutine. We have also moved closing the connection into the handler, as it now belongs there. The program is called threadedechoserver.go:

```
ch3$ vi threadedechoserver.go
```

```go
/* ThreadedEchoServer
 */
package main

import (
        "fmt"
        "log"
        "net"
)
```

```go
func main() {
        service := ":1201"
        tcpAddr, err := net.ResolveTCPAddr("tcp4", service)
        checkError(err)
        listener, err := net.ListenTCP("tcp", tcpAddr)
        checkError(err)
        for {
                conn, err := listener.Accept()
                if err != nil {
                        continue
                }
                // run as a goroutine
                go handleClient(conn)
        }
}
func handleClient(conn net.Conn) {
        // close connection on exit
        defer conn.Close()
        var buf [512]byte
        for {
                // read up to 512 bytes
                n, err := conn.Read(buf[0:])
                checkError(err)
                fmt.Println(string(buf[0:]))
                // write the n bytes read
                _, err = conn.Write(buf[0:n])
                checkError(err)
        }
}
func checkError(err error) {
        if err != nil {
                log.Fatal("Fatal error: %s", err.Error())
        }
}
```

This simple refactoring moves us to a much more interesting world. This book assumes knowledge of basic Go; it would still be remiss to not highlight areas to consider. After moving to a concurrent world, we should think of state management (if our applications require it), cross thread security, resource exhaustion, and more. No details are provided here, but something for your future consideration.

If you run the same scenario as the prior single-threaded version (server, two telnet clients), you will see either client can talk on demand.

Controlling TCP Connections
Timeout

The server may want to time out a client if it does not respond quickly enough; that is, it does not write a request to the server in time. This should be a long period (several minutes) because the users may be taking their time. Conversely, the client may want to time out the server (after a much shorter time). Both do this as follows:

```
func (c *IPConn) SetDeadline(t time.Time) error
```

This is done before any reads or writes on the socket.

Staying Alive

A client may want to stay connected to a server even if it has nothing to send. It can use this:

```
func (c *TCPConn) SetKeepAlive(keepalive bool) error
```

There are several other connection control methods, which are documented in the net package. To learn more about deadlines and keepalive, review the existing tests, and run them:

```
ch3$ go test -test.v -run "Timeout|KeepAlive" -count=1 $(go env GOROOT)/src/net
=== RUN    TestDialerKeepAlive
--- PASS: TestDialerKeepAlive (0.00s)
=== RUN    TestRetryTimeout
    dnsclient_unix_test.go:985: 192.0.2.1:53 {{16532 false 0 false false true false
RCodeSuccess} [{www.golang.org. TypeTXT ClassINET}] [] [] []} 2022-01-03 18:49:
09.787565 -0500 EST m=+5.003120852
    dnsclient_unix_test.go:985: 192.0.2.2:53 {{25591 false 0 false false true false
RCodeSuccess} [{www.golang.org. TypeTXT ClassINET}] [] [] []} 2022-01-03 18:49:
09.79893 -0500 EST m=+5.014486668
--- PASS: TestRetryTimeout (0.01s)
=== RUN    TestDNSTimeout
--- PASS: TestDNSTimeout (0.00s)
...

ch3$ go test -list "Timeout|KeepAlive" $(go env GOROOT)/src/net
TestDialerKeepAlive
TestRetryTimeout
TestDNSTimeout
...
```

UDP Datagrams

In a connectionless protocol, each message contains information about its origin and destination. There is no "session" established using a long-lived socket. UDP clients and servers make use of datagrams, which are individual messages containing source and destination information. There is no state maintained by these messages, unless the client or server does so. The messages are not guaranteed to arrive or may arrive out of order.

The most common situation for a client is to send a message and hope that a reply arrives. The most common situation for a server is to receive a message and then send one or more replies back to that client. In a peer-to-peer situation, though, the server may just forward messages to other peers.

The major difference between TCP and UDP handling for Go is how to deal with packets arriving from multiple clients, without the cushion of a TCP session to manage things. The major calls needed are as follows:

```
func ResolveUDPAddr(network, address string) (*UDPAddr, error)
func DialUDP(network string, laddr, raddr *UDPAddr) (*UDPConn, error)
func ListenUDP(network string, laddr *UDPAddr) (*UDPConn, error)
func (c *UDPConn) ReadFromUDP(b []byte) (n int, addr *UDPAddr, err error
func (c *UDPConn) WriteToUDP(b []byte, addr *UDPAddr) (int, error)
```

The client for a UDP time service doesn't need to make many changes; just change the ...TCP... calls to ...UDP... calls in the program udpdaytimeclient.go:

```
ch3$ vi udpdaytimeclient.go

/* UDPDaytimeClient
 */
package main

import (
        "fmt"
        "log"
        "net"
        "os"
)

func main() {
        if len(os.Args) != 2 {
                log.Fatalln("Usage: %s host:port", os.Args[0])
        }
        service := os.Args[1]
        udpAddr, err := net.ResolveUDPAddr("udp", service)
        checkError(err)
        conn, err := net.DialUDP("udp", nil, udpAddr)
        checkError(err)
        _, err = conn.Write([]byte("anything"))
        checkError(err)
        var buf [512]byte
        n, err := conn.Read(buf[0:])
        checkError(err)
        fmt.Println(string(buf[0:n]))
}
func checkError(err error) {
        if err != nil {
                log.Fatalln("Fatal error ", err.Error())
        }
}
```

The server has to make a few more changes in the program udpdaytimeserver.go:

```
ch3$ vi udpdaytimeserver.go

/* UDPDaytimeServer
 */
package main

import (
        "log"
        "net"
        "time"
)

func main() {
        service := ":1200"
        udpAddr, err := net.ResolveUDPAddr("udp", service)
        checkError(err)
        conn, err := net.ListenUDP("udp", udpAddr)
        checkError(err)
        for {
                handleClient(conn)
        }
}
func handleClient(conn *net.UDPConn) {
        var buf [512]byte
        _, addr, err := conn.ReadFromUDP(buf[0:])
        checkError(err)
        daytime := time.Now().String()
        conn.WriteToUDP([]byte(daytime), addr)
}
func checkError(err error) {
        if err != nil {
                log.Fatalln("Fatal error ", err.Error())
        }
}
```

The server is run as follows:

```
ch3$ go run udpdaytimeserver.go
```

A client on the same host is run as follows:

```
ch3$ go run udpdaytimeclient.go :1200
```

The client output will be something like this:

```
2022-01-03 18:57:00.616532 -0500 EST m=+8.044046910
```

Server Listening on Multiple Sockets

A server may be attempting to listen to multiple clients not just on one port, but on many. In this case, it has to use some sort of polling mechanism between the ports.

In C, the select() call lets the kernel do this work. The call takes a number of file descriptors. The process is suspended. When I/O is ready on one of these, a wakeup is done, and the process can continue. This is cheaper than busy polling. In Go, you can accomplish the same by using a different go routine for each port. A thread will become runnable when the lower-level select() discovers that I/O is ready for this thread.

The Conn, PacketConn, and Listener Types

So far, we have differentiated between the API for TCP and the API for UDP using, for example, DialTCP and DialUDP returning TCPConn and UDPConn, respectively. The Conn type is an interface, and both TCPConn and UDPConn implement this interface. To a large extent, you can deal with this interface rather than the two types.

Instead of separate dial functions for TCP and UDP, you can use a single function:

```
func Dial(network, address string) (Conn, error)
func DialIP(network string, laddr, raddr *IPAddr) (*IPConn, error)
```

The network can be any of tcp, tcp4 (IPv4-only), tcp6 (IPv6-only), udp, udp4 (IPv4-only), udp6 (IPv6-only), ip, ip4 (IPv4-only), and ip6 (IPv6-only) and several UNIX-specific ones such as unix for UNIX sockets. It will return an appropriate implementation of the Conn interface. Note that this function takes a string rather than address as the (r)addr argument so that programs using this can avoid working out the address type first.

Using this function makes minor changes to the programs. For example, the earlier program to get HEAD information from a web page can be rewritten as ipgetheadinfo.go:

```
ch3$ vi ipgetheadinfo.go

/* IPGetHeadInfo
 */
package main

import (
        "bytes"
        "fmt"
        "io"
        "log"
        "net"
        "os"
)

func main() {
        if len(os.Args) != 2 {
                log.Fatalln("Usage: %s host:port", os.Args[0])
        }
        service := os.Args[1]
        conn, err := net.Dial("tcp", service)
```

```
        checkError(err)
        _, err = conn.Write([]byte("HEAD / HTTP/1.0\r\n\r\n"))
        checkError(err)
        result, err := readFully(conn)
        checkError(err)
        fmt.Println(string(result))
}
func readFully(conn net.Conn) ([]byte, error) {
        defer conn.Close()
        result := bytes.NewBuffer(nil)
        var buf [512]byte
        for {
                n, err := conn.Read(buf[0:])
                result.Write(buf[0:n])
                if err != nil {
                        if err == io.EOF {
                                break
                        }
                        return nil, err
                }
        }
        return result.Bytes(), nil
}
func checkError(err error) {
        if err != nil {
                log.Fatalln("Fatal error: %s", err.Error())
        }
}
```

This can be run on my own machine as follows:

```
ch3$ go run ipgetheadinfo.go yahoo.com:80 # can't use go.dev as its on 443 w/TLS
```

It prints the following about the server running on port 80:

```
HTTP/1.0 200 OK
Date: Tue, 04 Jan 2022 00:02:13 GMT
Server: ATS
Cache-Control: no-store, no-cache, max-age=0, private
Content-Type: text/html
Content-Language: en
Expires: -1
X-Frame-Options: SAMEORIGIN
Content-Length: 12
```

Writing a server can be similarly simplified using this function:

```
func Listen(network, address string) (Listener, error)
```

This returns an object implementing the Listener interface. This interface has a method Accept:

```
type Listener interface {
        // Accept waits for and returns the next connection to the listener.
        Accept() (Conn, error)

        // Close closes the listener.
        // Any blocked Accept operations will be unblocked and return errors.
        Close() error

        // Addr returns the listener's network address.
        Addr() Addr
}
```

This will allow a server to be built. Using this, the multithreaded Echo server given earlier becomes threadedipechoserver.go:

```
ch3$ vi threadedipechoserver.go

/* ThreadedIPEchoServer
 */
package main

import (
        "log"
        "net"
)

func main() {
        service := ":1200"
        listener, err := net.Listen("tcp", service)
        checkError(err)
        for {
                conn, err := listener.Accept()
                if err != nil {
                        continue
                }
                go handleClient(conn)
        }
}
func handleClient(conn net.Conn) {
        defer conn.Close()
        var buf [512]byte
        for {
                n, err := conn.Read(buf[0:])
                checkError(err)

                _, err = conn.Write(buf[0:n])
                checkError(err)
        }
}
```

```
func checkError(err error) {
        if err != nil {
                log.Fatalln("Fatal error: %s", err.Error())
        }
}
```

If you want to write a UDP server, there is an interface called PacketConn and a method to return an implementation of this:

```
func ListenPacket(network, address string) (PacketConn, error)
```

This interface has the primary methods ReadFrom and WriteTo that handle packet reads and writes.

The Go net package recommends using these interface types rather than the concrete ones. But by using them, you lose specific methods such as SetKeepAlive of TCPConn and SetReadBuffer of UDPConn, unless you do a type cast. It is your choice.

Raw Sockets and the IPConn Type

This section covers advanced material that most programmers are unlikely to need. It deals with *raw sockets*, which allow programmers to build their own IP protocols or use protocols other than TCP or UDP.

TCP and UDP are not the only protocols built above the IP layer. The website (http://www.iana.org/assignments/protocol-numbers) lists about 140 of them (this list is often available on UNIX systems in the file /etc/protocols). TCP and UDP are only numbers 6 and 17, respectively, on this list.

Go allows you to build so-called raw sockets, to enable you to communicate using one of these other protocols, or even to build your own. But it gives minimal support: it will connect hosts and write and read packets between the hosts. In a later chapter, we look at designing and implementing your own protocols above TCP; this section considers the same type of problem, but at the IP layer.

To keep things simple, we use almost the simplest possible example: how to send an IPv4 ping message to a host. Ping uses the echo command from the ICMP protocol. This is a byte-oriented protocol, in which the client sends a stream of bytes to another host and the host replies. The format of the ICMP packet payload is as follows:

- The first byte is 8, standing for the echo message.

- The second byte is zero.

- The third and fourth bytes are a checksum on the entire message.

- The fifth and sixth bytes are an arbitrary identifier.

- The seventh and eight bytes are an arbitrary sequence number.

- The rest of the packet is user data.

The packet can be sent using the Conn.Write method, which prepares the packet with this payload. The replies received include the IPv4 header, which takes 20 bytes. (See, e.g., the Wikipedia article on the Internet Control Message Protocol, ICMP.)

The following program called ping.go will prepare an IP connection, send a ping request to a host, and get a reply. You may need root access in order to run it successfully:

```go
ch3$ vi ping.go

/* Ping
 */
package main

import (
        "fmt"
        "log"
        "net"
        "os"
)

// change this to your own IP address or leave set to 0.0.0.0
const myIPAddress = "0.0.0.0"
const ipv4HeaderSize = 20

func main() {
        if len(os.Args) != 2 {
                log.Fatalln("Usage: ", os.Args[0], "host")
        }
        localAddr, err := net.ResolveIPAddr("ip4", myIPAddress)
        checkError(err)

        remoteAddr, err := net.ResolveIPAddr("ip4", os.Args[1])
        checkError(err)

        conn, err := net.DialIP("ip4:icmp", localAddr, remoteAddr)
        checkError(err)

        var msg [512]byte
        msg[0] = 8  // echo
        msg[1] = 0  // code 0
        msg[2] = 0  // checksum, fix later
        msg[3] = 0  // checksum, fix later
        msg[4] = 0  // identifier[0]
        msg[5] = 13 // identifier[1] (arbitrary)
        msg[6] = 0  // sequence[0]
        msg[7] = 37 // sequence[1] (arbitrary)
        len := 8

        // now fix checksum bytes
        check := checkSum(msg[0:len])
        msg[2] = byte(check >> 8)
        msg[3] = byte(check & 255)

        // send the message
        _, err = conn.Write(msg[0:len])
```

```go
            checkError(err)
            fmt.Print("Message sent:    ")
            for n := 0; n < 8; n++ {
                    fmt.Print(" ", msg[n])
            }
            fmt.Println()

            // receive a reply
            size, err2 := conn.Read(msg[0:])
            checkError(err2)
            fmt.Print("Message received:")
            for n := ipv4HeaderSize; n < size; n++ {
                    fmt.Print(" ", msg[n])
            }
            fmt.Println()
}
func checkSum(msg []byte) uint16 {
            sum := 0
            // assume even for now
            for n := 0; n < len(msg); n += 2 {
                    sum += int(msg[n])*256 + int(msg[n+1])
            }
            sum = (sum >> 16) + (sum & 0xffff)
            sum += (sum >> 16)
            var answer uint16 = uint16(^sum)
            return answer
}
func checkError(err error) {
            if err != nil {
                    log.Fatalln("Fatal error: %s", err.Error())
            }
}
```

It is run using the destination address as an argument. The received message should differ from the sent message in only the first type byte and the third and fourth checksum bytes, as follows:

```
ch3$ sudo env "PATH=$PATH" go run ping.go google.com

Message sent:     8 0 247 205 0 13 0 37
Message received: 0 0 255 205 0 13 0 37
```

Notice we are using "sudo" (on Linux) since being root is required to use ICMP, as set in DialIP.

Conclusion

This chapter considered programming at the IP, TCP, and UDP levels. This is often necessary if you want to implement your own protocol or build a client or server for an existing protocol.

CHAPTER 4

■ ■ ■

Data Serialization

A client and a server need to exchange information via messages. TCP and UDP provide the transport mechanisms to do this. The two processes also need to have a protocol in place so that message exchange can take place meaningfully.

Messages are sent across the network as a sequence of bytes, which has no structure except as a linear stream of bytes. We address the various possibilities for messages and the protocols that define them in the next chapter. In this chapter, we concentrate on a component of messages – the data that is transferred.

A program will typically build complex data structures to hold the current program state. In conversing with a remote client or service, the program will be attempting to transfer such data structures across the network – that is, outside of the application's own address space.

Structured Data

Programming languages use structured data such as the following:

- Records/structures: A collection of fields of possibly different data types where the type is fixed, also known as a composition.

- Variant records: A record that contains a value potentially of differing types.

- Array: Fixed size or varying, also known as an aggregation.

- String: Fixed size or varying.

- Tables: Arrays of records; in data storage terms, a record is a row.

- Nonlinear structures such as

  - Circular linked lists

  - Binary trees

  - Objects with references to other objects

For our purpose, a composition is a data structure where nested elements do not exist without the parent. In aggregation, the stored/nested elements can potentially exist on their own.

None of the IP, TCP, or UDP packets know the meaning of any of these data types. All that they (packets) can contain is a sequence of bytes. Thus, an application has to *serialize* any data into a stream of bytes in order to write it and *deserialize* the stream of bytes back into suitable data structures on reading it. These two operations are known as *marshalling* and *unmarshalling,* respectively.[1]

For example, consider sending the following variable length table of two columns of variable length strings:

fred	programmer
liping	analyst
sureerat	manager

This could be done in various ways. For example, suppose that it is known that the data will be an unknown number of rows in a two-column table. Then a marshalled form could be

```
3                   // 3 rows, 2 columns (assumed from above table)
4 fred              // 4 char string, col 1
10 programmer       // 10 char string, col 2
6 liping            // 6 char string, col 1
7 analyst           // 7 char string, col 2
8 sureerat          // 8 char string, col 1
7 manager           // 7 char string, col 2
```

Variable length things can alternatively have their length indicated by terminating them with an "illegal" value, such as \0 for strings. The previous table could also be written with the number of rows again, but each string terminated by \0 (the newlines are for readability, not part of the serialization):

```
3
fred\0
programmer\0
liping\0
analyst\0
sureerat\0
manager\0
```

Alternatively, it may be known that the data is a three-row fixed table of two columns of strings of length 8 and 10, respectively. Then a serialization of the table could be (again, the newlines are not part of the serialization)

```
fred\0\0\0\0
programmer
liping\0\0
analyst\0\0\0
sureerat
manager\0\0\0
```

Any of these formats (and others) is okay, but the message exchange protocol must specify which one is used or allow it to be determined at runtime.

---

[1] I'm treating serialization and marshalling as synonymous. There are a variety of opinions on this, some more language specific than others. See, search for example, "What is the difference between Serialization and Marshaling?" on Stack Overflow or Google.

Mutual Agreement

The previous section gave an overview of the issue of data serialization. In practice, the details can be considerably more complex. For example, consider the first possibility, marshalling a table into the byte stream:

```
3
4 fred
10 programmer
6 liping
7 analyst
8 sureerat
7 manager
```

Many questions arise. For example, how many rows are possible for the table – that is, how big an integer do we need to describe the row size? If it is 255 or less, then a single byte will do, but if it is more, then a short, integer, or long may be needed. A similar problem occurs for the length of each string. With the characters themselves, to which character set do they belong? 7-bit ASCII? 16-bit Unicode? The question of character sets is discussed at length in a later chapter.

This serialization is *opaque* or *implicit*. If data is marshalled using this format, then there is nothing in the serialized data to say how it should be unmarshalled. The unmarshalling side has to know exactly how the data is serialized in order to unmarshal it correctly. For example, if the number of rows is marshalled as an 8-bit integer but unmarshalled as a 16-bit integer, then an incorrect result will occur as the receiver tries to unmarshal 3 and 4 as a 16-bit integer, and the receiving program will almost certainly fail later.

An early well-known serialization method is XDR (external data representation) used by Sun's RPC, later known as ONC (Open Network Computing). XDR is defined by RFC 1832, and it is instructive to see how precise this specification is. Even so, XDR is inherently type unsafe as serialized data contains no type information. The correctness of its use in ONC is ensured primarily by compilers generating code for both marshalling and unmarshalling.

Go contains no explicit support for marshalling or unmarshalling opaque serialized data. The RPC package in Go does not use XDR but instead uses *Gob* serialization (also part of Go), described later in this chapter.

Self-Describing Data

Self-describing data carries type information along with the data. For example, the previous data might get encoded as follows:

```
table
    uint8 3
    uint 2
string
    uint8 4
    []byte fred
string
    uint8 10
    []byte programmer
string
    uint8 6
    []byte liping
```

```
string
    uint8 7
    []byte analyst
string
    uint8 8
    []byte sureerat
string
    uint8 7
    []byte manager
```

Of course, a real encoding would not normally be as cumbersome and verbose as in the example: Small integers would be used as type markers, and the whole data would be packed in as small a byte array as possible (XML provides a counterexample, though). However, the principle is that the marshaller will generate such type information in the serialized data. The unmarshaller will know the type-generation rules and will be able to use them to reconstruct the correct data structure.

Encoding Packages

As mentioned earlier, there is more than one way to encode/decode data. Go provides high level interfaces in the "encoding" package. Additionally, Go includes several specialized packages for well-known data formats including JSON and XML in subpackages. Take a moment to review the "encoding" package documentation; we will cross these and related interfaces throughout this chapter.

```
$ mkdir ch4
$ cd ch4
ch4$ go doc -all encoding

package encoding // import "encoding"

Package encoding defines interfaces shared by other packages that convert
data to and from byte-level and textual representations. Packages that check
for these interfaces include encoding/gob, encoding/json, and encoding/xml.
As a result, implementing an interface once can make a type useful in
multiple encodings. Standard types that implement these interfaces include
time.Time and net.IP. The interfaces come in pairs that produce and consume
encoded data.

TYPES

type BinaryMarshaler interface {
        MarshalBinary() (data []byte, err error)
}
    BinaryMarshaler is the interface implemented by an object that can marshal
    itself into a binary form.

    MarshalBinary encodes the receiver into a binary form and returns the
    result.

type BinaryUnmarshaler interface {
        UnmarshalBinary(data []byte) error
}
```

BinaryUnmarshaler is the interface implemented by an object that can unmarshal a binary representation of itself.

UnmarshalBinary must be able to decode the form generated by MarshalBinary. UnmarshalBinary must copy the data if it wishes to retain the data after returning.

```
type TextMarshaler interface {
        MarshalText() (text []byte, err error)
}
```

TextMarshaler is the interface implemented by an object that can marshal itself into a textual form.

MarshalText encodes the receiver into UTF-8-encoded text and returns the result.

```
type TextUnmarshaler interface {
        UnmarshalText(text []byte) error
}
```

TextUnmarshaler is the interface implemented by an object that can unmarshal a textual representation of itself.

UnmarshalText must be able to decode the form generated by MarshalText. UnmarshalText must copy the text if it wishes to retain the text after returning.

As mentioned in the above documentation, we can confirm the usage of these interfaces by reviewing the mentioned samples.

```
ch4$ go doc net.IP.MarshalText

package net // import "net"

func (ip IP) MarshalText() ([]byte, error)
    MarshalText implements the encoding.TextMarshaler interface. The encoding is
    the same as returned by String, with one exception: When len(ip) is zero, it
    returns an empty slice.
```

You can do the same to read about the UnmarshalText implementation. Unlike net.IP, time.Time does use the binary marshaller interface. "go doc" provides an easy and powerful way to learn how Go's network related interfaces are defined and consumed.

You can list the available encoding packages as follows:

```
ch4$ go list encoding/...

encoding
encoding/ascii85
encoding/asn1
encoding/base32
encoding/base64
encoding/binary
encoding/csv
```

```
encoding/gob
encoding/hex
encoding/json
encoding/pem
encoding/xml
```

ASN.1

Abstract Syntax Notation One (ASN.1) was originally designed in 1984 for the telecommunications industry. ASN.1 is a complex standard, and a subset of it is supported by Go in the package asn1. It builds self-describing serialized data from complex data structures. Its primary use in current networking systems is as the encoding for X.509 certificates, which are heavily used in authentication systems. The support in Go is based on what is needed to read and write X.509 certificates.

Structured data in ASN has similar purpose but differing names; for example, a struct is called a "SET" in ASN, a "SEQUENCE OF" is an array, and a "CHOICE" is like a variant. ASN has sets encoding rules that provide various levels of complexity vs. performance (i.e., size), including

- Basic Encoding Rules (BER)

- Distinguished Encoding Rules (DER)

- Basic XML Encoding Rules (XER)

- And others

ASN.1 support in Go is based on what is needed to read and write X.509 certificates. X.509 uses the DER encoding rules, which in turn are a subset of BER.[2] A value can often be encoded in more than one way with BER, where in DER, it can only have a single encoding. DER offers less chances of misencoding a value, a feature good for security.

The documentation not only highlights the interface used but also includes links to learn more about the encoding.

```
ch4$ go doc encoding/asn1

package asn1 // import "encoding/asn1"

Package asn1 implements parsing of DER-encoded ASN.1 data structures, as
defined in ITU-T Rec X.690.

See also "A Layman's Guide to a Subset of ASN.1, BER, and DER,"
http://luca.ntop.org/Teaching/Appunti/asn1.html.

const TagBoolean = 1 ...
const ClassUniversal = 0 ...
var NullBytes = []byte{ ... }
var NullRawValue = RawValue{ ... }
func Marshal(val interface{}) ([]byte, error)
func MarshalWithParams(val interface{}, params string) ([]byte, error)
func Unmarshal(b []byte, val interface{}) (rest []byte, err error)
func UnmarshalWithParams(b []byte, val interface{}, params string) (rest []byte, err error)
```

---

[2] You can review the ASN.1 encoding rules for BEF, CER, and DER in document X.690-202102 –
https://www.itu.int/rec/T-REC-X.690-202102-I/en

```
type BitString struct{ ... }
type Enumerated int
type Flag bool
type ObjectIdentifier []int
type RawContent []byte
type RawValue struct{ ... }
type StructuralError struct{ ... }
type SyntaxError struct{ ... }
```

As with other encoding packages, there are functions that allow us to marshal and unmarshal data:

```
func Marshal(val interface{}) ([]byte, error)
func Unmarshal(b []byte, val interface{}) (rest []byte, err error)
```

The Marshal function converts a data value into a serialized byte array, and the Unmarshal function converts a byte array back into a local variable. The second argument of Unmarshal function deserves further examination. Given a variable of any type, we can marshal it by just passing its value to Marshal. To unmarshal it, we need a variable of a named type that will match the serialized data. The precise details of this are discussed later. But we also need to make sure that the variable is allocated to memory for that type so that there is actually existing memory for the unmarshalling to write values into.

We illustrate with an almost trivial example in asn1.go of marshalling and unmarshalling an integer. We can pass an integer value to marshal to return a byte array and unmarshal the array into an integer variable, as in this program in file asn1.go:

```
ch4$ vi asn1.go

/* ASN1 example
*/
package main

import (
        "encoding/asn1"
        "fmt"
)

func thirteen() {
        val := 13
        mdata, _ := asn1.Marshal(val)
        var n int
        asn1.Unmarshal(mdata, &n)
        fmt.Printf("Before marshal: %v, After unmarshal: %v\n", val, n)
}
func main() {
        thirteen()
}
```

Execute the program as follows:

```
ch4$ go run asn1.go

Before marshal: 13, After unmarshal: 13
```

As expected, the marshalled to unmarshalled cycle results in 13.

Once we move beyond this, things get harder. In order to manage more complex data types, we have to look more closely at the data structures supported by ASN.1 and how ASN.1 support is done in Go.

Any serialization method will be able to handle certain data types and not handle some others. So in order to determine the suitability of any serialization such as ASN.1, you have to look at the possible data types supported vs. those you want to use in your application. The following ASN.1 types are taken from `http://www.obj-sys.com/asn1tutorial/node4.html`.

The simple types are as follows:

- `BOOLEAN`: Two-state variable values

- `INTEGER`: Models integer variable values

- `BIT STRING`: Models binary data of arbitrary length

- `OCTET STRING`: Models binary data whose length is a multiple of eight

- `NULL`: Indicates effective absence of a sequence element

- `OBJECT IDENTIFIER`: Names information objects

- `REAL`: Models real variable values

- `ENUMERATED`: Models values of variables with at least three states

- `CHARACTER STRING`: Models values that are strings of characters from a specified character set

Character strings can be from certain character sets:

- `NumericString`: 0,1,2,3,4,5,6,7,8,9, and space.

- `PrintableString`: Upper- and lowercase letters, digits, space, apostrophe, left/right parenthesis, plus sign, comma, hyphen, full stop, solidus, colon, equal sign, and question mark.

- `TeletexString (T61String)`: The Teletex character set in CCITT's T61, space, and delete.

- `VideotexString`: The Videotex character set in CCITT's T.100 and T.101, space, and delete.

- `VisibleString (ISO646String)`: Printing character sets of international ASCII and space.

- `IA5String`: International Alphabet 5 (International ASCII).

- `GraphicString 25`: All registered G sets and space `GraphicString`.

- There are additional string types as well as these, notably `UTF8String`.

And finally, there are the structured types:

- `SEQUENCE`: Models an ordered collection of variables of different types

- `SEQUENCE OF`: Models an ordered collection of variables of the same type

- `SET`: Models an unordered collection of variables of different types

- `SET OF`: Models an unordered collection of variables of the same type

- `CHOICE`: Specifies a collection of distinct types from which to choose one type

- SELECTION: Selects a component type from a specified CHOICE type

- ANY: Enables an application to specify the type

■ **Note**   ANY is a deprecated ASN.1 Structured Type. It has been replaced with X.680 Open Type.

Not all of these are supported by Go. Not all possible values are supported by Go. The rules, as given by "go doc encoding/asn1.Unmarshal", are as follows:

- An ASN.1 INTEGER can be written to an int, int32, int64, or *big.Int (from the math/big package). If the encoded value does not fit in the Go type, Unmarshal returns a parse error.

- An ASN.1 BIT STRING can be written to a BitString.

- An ASN.1 OCTET STRING can be written to a []byte.

- An ASN.1 OBJECT IDENTIFIER can be written to an ObjectIdentifier.

- An ASN.1 ENUMERATED can be written to an Enumerated.

- An ASN.1 UTCTIME or GENERALIZEDTIME can be written to a time.Time.

- An ASN.1 PrintableString, IA5String, or NumericString can be written to a string.

- Any of the preceding ASN.1 values can be written to an interface{}. The value stored in the interface has the corresponding Go type. For integers, that type is int64.

- An ASN.1 SEQUENCE OF x or SET OF x can be written to a slice if an x can be written to the slice's element type.

- An ASN.1 SEQUENCE or SET can be written to a struct if each of the elements in the sequence can be written to the corresponding element in the struct.

Go places real restrictions on ASN.1. For example, ASN.1 allows integers of any size (per ASN.1 – "Type INTEGER takes any of the infinite set of integer values"), while the Go implementation will only allow up to limit of big.Int (which is larger than int64 but not infinite). On the other hand, Go distinguishes between signed and unsigned types, while ASN.1 doesn't. So, for example, transmitting a value of uint64 may fail if it is too large for int64.

In a similar vein, ASN.1 allows several different character sets, while the Go package states that it supports PrintableString, IA5String (ASCII), NumericString, and utf8.

We have seen that a value such as an integer can be easily marshalled and unmarshalled. Other basic types such as booleans and reals can be similarly dealt with. Strings composed entirely of ASCII characters or UTF8 characters can be marshalled and unmarshalled. This code works as long as the string is composed only of ASCII or UTF8 characters:

```go
func ascii() {
        s := "hello"
        mdata, _ := asn1.Marshal(s)
        var newstr string
        _,_ =asn1.Unmarshal(mdata, &newstr)
        fmt.Printf("Before marshal: %v, After unmarshal%v\n", s, newstr)
}
```

Update asn1.go to include the preceding function, and call it from main.

```
ch4$ vi asn1.go

... prior code ...

func ascii() {
        s := "hello"
        mdata, _ := asn1.Marshal(s)
        var newstr string
        _,_ =asn1.Unmarshal(mdata, &newstr)
        fmt.Printf("Before marshal: %v, After unmarshal: %v\n", s, newstr)
}

func main() {
        thirteen()
        ascii() // call new function
}

ch4$ go run asn1.go

Before marshal: 13, After unmarshal: 13
Before marshal: hello, After unmarshal: hello
```

ASN.1 also includes some "useful types" not in this list, such as UTC time. Go supports this UTC time type. This means that you can pass time values in a way that is not possible for other data values. ASN.1 does not support pointers, but Go has special code to manage pointers to time values. The function Now() returns time.Time. The special code marshals this, and it can be unmarshalled into a pointer variable to a time.Time object. Add the following code to asn1.go and trigger from main:

```
ch4$ vi asn1.go

... prior code ...

func myTime() {
        t := time.Now()
        mdata, _ := asn1.Marshal(t)
        var newtime = new(time.Time)
        _, _ = asn1.Unmarshal(mdata, newtime)
        fmt.Printf("Before marshal: %v, After unmarshal: %v\n", t, newtime)
}

func main() {
        thirteen()
        ascii()
        myTime() // call new function
}

ch4$ go run asn1.go
```

```
Before marshal: 13, After unmarshal: 13
Before marshal: hello, After unmarshal: hello
Before marshal: 2022-01-03 21:02:19.134959 -0500 EST m=+0.000178450, After unmarshal:
2022-01-03 21:02:19 -0500 EST
```

In general, value types are preferred over pointers. One reason to use pointers (i.e., *time.Time or new(time.Time)) is serialization may not ignore zero values when using tags (like the json package).

Here, we show a time value restored to time pointer; Go looks after this special case. Additionally, we see a string with a Unicode sequence. The program asn1basic.go illustrates these:

```
ch4$ vi asn1basic.go

/* ASN.1 Basic
 */

package main

import (
        "encoding/asn1"
        "fmt"
        "time"
)

func main() {
        // time pointer to time value
        t := time.Now()
        fmt.Println("Before marshalling: ", t.String())
        mdata, _ := asn1.Marshal(t)
        var newtime = new(time.Time)
        asn1.Unmarshal(mdata, newtime)
        fmt.Println("After marshal/unmarshal: ", newtime.String())

        // vulgar fraction, string to string
        s := "hello \u00bc"
        fmt.Println("Before marshalling: ", s)
        mdata2, _ := asn1.Marshal(s)
        var newstr string
        asn1.Unmarshal(mdata2, &newstr)
        fmt.Println("After marshal/unmarshal: ", newstr)
}
```

When it runs as follows:

```
ch4$ go run asn1basic.go

Before marshalling:  2022-01-03 21:02:50.268961 -0500 EST m=+0.000121092
After marshal/unmarshal:  2022-01-03 21:02:50 -0500 EST
Before marshalling:  hello ¼
After marshal/unmarshal:  hello ¼
```

Review go doc time.Time; the first couple of paragraphs mention considerations when using time. Time and pointers.

In general, you will probably want to marshal and unmarshal structures. Apart from the special case of time, Go will happily deal with structures, but not with pointers to structures. Operations such as new create pointers, so you have to dereference them before marshalling/unmarshalling them. Go normally dereferences pointers for you when needed, but not in this case, so you have to dereference them explicitly. These both work for a type T, create asn1pointers.go:

```
ch4$ vi asn1pointers.go

package main

import (
        "encoding/asn1"
        "fmt"
)

type T struct {
        S string
        I int
}

func main() {
        // using variables
        t1 := T{"ok", 1}
        mdata1, _ := asn1.Marshal(t1)
        var newT1 T
        asn1.Unmarshal(mdata1, &newT1)
        fmt.Printf("Before marshal: %v, after unmarshal: %v\n", t1, newT1)

        // using pointers
        var t2 = new(T)
        t2.S = "still ok"
        t2.I = 2
        mdata2, _ := asn1.Marshal(*t2)
        var newT2 = new(T)
        asn1.Unmarshal(mdata2, newT2)
        fmt.Printf("Before marshal: %v, after unmarshal: %v\n", t2, newT2)
}

ch4$ go run asn1pointers.go

Before marshal: {ok 1}, after unmarshal: {ok 1}
Before marshal: &{still ok 2}, after unmarshal: &{still ok 2}
```

Any suitable mix of pointers and variables will work as well.

The fields of a structure must all be exportable, that is, field names must begin with an uppercase letter. Go uses the reflect package to marshal/unmarshal structures, so it must be able to examine all fields. This type cannot be marshalled:

```
type T struct {
    Field1 int
    field2 int // not exportable
}
```

Both Marshal and Unmarshal produce related errors for the prior condition. We next create an example showing this condition; first, create driver.go.

```
ch4$ vi driver.go

/* driver.go
 */
package main

import (
        "encoding/asn1"
        "fmt"
        "badtype"
)

func main() {
        // using variables
        t1 := p.T{F:1}
        mdata1, err := asn1.Marshal(t1)
        fmt.Println(err)
        var newT1 p.T
        _, err = asn1.Unmarshal(mdata1, &newT1)
        fmt.Println(err)
}
```

Next, we create our malformed struct in a package called badtype; create the badtype directory and the file mytype.go.

```
ch4$ mkdir badtype
ch4$ vi ./badtype/mytype.go

/* ./badtype/mytype.go
 */
package p

type T struct {
        f int
        F int
}

ch4$ cd badtype
badtype$ go mod init badtype
badtype$ cd ..
```

If you run the preceding code as follows, you will see the related errors:

```
ch4$ go mod init example.com
ch4$ go mod edit -replace badtype=$(pwd)/badtype
ch4$ go mod tidy
```

```
ch4$ go run driver.go

asn1: structure error: struct contains unexported fields
asn1: syntax error: sequence truncated
```

While we are using the command line, most IDEs will handle dependencies (e.g., replace) for you.

Next, we show some (in)flexibility of ASN coding. ASN.1 only deals with the data's types. It does not consider the data's names (i.e., the structure field names). So the following type T1 can be marshalled/unmarshalled into type T2 as the corresponding fields are the same types.

Not only must the types of each field match, but the number must match as well. Here, we demo both types of errors:

* asn1.SyntaxError – missing fields

* asn1.StructuralError – incorrect type

Place the following code in asn1fields.go; notice the structs and how they differ.

```
ch4$ vi asn1fields.go

package main

import (
        "encoding/asn1"
        "fmt"
        "log"
)

type MyType struct {
        F1 rune
        F2 int
}

type YourType struct {
        F3 rune
}

type TheirType struct {
        F4 byte
}

func main() {
        // this first example works
        t1 := MyType{'▢', 1}
        mdata1, _ := asn1.Marshal(t1)

        t2 := new(YourType)
        _, err := asn1.Unmarshal(mdata1, t2)
        fmt.Printf("Before marshal: %v, after unmarshal: %v\n", t1, t2)
        checkError(err)

        // syntax error (fails to fill all fields)
        y := YourType{'▢'}
```

```
        mdata2, _ := asn1.Marshal(y)
        z := new(MyType)
        _, err = asn1.Unmarshal(mdata2, z)
        fmt.Printf("Before marshal: %v, after unmarshal: %v\n", y, z)
        checkError(err)

        // structural error (incorrect Go type byte != rune)
        t3 := new(TheirType)
        _, err = asn1.Unmarshal(mdata1, t3)
        fmt.Printf("Before marshal: %v, after unmarshal: %v\n", t1, t3)
        checkError(err)
}

func checkError(err error) {
        if err != nil {
                log.Println(err.Error()) // prevent early termination
        }
}
```

As we run, take note of the outcome and associated errors.

```
ch4$ go run asn1fields.go

Before marshal: {12525 1}, after unmarshal: &{12525}
Before marshal: {12525}, after unmarshal: &{12525 0}
2022/03/29 21:33:20 asn1: syntax error: sequence truncated
Before marshal: {12525 1}, after unmarshal: &{0}
2022/03/29 21:33:20 asn1: structure error: unknown Go type: uint8
```

Review the related error documentation to confirm.

```
ch4$ go doc asn1.SyntaxError

package asn1 // import "encoding/asn1"

type SyntaxError struct {
    Msg string
}
    A SyntaxError suggests that the ASN.1 data is invalid.

func (e SyntaxError) Error() string

ch4$ go doc asn1.StructuralError

package asn1 // import "encoding/asn1"

type StructuralError struct {
    Msg string
}
    A StructuralError suggests that the ASN.1 data is valid, but the Go type
    which is receiving it doesn't match.

func (e StructuralError) Error() string
```

ASN.1 illustrates many of the choices that can be made by those implementing a serialization method. Pointers could have been given special treatment by using more code, such as the enforcement of name matches. The order and number of strings will depend on the details of the serialization specification, the flexibility it allows, and the coding effort needed to exploit that flexibility. It is worth noting that other serialization formats will make different choices, and implementations in different languages will also enforce different rules.

ASN.1 Daytime Client and Server

Now (finally) let's turn to using ASN.1 to transport data across the network.

We can write a TCP server that delivers the current time as an ASN.1 Time type using the techniques of the last chapter.

```
ch4$ vi asndaytimeserver.go

/* ASN1 DaytimeServer
 */
package main

import (
        "encoding/asn1"
        "log"
        "net"
        "time"
)

func main() {
        service := ":1200"
        tcpAddr, err := net.ResolveTCPAddr("tcp", service)
        checkError(err)
        listener, err := net.ListenTCP("tcp", tcpAddr)
        checkError(err)
        for {
                conn, err := listener.Accept()
                if err != nil {
                        continue
                }
                daytime := time.Now()
                // ignore returned errors
                mdata, _ := asn1.Marshal(daytime)
                conn.Write(mdata)
                conn.Close() // we're finished
        }
}

func checkError(err error) {
        if err != nil {
                log.Fatalln("Fatal error: %s", err.Error())
        }
}
```

This can be compiled to an executable such as ASN1DaytimeServer and run with no arguments. It will wait for connections and then send the time as an ASN.1 string to the client.

Store our client in asndaytimeclient.go:

```
ch4$ vi asndaytimeclient.go

/* ASN.1 DaytimeClient
 */
package main

import (
        "bytes"
        "encoding/asn1"
        "fmt"
        "io"
        "log"
        "net"
        "os"
        "time"
)

func main() {
        if len(os.Args) != 2 {
                log.Fatalln("Usage: %s host:port", os.Args[0])
        }
        service := os.Args[1]
        conn, err := net.Dial("tcp", service)
        checkError(err)
        result, err := readFully(conn)
        checkError(err)
        var newtime time.Time
        _, err1 := asn1.Unmarshal(result, &newtime)
        checkError(err1)
        fmt.Println("After marshal/unmarshal: ", newtime.String())
}

func readFully(conn net.Conn) ([]byte, error) {
        defer conn.Close()
        result := bytes.NewBuffer(nil)
        var buf [512]byte
        for {
                n, err := conn.Read(buf[0:])
                result.Write(buf[0:n])
                if err != nil {
                        if err == io.EOF {
                                break
                        }
                        return nil, err
                }
        }
        return result.Bytes(), nil
}
```

```
func checkError(err error) {
        if err != nil {
                log.Fatalln("Fatal error: %s", err.Error())
        }
}
```

In one terminal, run the server.

```
ch4$ go run asndaytimeserver.go
```

In a second terminal, run the client.

```
ch4$ go run asndaytimeclient.go localhost:1200
```

```
After marshal/unmarshal:  2022-01-03 21:11:32 -0500 EST
```

This connects to the service given in a form such as localhost:1200, reads the TCP packet, and decodes the ASN.1 content back into a string, which it prints.

Note that neither of these two – the client or the server – is compatible with the text-based clients and servers of the last chapter. This client and server are exchanging ASN.1 encoded data values, not textual strings.

JSON

JSON[3] stands for JavaScript Object Notation. It was designed to be a lightweight means of passing data between JavaScript systems (i.e., browser/web server). It uses a text-based format and is sufficiently general that it has become used as a general-purpose serialization method for many programming languages.

JSON serializes objects, arrays, and basic values. The basic values include string, number, boolean values, and the null value. Arrays are a comma-separated list of values that can represent arrays, vectors, lists, or sequences of various programming languages. They are delimited by square brackets [...]. Objects are represented by a list of "field: value" pairs enclosed in curly braces { ... }.

For example, the table of employees given earlier could be written as an array of employee objects:

```
[
   {"Name": "fred", "Occupation": "programmer"},
   {"Name": "liping", "Occupation": "analyst"},
   {"Name": "sureerat", "Occupation": "manager"}
]
```

There is no special support for complex data types such as dates, no distinction between number types, no recursive types, etc. JSON is a very simple format but nevertheless can be quite useful. Its text-based format makes it easy to use and debug, even though it has the overheads of string handling. Go's implementation is based on https://www.rfc-editor.org/rfc/rfc7159.html.

From the Go encoding/json package documentation, marshalling uses the following type-dependent default encodings:

- Boolean values encode as JSON Booleans.

- Floating point, integer, and Number values encode as JSON numbers.

---

[3] "Introducing JSON" (https://www.json.org/json-en.html) and RFC 7159 (https://www.rfc-editor.org/rfc/rfc7159.html)

- String values encode as JSON strings coerced to valid UTF-8, where each invalid UTF-8 sequence is replaced by the encoding of the Unicode replacement character U+FFFD (potentially rendered as ◆).

  - Disable HTML tag encoding via SetEscapeHTML(false).

- Array and slice values encode as JSON arrays, except that []byte encodes as a base64-encoded string.

- Struct values encode as JSON objects. Each struct field becomes a member of the object. By default, the object's key name is the struct field name converted to lowercase.

  - If the struct field has a tag, that tag will be used as the name instead.

- Map values encode as JSON objects. The map's key type must be string; the object keys are used directly as map keys.

- Pointer values encode as the value pointed to. (Note: This allows trees but not graphs!). A nil pointer encodes as the null JSON object.

- Interface values encode as the value contained in the interface. A nil interface value encodes as the null JSON object.

- Channel, complex, and function values cannot be encoded in JSON. Attempting to encode such a value causes Marshal to return json.UnsupportedTypeError.

- JSON cannot represent cyclic data structures, and Marshal does not handle them. Passing cyclic structures to Marshal will result in an infinite recursion.

A program to store JSON serialized data into the file person.json is savejson.go:

```
ch4$ vi savejson.go

/* SaveJSON
 */
package main

import (
        "encoding/json"
        "log"
        "os"
)

type Person struct {
        Name    Name
        Email []Email
}

type Name struct {
        Family    string
        Personal string
}

type Email struct {
        Kind      string
```

```
        Address string
}

func main() {
        person := Person{
                Name: Name{Family: "Newmarch", Personal: "Jan"},
                Email: []Email{
                        Email{Kind: "home", Address: "jan@newmarch.name"},
                        Email{Kind: "work", Address: "j.newmarch@boxhill.edu.au"},
                },
        }
        saveJSON("person.json", person)
}

func saveJSON(fileName string, key interface{}) {
        data, err := json.Marshal(key)
        checkError(err)
        err = os.WriteFile(fileName, data, 0600)
        checkError(err)
}

func checkError(err error) {
        if err != nil {
                log.Fatalln("Fatal error ", err.Error())
        }
}
```

After running the preceding program, we can view the serialized results.

```
ch4$ go run savejson.go

ch4$ cat person.json

{"Name":{"Family":"Newmarch","Personal":"Jan"},"Email":[{"Kind":"home","Address":"jan@
newmarch.name"},{"Kind":"work","Address":"j.newmarch@boxhill.edu.au"}]}
```

Here, we used the "cat" utility to view.
To load it back into memory, use loadjson.go:

```
ch4$ vi loadjson.go

/* LoadJSON
 */
package main

import (
        "encoding/json"
        "fmt"
        "log"
        "os"
)
```

```go
type Person struct {
        Name    Name
        Email []Email
}

type Name struct {
        Family   string
        Personal string
}

type Email struct {
        Kind     string
        Address string
}

func main() {
        var person Person
        loadJSON("person.json", &person)
        fmt.Printf("%v\n", person)
}

func loadJSON(fileName string, key interface{}) {

        data, err := os.ReadFile(fileName)
        checkError(err)
        err = json.Unmarshal(data, key)
        checkError(err)
}

func checkError(err error) {
        if err != nil {
                log.Fatalln("Fatal error ", err.Error())
        }
}
```

Running our loader, the serialized form is

```
ch4$ go run loadjson.go

{{Newmarch Jan} [{home jan@newmarch.name} {work j.newmarch@boxhill.edu.au}]}
```

The output is the rendering of a Go struct, not pure JSON. The json package provides a related function to pretty print. If you wish to pretty print, copy savejson.go to prettyjson.go and modify saveJSON as follows:

```
ch4$ vi prettyjson.go

...

func main() {
        person := Person{
                Name: Name{Family: "Newmarch", Personal: "Jan"},
                Email: []Email{
```

```
                          Email{Kind: "home", Address: "jan@newmarch.name"},
                          Email{Kind: "work", Address: "j.newmarch@boxhill.edu.au"},
                },
                }
        saveJSON("pretty_person.json", person)
}
func saveJSON(fileName string, key interface{}) {
        data, err := json.MarshalIndent(key, "   ", "    ")
        checkError(err)
        err = os.WriteFile(fileName, data, 0600)
        checkError(err)
}
...
```

If we run the preceding code, our output is much prettier.

```
ch4$ go run prettyjson.go

ch4$ cat pretty_person.json
{
    "Name": {
        "Family": "Newmarch",
        "Personal": "Jan"
    },
    "Email": [
        {
            "Kind": "home",
            "Address": "jan@newmarch.name"
        },
        {
            "Kind": "work",
            "Address": "j.newmarch@boxhill.edu.au"
        }
    ]
  }
```

If you update loadjson.go to read this file (pretty_json.json), you will see it is still valid JSON.

A Client and A Server

We now send JSON for a round trip. A client to send a person's data and read it back ten times is jsonechoclient.go:

```
ch4$ vi jsonechoclient.go

/* JSON EchoClient
 */
package main

import (
        "bytes"
```

```go
        "encoding/json"
        "fmt"
        "io"
        "log"
        "net"
        "os"
)

type Person struct {
        Name    Name
        Email   []Email
}

type Name struct {
        Family   string
        Personal string
}

type Email struct {
        Kind    string
        Address string
}

func main() {
        if len(os.Args) != 2 {
                log.Fatalln("Usage: ", os.Args[0], "host:port")
        }
        person := Person{
                Name: Name{Family: "Newmarch", Personal: "Jan"},
                Email: []Email{
                        Email{Kind: "home", Address: "jan@newmarch.name"},
                        Email{Kind: "work", Address: "j.newmarch@boxhill.edu.au"},
                },
        }
        service := os.Args[1]
        conn, err := net.Dial("tcp", service)
        checkError(err)
        defer conn.Close()
        for n := 0; n < 10; n++ {
                data, _ := json.Marshal(person)
                conn.Write(data)

                var newPerson Person
                buf, _ := readFully(conn)
                err = json.Unmarshal(buf, &newPerson)
                fmt.Println(newPerson)
        }
}

func readFully(conn net.Conn) ([]byte, error) {
        result := bytes.NewBuffer(nil)
        var buf [512]byte
        for {
```

```
                n, err := conn.Read(buf[0:])
                result.Write(buf[0:n])

                if err != nil {
                        if err == io.EOF {
                                break
                        }
                        return nil, err
                }
                if n < 512 {
                        break
                }
        }
        return result.Bytes(), nil
}

func checkError(err error) {
        if err != nil {
                log.Fatalln("Fatal error ", err.Error())
        }
}
```

The corresponding server is jsonechoserver.go:

```
ch4$ vi jsonechoserver.go
/* JSON EchoServer
 */
package main

import (
        "bytes"
        "encoding/json"
        "fmt"
        "io"
        "net"
        "log"
)

type Person struct {
        Name   Name
        Email  []Email
}

type Name struct {
        Family   string
        Personal string
}

type Email struct {
        Kind    string
        Address string
}
```

```go
func main() {
        service := "0.0.0.0:1200"
        tcpAddr, err := net.ResolveTCPAddr("tcp", service)
        checkError(err)
        listener, err := net.ListenTCP("tcp", tcpAddr)
        checkError(err)
        for {
                conn, err := listener.Accept()
                if err != nil {
                        continue
                }
                for n := 0; n < 10; n++ {
                        var person Person
                        buf, _ := readFully(conn)
                        err = json.Unmarshal(buf, &person)

                        fmt.Println(person)

                        data, _ := json.Marshal(person)
                        conn.Write(data)
                }
                conn.Close() // we're finished
        }
}

func readFully(conn net.Conn) ([]byte, error) {
        result := bytes.NewBuffer(nil)
        var buf [512]byte
        for {
                n, err := conn.Read(buf[0:])
                result.Write(buf[0:n])

                if err != nil {
                        if err == io.EOF {
                                break
                        }
                        return nil, err
                }
                if n < 512 {
                        break
                }
        }
        return result.Bytes(), nil
}

func checkError(err error) {
        if err != nil {
                log.Fatalln("Fatal error ", err.Error())
        }
}
```

In one terminal, we run the server:

```
ch4$ go run jsonechoserver.go
<waits for connections>
```

In a second terminal, we run the client:

```
ch4$ go run jsonechoclient.go localhost:1200
{{Newmarch Jan} [{home jan@newmarch.name} {work j.newmarch@boxhill.edu.au}]}
... (8 more duplicated lines) ...
{{Newmarch Jan} [{home jan@newmarch.name} {work j.newmarch@boxhill.edu.au}]}
```

Here is what is happening:

- On the server, the inner loop creates a new Person, waiting for a serialized instance.

- On the client, a single instance of Person is created:

    - Enter a loop that does the following:

        - Serializes and sends Person to server

        - Creates a new Person and waits for server

    - Back on server:

        - The data is consumed and deserialized, populating a new Person instance.

        - Printed.

        - The Person is again serialized and sent back.

This process repeats ten times until the client loop finishes, while the server remains waiting with outer loop.

There is more to consider when parsing JSON. Go even provides additional APIs including one to tokenize a JSON stream. We cover JSON in more detail in later sections.

The Gob Package

Gob is a serialization technique specific to Go. It is designed to encode Go data types specifically and does not at present have substantial support for or by any other languages. It supports all Go data types except for channels, functions, and interfaces. It supports integers of all types and sizes, strings and Booleans, structs, arrays, and slices. At present, it has some problems with circular structures such as rings, but that will improve over time. The purpose was to allow pure Go client and servers to work together without the need of a third-party package.

Gob encodes type information into its serialized forms. This is far more extensive than the type information in, say, an X.509 serialization but far more efficient than the type information contained in an XML document. Type information is only included once for each piece of data but includes, for example, the names of struct fields.

This inclusion of type information makes Gob marshalling and unmarshalling fairly robust to changes or differences between the marshaller and unmarshaller. For example, this struct

```
struct T {
    a int
    b int
}
```

Can be marshalled and then unmarshalled into a different struct, where the order of fields has changed:

```
struct T {
    b int
    a int
}
```

It can also cope with missing fields (the values are ignored) or extra fields (the fields are left unchanged). It can cope with pointer types so that the previous struct could be unmarshalled into this one:

```
struct T {
    *a int
    **b int
}
```

To some extent, it can cope with type coercions so that an int field can be broadened/widened into an int64, but not incompatible types such as int to uint.

To use Gob to marshal a data value, you first need to create an Encoder. This takes an io.Writer as a parameter, and marshalling will be done to this writable stream. The encoder has a method called Encode, which marshals the value to the stream. This method can be called multiple times on multiple pieces of data. Type information for each data type is only written once, though.

You use a Decoder to unmarshal the serialized data stream. This takes an io.Reader, and each read returns an unmarshalled data value.

A program to store Gob serialized data into the file person.gob is savegob.go:

```
ch4$ vi savegob.go

/* SaveGob
 */
package main

import (
        "encoding/gob"
        "os"
        "log"
)

type Person struct {
        Name   Name
        Email []Email
}

type Name struct {
        Family   string
        Personal string
}

type Email struct {
        Kind    string
        Address string
}
```

```go
func main() {
        person := Person{
                Name: Name{Family: "Newmarch", Personal: "Jan"},
                Email: []Email{
                        Email{Kind: "home", Address: "jan@newmarch.name"},
                        Email{Kind: "work", Address: "j.newmarch@boxhill.edu.au"},
                },
        }
        saveGob("person.gob", person)
}

func saveGob(fileName string, key interface{}) {
        outFile, err := os.Create(fileName)
        checkError(err)
        encoder := gob.NewEncoder(outFile)
        err = encoder.Encode(key)
        checkError(err)
        outFile.Close()
}

func checkError(err error) {
        if err != nil {
                log.Fatalln("Fatal error ", err.Error())
        }
}
```

By running our savegob.go code, we see a serialized version of our Person stored in person.gob on disk.

```
ch4$ go run savegob.go

ch4$ cat -t person.gob
```

```
)?M-^A^C^A^A^FPerson^A?M-^B^@^A^B^A^DName^A?M-^D^@^A^EEmail^A?M-^H^@^@^@*?M-
^C^C^A^A^DName^A?M-^D^@^A^B^A^FFamily^A^L^@^A^HPersonal^A^L^@^@^@^[?M-^G^B^A^A^L[]main.
Email^A?M-^H^@^A?M-^F^@^@(?M-^E^C^A^A^EEmail^A?M-^F^@^A^B^A^DKind^A^L^@^A^GAddress^A^L^@^@
^@R?M-^B^A^A^HNewmarch^A^CJan^@^A^B^A^Dhome^A^Qjan@newmarch.name^@^A^Dwork^A^Yj.newmarch@
boxhill.edu.au^@^@%
```

In the aforementioned, we used the "cat" command-line tool to show our Gob serialized output. Better tools exist, including "xxd" to "dump" and review, but are lesser known.

To load it back into memory, use loadgob.go:

```
ch4$ vi loadgob.go
```

```go
/* LoadGob
 */
package main
```

```go
import (
        "encoding/gob"
        "fmt"
        "log"
        "os"
)

type Person struct {
        Name   Name
        Email []Email
}

type Name struct {
        Family   string
        Personal string
}

type Email struct {
        Kind    string
        Address string
}

func main() {
        var person Person
        loadGob("person.gob", &person)
        fmt.Println(person)
}

func loadGob(fileName string, key interface{}) {
        inFile, err := os.Open(fileName)
        checkError(err)
        decoder := gob.NewDecoder(inFile)
        err = decoder.Decode(key)
        checkError(err)
        inFile.Close()
}

func checkError(err error) {
        if err != nil {
                log.Fatalln("Fatal error ", err.Error())
        }
}
```

Running loadgob.go shows the deserialized Person from person.gob.

ch4$ go run loadgob.go

{{Newmarch Jan} [{home jan@newmarch.name} {work j.newmarch@boxhill.edu.au}]}

A Client and A Server

Next, we place our Gob serialization on the network. A client to send a person's data and read it back ten times is gobechoclient.go:

```
ch4$ vi gobechoclient.go

/* Gob EchoClient
 */
package main

import (
        "encoding/gob"
        "log"
        "net"
        "os"
)

type Person struct {
        Name   Name
        Email []Email
}

type Name struct {
        Family   string
        Personal string
}

type Email struct {
        Kind    string
        Address string
}

func main() {
        if len(os.Args) != 2 {
                log.Fatalln("Usage: ", os.Args[0], "host:port")
        }
        person := Person{
                Name: Name{Family: "Newmarch", Personal: "Jan"},
                Email: []Email{
                        Email{Kind: "home", Address: "jan@newmarch.name"},
                        Email{Kind: "work", Address: "j.newmarch@boxhill.edu.au"},
                },
        }
        service := os.Args[1]
        conn, err := net.Dial("tcp", service)
        checkError(err)
        encoder := gob.NewEncoder(conn)
        decoder := gob.NewDecoder(conn)
        for n := 0; n < 10; n++ {
                encoder.Encode(person)
```

```
                var newPerson Person
                decoder.Decode(&newPerson)

        }
}

func checkError(err error) {
        if err != nil {
                log.Fatalln("Fatal error ", err.Error())
        }
}
```

The corresponding server is gobechoserver.go:

```
ch4$ vi gobechoserver.go

/* Gob EchoServer
 */
package main

import (
        "encoding/gob"
        "fmt"
        "log"
        "net"
)

type Person struct {
        Name   Name
        Email []Email
}

type Name struct {
        Family   string
        Personal string
}
type Email struct {
        Kind    string
        Address string
}

func main() {
        service := "0.0.0.0:1200"
        tcpAddr, err := net.ResolveTCPAddr("tcp", service)
        checkError(err)
        listener, err := net.ListenTCP("tcp", tcpAddr)
        checkError(err)
        for {
                conn, err := listener.Accept()
                if err != nil {
                        continue
                }
```

```
                encoder := gob.NewEncoder(conn)
                decoder := gob.NewDecoder(conn)
                for n := 0; n < 10; n++ {
                        var person Person
                        decoder.Decode(&person)
                        fmt.Println(person)
                        encoder.Encode(person)
                }
                conn.Close() // we're finished
        }
}

func checkError(err error) {
        if err != nil {
                log.Fatalln("Fatal error ", err.Error())
        }
}
```

Similar to our JSON example, we serialize data back and forth, starting from the client to the server. Launch the server in one terminal.

```
ch4$ go run gobechoserver.go

<waits for client connection>
```

Launch the client in the second terminal.

```
ch4$ go run gobechoclient.go localhost:1200

{{Newmarch Jan} [{home jan@newmarch.name} {work j.newmarch@boxhill.edu.au}]}

... (8 more duplicate lines) ...

{{Newmarch Jan} [{home jan@newmarch.name} {work j.newmarch@boxhill.edu.au}]}
```

Like the json package, the Gob package provides an interface (i.e., GobEncoder) allowing you to customize the Gob serialization process.

Many serialization libraries exist (e.g., json package). Why have gob? In Rob Pike's blog post, "Gobs of data",[4] the gob package presented an opportunity to have a Go specific library, one that in theory has less complications and more optimizations for Go-only use cases compared to other serialization libraries.

Encoding Binary Data As Strings

Once upon a time, transmitting 8-bit data was problematic. It was often transmitted over noisy serial lines and could easily become corrupted. Seven-bit data, on the other hand, could be transmitted more reliably because the 8th bit could be used as check digit. For example, in an "even parity" scheme, the check digit would be set to one or zero to make an even number of 1s in a byte. This allows detection of errors of a single bit in each byte.

---

[4] Gobs of data – https://go.dev/blog/gob

ASCII is a 7-bit character set. A number of schemes have been developed that are more sophisticated than simple parity checking but which involve translating 8-bit binary data into a 7-bit ASCII format. Essentially, the 8-bit data is stretched out in some way over the 7-bit bytes.

Binary data transmitted in HTTP responses and requests is often translated into an ASCII form. This makes it easy to inspect the HTTP messages with a simple text reader without worrying about what strange 8-bit bytes might do to your display!

One common format is Base64 (go doc base64). Go has support for many binary-to-text formats, including Base64, via the encoding/base64 package. This package is based on the RFC "The Base16, Base32, and Base64 Data Encodings."[5]

There are two principal functions to use for Base64 encoding and decoding:

```
ch4$ go doc encoding/base64 NewEncoder

package base64 // import "encoding/base64"

func NewEncoder(enc *Encoding, w io.Writer) io.WriteCloser
    NewEncoder returns a new base64 stream encoder. Data written to the returned
    writer will be encoded using enc and then written to w. Base64 encodings
    operate in 4-byte blocks; when finished writing, the caller must Close the
    returned encoder to flush any partially written blocks.

ch4$ go doc encoding/base64 NewDecoder

package base64 // import "encoding/base64"

func NewDecoder(enc *Encoding, r io.Reader) io.Reader
    NewDecoder constructs a new base64 stream decoder.
```

A simple program just to encode and decode a set of eight binary digits is base64.go:

```
ch4$ vi base64.go

/*
  Base64
*/
package main

import (
        "encoding/base64"
        "fmt"
)

func main() {
        eightBitData := []byte{1, 2, 3, 4, 5, 6, 7, 8}
        enc := base64.StdEncoding.EncodeToString(eightBitData)
        dec, _ := base64.StdEncoding.DecodeString(enc)
        fmt.Println("Original data ", eightBitData)
        fmt.Println("Encoded string ", enc)
```

---

[5] The Base16, Base32, and Base64 Data Encodings – https://datatracker.ietf.org/doc/html/rfc4648

```
            fmt.Println("Decoded data ", dec)
}

ch4$ go run base64.go

Original data  [1 2 3 4 5 6 7 8]
Encoded string  AQIDBAUGBwg=
Decoded data  [1 2 3 4 5 6 7 8]
```

The = character is used as an optional padding. Base64 encoding is a gold standard in data encoding. Variants of Base64 include Base58 (used by Bitcoin). Base64 encoding/decoding is used by Go's built-in http networking code; see "GOROOT/src/net/http/client.go" for an example.

The preceding example shows a typical usage of the base64 interface. The next example shows using the aforementioned builders NewDecoder and NewEncoder. Things to consider when using these functions (for any encoding/decoding) include how much memory is used and which interface your code expects, like an io.Reader.

Save the following as newbase64coders.go.

```
ch4$ vi newbase64coders.go

package main

import (
        "bytes"
        "encoding/base64"
        "fmt"
        "io"
)

var (
        enc    *base64.Encoding = base64.StdEncoding.WithPadding('|')
        input []byte           = []byte("∞a∞\x02ab")
        w      bytes.Buffer
)

func restoreViaDecoder() {
        var buf *bytes.Buffer = bytes.NewBuffer(w.Bytes())
        var ior io.Reader = base64.NewDecoder(enc, buf)
        l := len(input)

        // adjust for unknown padding
        if l > 3 && l%3 != 0 {
                l = l + 2
        }

        restored := make([]byte, l)
        ior.Read(restored)
        fmt.Printf("%11s: %s %v\n", "viaDecoder", string(restored), restored)
}

func restoreViaEncoding() {
        var dst []byte = make([]byte, len(input))
```

```
        enc.Decode(dst, w.Bytes())
        fmt.Printf("%11s: %s %v\n", "viaEncoding", string(dst), dst)
}

func main() {
        fmt.Printf("%11s: %s %v\n", "input", string(input), input)

        var wc io.WriteCloser = base64.NewEncoder(enc, &w)

        wc.Write(input)
        wc.Close()

        fmt.Printf("%11s: %s %v\n", "ecoded", string(w.Bytes()), w.Bytes())

        restoreViaDecoder()
        restoreViaEncoding()
}
```

The code uses the same encoder but decodes in two styles; again choose which based on your needs.

```
ch4$ go run newbase64coders.go
      input: ∞a∞ab [226 136 158 97 226 136 158 2 97 98]
    encoded: 4oieYeKIngJhYg|| [52 111 105 101 89 101 75 73 110 103 74 104 89 103 124 124]
  viaDecoder: ∞a∞ab [226 136 158 97 226 136 158 2 97 98 0 0]
viaEncoding: ∞a∞ab [226 136 158 97 226 136 158 2 97 98]
```

Protocol Buffers

The serialization methods considered so far fall into various types:

- ASN.1 encodes the different types using binary tags in the data. In that sense, an ASN.1 encoded data structure is a self-describing structure.

- JSON similarly is a self-describing format using the rules of JavaScript data structures: lists, dictionaries, etc.

- Gob similarly encodes type information into its encoded form. This is far more detailed than the JSON format.

A separate class of serialization techniques rely on an external specification of the data type to be encoded. There are several major ones, such as the encoding used by ONC RPC.

ONC RPC is an old encoding, targeted toward the C language. A recent one is from Google, known as *protocol buffers*. This is not supported in the Go Standard Libraries but is supported by the Google Protocol Buffers developer group (https://developers.google.com/protocol-buffers/) and is apparently very popular within Google. For that reason, we include a section on protocol buffers, although in the rest of the book, we typically deal with the Go Standard Libraries.

Protocol buffers are a binary encoding of data intended to support the data types of a large variety of languages. They rely on an external specification of a data structure, which is used to encode data (in a source language) and also to decode the encoded data back into a target language. (Note: Protocol buffers transitioned to version 3 in July 2016. It is not compatible with version 2. Version 2 will be supported for a long time but will eventually be obsoleted. See Protocol Buffers v3.0.0 at (`https://github.com/google/protobuf/releases/tag/v3.0.0`).

The data structure to be serialized is known as a *message*. The data types supported in each message include

- Numbers (integers or floats)

- Booleans

- Strings (in UTF-8)

- Raw bytes

- Maps

- Other messages, allowing complex data structures to be built

The fields of a message are all optional (this is a change from proto2 where fields were required or optional). A field can stand for a list or array by the keyword repeated or a map using the keyword map. Each field has a type, followed by a name, followed by a tag index value. The full language guide is called the "Protocol Buffers Language Guide" (see `https://developers.google.com/protocol-buffers/docs/proto`).

Messages are defined independent of the possible target language. A version of the Person type in the syntax of Protocol Buffers version 3 is personv3.proto. Note that the file includes specific tags (1, 2) on each type.

```
ch4$ vi personv3.proto

syntax = "proto3";

option go_package = "/protos";

package person;

message Person {
        message Name {
                string family = 1;
                string personal = 2;
        }
        message Email {
                string kind = 1;
                string address = 2;
        }
        Name   name = 1;
        repeated Email email = 2;
}
```

Installing and Compiling Protocol Buffers

Protocol buffers are compiled using a program called protoc. This is unlikely to be installed on your system.

Install the latest version from the Protocol Buffers v3 page. For 64-bit Linux, for example, download protoc-3.19.4-linux-x86_64.zip (or later) from GitHub and unzip it to a suitable place (it includes the binary bin/protoc, which should be placed somewhere in your PATH). You can find the compiler here: https://github.com/protocolbuffers/protobuf/releases/latest.

After, install the "protoc" binary. You also need the "back end" to generate Go files. To do this, fetch it from GitHub:

```
ch4$ go install google.golang.org/protobuf/cmd/protoc-gen-go@latest
```

This will install protoc-gen-go into $GOPATH/bin, so make sure your path is set up to use it. Each language has a specific "back end" that works with protoc. Other tools can ease the installation like a package manager.

You are nearly ready to compile a .proto file. The previous example of personv3.proto declares the package person. In your GOPATH, you should have a directory called src. Create a subdirectory called src/person.

Then compile the personv3.proto as follows:

```
ch4$ mkdir myapp
ch4$ protoc --go_out=./myapp ./personv3.proto
```

This should create the ./myapp/protos/personv3.pb.go file.

The Generated personv3.pb.go File

The compiled file will declare a number of types and methods on these types. The types are as follows:

```
type Person struct {
        ...

        Name    *Person_Name       `protobuf:"bytes,1,opt,name=name,proto3"
json:"name,omitempty"`
        Email []*Person_Email `protobuf:"bytes,2,rep,name=email,proto3"
json:"email,omitempty"`
}

type Person_Name struct {
        ...

        Family    string `protobuf:"bytes,1,opt,name=family,proto3" json:"family,omitempty"`
        Personal string `protobuf:"bytes,2,opt,name=personal,proto3"
json:"personal,omitempty"`
}

type Person_Email struct {
        ...
```

```
    Kind    string `protobuf:"bytes,1,opt,name=kind,proto3" json:"kind,omitempty"`
    Address string `protobuf:"bytes,2,opt,name=address,proto3" json:"address,omitempty"`
}
```

They are in the package called person. (Note: Simple types such as strings are encoded directly. In Protocol Buffers v2, a pointer was used. For compound types, a pointer is required, as in v2.)

Using the Generated Code

There is essentially no difference between the coding used in the JSON example and this one. A simple program just to marshal and unmarshal a Person follows. We create an app called protocolbuffer.go. This app will be in a module, which in turn houses the generated protobuf package.

```
ch4$ cd myapp
ch4/myapp$
```

Create the following file: protocolbuffer.go.

```
ch4/myapp$ vi protocolbuffer.go

/* ProtocolBuffer
 */

package main

import (
    "myapp/protos"

    "google.golang.org/protobuf/proto"

    "fmt"
)

func main() {
    name := protos.Person_Name{
        Family:   "newmarch",
        Personal: "jan",
    }
    email1 := protos.Person_Email{
        Kind:    "home",
        Address: "jan@newmarch.name",
    }
    email2 := protos.Person_Email{
        Kind:    "work",
        Address: "j.newmarch@boxhill.edu.au",
    }
    emails := []*protos.Person_Email{&email1, &email2}
    p := protos.Person{
        Name:  &name,
        Email: emails,
    }
```

```
fmt.Println(p)

data, _ := proto.Marshal(&p)

newP := protos.Person{}

proto.Unmarshal(data, &newP)

fmt.Printf("%v\n", newP)

if p.Name.Personal == newP.Name.Personal && p.Email[0].Address == newP.Email[0].
Address {
    fmt.Println("same")
}
}
```

With the generated code inside of ./myapp/protos/personv3.pb.go and the above main application protocolbuffer.go, we can retrieve the remaining dependencies using Go modules. In the myapp directory, create the following go.mod:

```
ch4/myapp$ go mod init myapp

ch4/myapp$ go mod edit -replace myapp=./protos
ch4/myapp$ go mod tidy
```

The output should be a Person before and after marshalling and should be the same by running the following:

```
ch4/myapp$ go run protocolbuffer.go
```

```
{{{} [] [] <nil>} 0 [] family:"newmarch"  personal:"jan" [kind:"home"  address:"jan@
newmarch.name" kind:"work"  address:"j.newmarch@boxhill.edu.au"]}
{{{} [] [] 0xc00012a000} 0 [] family:"newmarch"  personal:"jan" [kind:"home"  address:"jan@
newmarch.name" kind:"work"  address:"j.newmarch@boxhill.edu.au"]}
same
```

While not pretty to look at, the content is the same. The comparison at the end is a warning that you can't simply compare two structs. Here, we simply compared a couple of fields. Pretty printing is available, for example, via protojson: https://pkg.go.dev/google.golang.org/protobuf/encoding/protojson.

We haven't done much with the marshalled object. However, it could be saved to a file or sent across the network and unmarshalled by any of the supported languages: C++, C#, Java, Python, as well as Go.

Conclusion

This chapter discussed the general properties of serializing data types and showed a number of common encodings. There are many more, including XML (included in the Go libraries), CBOR (a binary form of JSON), and YAML (similar to XML), as well as many language-specific ones such as Java Object Serialization and Python's Pickle. Those not in the Go standard packages may often be found on GitHub.

CHAPTER 5

Application-Level Protocols

A client and a server need to exchange information via messages. TCP and UDP provide the transport mechanisms to do this. The two processes also need to have a protocol in place so that message exchange can take place meaningfully. A protocol defines what type of conversation can take place between two components of a distributed application by specifying messages and data types, encoding formats, and so on. This chapter looks at some of the issues involved in this process and gives a complete example of a simple client-server application.

Protocol Design

There are many possibilities and issues to be decided on when designing a protocol. Some of the issues include the following:

- Is it to be broadcast or point to point? Broadcast can be UDP, local multicast, or the more experimental MBONE. Point to point could be either TCP or UDP. In general, at the IP level, often, we consider the following topologies; unicast, multicast, broadcast, and anycast.

- Is it to be stateful or stateless? Is it reasonable for one side to maintain state about the other side? It is often simpler for one side to maintain state about the other, but what happens if something crashes?

- Is the transport protocol reliable or unreliable? Reliable is often slower, but then you don't have to worry so much about lost messages. For example, decisions around reliability have influenced HTTP's evolution.

- Are replies needed? If a reply is needed, how do you handle a lost reply? Timeouts may be used. RPC functions that return void are an example of this.

- What data format do you want? Several possibilities were discussed in the last chapter.

- Is your communication bursty or steady stream? Ethernet and the Internet are best at bursty traffic. Steady stream is needed for video streams and particularly for voice. If required, how do you manage Quality of Service (QoS)?

- Are there multiple streams with synchronization required? Does the data need to be synchronized with anything, such as video and voice?

- Are you building a stand-alone application or a library to be used by others? The standards of documentation required might vary.

© Jan Newmarch and Ronald Petty 2022
J. Newmarch and R. Petty, *Network Programming with Go Language*,
https://doi.org/10.1007/978-1-4842-8095-9_5

Why Should You Worry?

Jeff Bezos, the CEO of Amazon, reportedly made the following statements in 2002:

- All teams will henceforth expose their data and functionality through service interfaces.

- Teams must communicate with each other through these interfaces.

- There will be no other form of interprocess communication allowed: no direct linking, no direct reads of another team's data store, no shared-memory model, no backdoors whatsoever. The only communication allowed is via service interface calls over the network.

- It doesn't matter what technology they use. HTTP, Corba, Pubsub, custom protocols – it doesn't matter. Bezos doesn't care.

- All service interfaces, without exception, must be designed from the ground up to be externalizable. That is to say, the team must plan and design to be able to expose the interface to developers on the outside world. No exceptions.

- Anyone who doesn't do this will be fired.

(Source: Repost of Steve Yegge's posting at `https://gist.github.com/chitchcock/1281611`)

What Bezos was doing was orienting one of the world's most successful Internet companies around service architectures, and interfaces must be clear enough that *all* communication must be through those interfaces alone – without confusion or errors.

Version Control

A protocol used in a client-server system will evolve over time, changing as the system expands. This raises compatibility problems: A version 2 client will make requests that a version 1 server doesn't understand, whereas a version 2 server will send replies that a version 1 client won't understand.

Each side should ideally be able to understand messages from its own version and all earlier ones. It should be able to write replies to old-style queries in old-style response formats. See Figure 5-1.

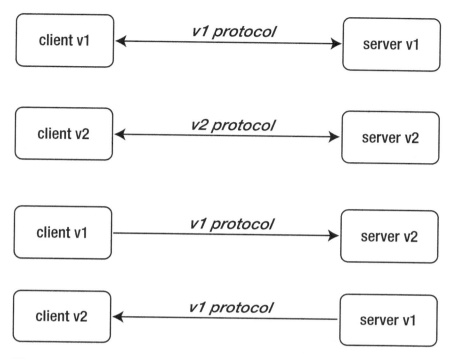

Figure 5-1. *Compatibility vs. version control*

The ability to talk earlier version formats may be lost if the protocol changes too much. In this case, you need to be able to ensure that no copies of the earlier version still exist, which is generally impossible.

Preferences can change with experience regarding versioning. For example, Protocol buffers dropped the *required* syntax from the v3 release to favor simplicity.[1]

Part of the protocol setup often involves version information. Versioning a protocol (or API) is a mechanism that lets clients and servers agree on a set of endpoints, requests, and responses (or messages). Overt versioning maybe clear but often can limit interaction between components as the protocol changes. Alternatives exist including versionless APIs (sometimes called open APIs), where the goal is to maintain backward and forward compatibility. Protocols such as HTTP have evolved in their use (and not so much in their design) in these regards. Recently, GraphQL and similar tools show promise in the versionless space. One final point, versionless, doesn't mean there is no versioning at all; it just implies there is more compatibility over the various releases of a protocol.

The Web

The Web is a good example of a system that has been through multiple different versions. The underlying HTTP protocol manages version control in an excellent manner, even though it has been through multiple versions. Most servers/browsers support the HTTP/3 version but also support the earlier versions. Version HTTP/2 appears to account for just over 60% of web traffic in 2021, HTTP/3 (QUIC) is around 5%, and HTTP/1.1 accounts for almost all the rest. We can see one type of change over the HTTP versions pertaining to the GET requests:

---

[1] "why messge type remove 'required,optional'?" – https://github.com/protocolbuffers/protobuf/issues/2497

Request	Version
GET /	Pre 1.0
GET / HTTP/1.0	HTTP 1.0
GET / HTTP/1.1	HTTP 1.1
GET / HTTP/1.1 Connection: Upgrade, HTTP2-Settings Upgrade: h2c	HTTP 2
QUIC version 1Alt-Svc: h3=":50123"	HTTP 3

HTTP/2 is a binary format and is not compatible with earlier versions. Nevertheless, there is a negotiation mechanism of sending an HTTP/1.1 request with upgrade fields to HTTP/2. If the client accepts it, the upgrade can be made. If the client doesn't understand the upgrade parameters, the connection continues with HTTP/1.1.

HTTP/3 is also a binary format, one that replaces the TCP transport with UDP. Additional improvements include secure by default. While not 100% finished, HTTP/3 is in the final stages of becoming the new HTTP standard.[2]

While originally designed for HTML, HTTP can carry any content. If we just look at HTML, this has been through a large number of versions with, at times, little attempt to ensure compatibility between versions:

- HTML5, which has abandoned any version signaling between dot revisions.

- HTML versions 1–4 (all different), with versions in the "browser wars" particularly problematic.

- Nonstandard tags recognized by different browsers.

- Non-HTML documents often require content handlers that may not be present. Does your browser have a handler for Flash?

- Inconsistent treatment of document content (e.g., some stylesheet content will crash some browsers).

- Different support for JavaScript (and different versions of JavaScript).

- Different runtime engines for Java.

- Many pages do not conform to *any* HTML versions (e.g., with syntax errors).

HTML5 (and indeed many earlier versions) is an excellent example of how *not* to do version control. The latest revision at the time of writing is Revision 5. "In this version, new features are introduced to help web application authors, new elements are introduced based on research into prevailing authoring practices,…." Not only are some new features added, but some older ones (which should not be in much use anymore) have also been removed and no longer work. There is no means for an HTML5 document to signal which revision it uses. For more on this topic, check out the "HTML – Living Standard" (https://html.spec.whatwg.org/).

---

[2] "Last Call: <draft-ietf-quic-transport-32.txt> (QUIC: A UDP-Based Multiplexed and Secure Transport) to Proposed Standard" – https://mailarchive.ietf.org/arch/msg/quic/ye1LeRl7oEz898RxjE6D3koWhnO/

Message Format

In the last chapter, we discussed some possibilities for representing data to be sent across the wire. Now we look one level up, to the messages that may contain such data.

- The client and server will exchange messages with different meanings:
  - Login request.
  - Login reply.
  - Get record request.
  - Record data reply.
- The client will prepare a request, which must be understood by the server.
- The server will prepare a reply, which must be understood by the client.

Commonly, the first part of the message will be a message type.

- Client to server:

```
LOGIN <name> <passwd>
GET <subject> grade
```

- Server to client:

```
LOGIN succeeded
GRADE <subject> <grade>
```

The message types can be strings or integers. For example, HTTP uses integers such as 404 to mean "not found" (although these integers are written as strings). The messages from client to server and vice versa are disjoint. The LOGIN message from the client to the server is a different message than the LOGIN message from the server to the client, and they will probably play complementary roles in the protocol.

Data Format

There are two main format choices for messages: byte encoded or character encoded.

Byte Format

In the byte format:

- The first part of the message is typically a byte to distinguish between message types.
- The message handler examines this first byte to distinguish the message type and then performs a switch to select the appropriate handler for that type.
- Further bytes in the message contain message content according to a predefined format (as discussed in the previous chapter).

The advantages are compactness and hence speed. The disadvantages are caused by the opaqueness of the data: it may be harder to spot errors, harder to debug, and require special purpose decoding functions. There are many examples of byte-encoded formats, including major protocols such as DNS and NFS, up to recent ones such as Skype. Of course, if your protocol is not publicly specified, then a byte format can also make it harder for others to reverse-engineer it!

Pseudocode for a byte-format server is as follows:

```
handleClient(conn) {
    while (true) {
        byte b = conn.readByte()
        switch (b) {
            case MSG_1: ...
            case MSG_2: ...
            ...
        }
    }
}
```

Go net package has basic support for managing byte streams. The interface net.Conn includes the following methods among others:

```
Read(b []byte) (n int, err error)
Write(b []byte) (n int, err error)
```

These methods are implemented by net.TCPConn and net.UDPConn.

Character Format

In this mode, everything is sent as characters if possible. For example, an integer 234 would be sent as, say, the three characters 2, 3, and 4 instead of as the one byte 234. Data that is inherently binary may be Base64 encoded to change it into a 7-bit format and then sent as ASCII characters, as discussed in the previous chapter.

In character format:

- A message is a sequence of one or more lines. The start of the first line of the message is typically a word that represents the message type.

- String-handling functions may be used to decode the message type and data.

- The rest of the first line and successive lines contain the data.

- Line-oriented functions and line-oriented conventions are used to manage this.

The pseudocode is as follows:

```
handleClient() {
    line = conn.readLine()
    if (line.startsWith(...) {
        ...
    } else if (line.startsWith(...) {
        ...
    }
}
```

Character formats are easier to set up and easier to debug. For example, you can use telnet to connect to a server on any port and send client requests to that server. There isn't a simple tool like telnet to send server responses to a client, but you can use tools like tcpdump or wireshark to snoop on TCP traffic and see immediately what clients are sending to, and receiving from, the servers.

There is not the same level of support in Go for managing character streams. There are significant issues with character sets and character encodings, and we will explore these issues in a later chapter.

If we just pretend everything is ASCII, like it was once upon a time, then character formats are quite straightforward to deal with. The principal complication at this level is the varying status of "newline" across different operating systems. UNIX uses the single character \n. Windows and others (more correctly) use the pair \r\n. On the Internet, the pair \r\n is most common. UNIX systems just need to take care that they don't assume \n.

A Simple Example

This example deals with a directory browsing protocol, which is basically a stripped-down version of FTP, but without even the file transfer part. We only consider listing a directory name, listing the contents of a directory, and changing the current directory – all on the server side, of course. This is a complete worked example of creating all components of a client-server application. It is a simple program that includes messages in both directions, as well as a design of messaging protocol.

A Stand-Alone Application

Look at a simple non-client-server program that allows you to list files in a directory and change and print the name of the directory on the server. We omit copying files, as that adds to the length of the program without introducing important concepts. For simplicity, all file names will be assumed to be in 7-bit ASCII. If we just looked at a stand-alone application first, it would look like Figure 5-2.

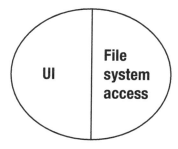

Figure 5-2. *The stand-alone application*

The pseudocode would be as follows:

```
read line from user
while not eof do
  if line == dir
    list directory // local function call
  else
  if line == cd <directory>
    change directory // local function call
```

```
else
if line == pwd
  print directory // local function call
else
if line == quit
  quit
else
  complain
read line from user
```

A nondistributed application would simply link the UI and file access code by local function calls.

The Client-Server Application

In a client-server situation, the client would be at the user end, talking to a server somewhere else. Aspects of this program belong solely at the presentation end, such as getting the commands from the user. Some are messages from the client to the server; some are solely at the server end. See Figure 5-3.

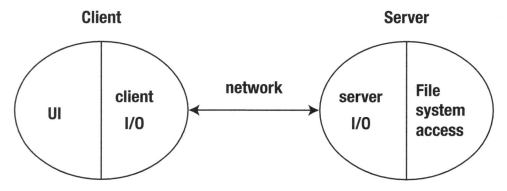

Figure 5-3. *The client-server situation*

The Client Side

For a simple directory browser, assume that all directories and files are at the server end and we are transferring file information only from the server to the client. The client side (including presentation aspects) will become

```
read line from user
while not eof do
  if line == dir
    list directory // network call to server
  else
  if line == cd <directory>
    change directory // network call to server
  else
```

```
if line == pwd
  print directory // network call to server
else
if line == quit
  quit
else
  complain
read line from user
```

where the calls `list directory`, `change directory`, and `print directory` now all involve network calls to the server. The details are not shown yet and will be discussed later.

Alternative Presentation Aspects

A GUI program would allow directory contents to be displayed as lists, for files to be selected and actions such as change directory to be performed on them. The client would be controlled by actions associated with various events that take place on graphical objects. The pseudocode might look like this:

```
change dir button:
  if there is a selected file
    change directory // remote call to server
  if successful
    update directory label
    list directory // remote call to server
    update directory list
```

The functions called from the different UIs should be the same – changing the presentation should not change the networking code.

The Server Side

The server side is independent of whatever presentation is used by the client. It is the same for all clients:

```
while read command from client
  if command == dir
    send list directory // local call on server
  else
  if command == cd <directory>
    change directory // local call on server
  else
  if command == pwd
    send print directory // local call on server
  else
```

Protocol: Informal

Client Request	Server Response
dir	Send list of files
cd <directory>	Change dir Send an error if failed Send ok if succeed
pwd	Send current directory
quit	Quit

Text Protocol

This is a simple protocol. The most complicated data structure that we need to send is an array of strings for a directory listing. In this case, we don't need the heavy-duty serialization techniques of the last chapter. In this case, we can use a simple text format.

But even if we make the protocol simple, we still have to specify it in detail. We choose the following message format:

- All messages are in 7-bit US-ASCII.

- The messages are case-sensitive.

- Each message consists of a sequence of lines.

- The first word on the first line of each message describes the message type. All other words are message data.

- All words are separated by exactly one space character.

- Each line is terminated by CR-LF.

Some of the choices made previously are weaker in real-life protocols. For example:

- Message types could be case-insensitive. This just requires mapping message type strings down to lowercase before decoding.

- An arbitrary amount of whitespace could be left between words. This just adds a little more complication, compressing whitespace.

- Continuation characters such as \ can be used to break long lines over several lines. This starts to make processing more complex.

- Just a \n could be used as line terminator, \r\n can too. This makes recognizing the end of line a bit harder.

All of these variations exist in real protocols. Cumulatively, they make string processing more complex than in this case.

Client Request	Server Response
send "DIR"	Send list of files, one per line, terminated by a blank line
send "CD <directory>"	Change dir Send "ERROR" if failed Send "OK" if succeeded
send "PWD"	Send current working directory

We should also specify the transport:

- All messages are sent over a TCP connection established from the client to the server.

Server Code

The server is ftpserver.go:

```
$ mkdir ch5
$ cd ch5
ch5$ vi ftpserver.go

/* FTP Server
 */
package main

import (
        "log"
        "net"
        "os"
        "strings"
)
const (
        DIR = "DIR"
        CD  = "CD"
        PWD = "PWD"
)

func main() {
        service := "0.0.0.0:1202"
        tcpAddr, err := net.ResolveTCPAddr("tcp", service)
        checkError(err)
        listener, err := net.ListenTCP("tcp", tcpAddr)
        checkError(err)
        for {
                conn, err := listener.Accept()
                if err != nil {
                        continue
                }
                go handleClient(conn)
        }
}
```

```go
func handleClient(conn net.Conn) {
        defer conn.Close()
        var buf [512]byte
        for {
                n, err := conn.Read(buf[0:])
                if err != nil {
                        conn.Close()
                        return
                }
                s := strings.Split(string(buf[0:n]), " ")
log.Println(s)
                // decode request
                switch s[0] {
                case CD:
                        chdir(conn, s[1])
                case DIR:
                        dirList(conn)
                case PWD:
                        pwd(conn)
                default:
                        log.Println("Unknown command ", s)
                }
        }
}

func chdir(conn net.Conn, s string) {
        if os.Chdir(s) == nil {
                conn.Write([]byte("OK"))
        } else {
                conn.Write([]byte("ERROR"))
        }
}
func pwd(conn net.Conn) {
        s, err := os.Getwd()
        if err != nil {
                conn.Write([]byte(""))
                return
        }
        conn.Write([]byte(s))
}

func dirList(conn net.Conn) {
        // send a blank line on termination
        defer conn.Write([]byte("\r\n"))
        dir, err := os.Open(".")
        if err != nil {
                return
        }
        names, err := dir.Readdirnames(-1)
        if err != nil {
                return
        }
```

```
        for _, nm := range names {
                conn.Write([]byte(nm + "\r\n"))
        }
}

func checkError(err error) {
        if err != nil {
                log.Fatalln("Fatal error ", err.Error())
        }
}
```

Client Code

A command-line client is ftpclient.go:

ch5$ vi ftpclient.go

```
/* FTPClient
 */
package main

import (
        "bufio"
        "bytes"
        "fmt"
        "log"
        "net"
        "os"
        "strings"
)

// strings used by the user interface
const (
        uiDir  = "dir"
        uiCd   = "cd"
        uiPwd  = "pwd"
        uiQuit = "quit"
)

// strings used across the network
const (
        DIR = "DIR"
        CD  = "CD"
        PWD = "PWD"
)

func main() {
        if len(os.Args) != 2 {
                log.Fatalln("Usage: ", os.Args[0], "host")
        }
```

```go
        host := os.Args[1]
        conn, err := net.Dial("tcp", host+":1202")
        checkError(err)
        reader := bufio.NewReader(os.Stdin)
        for {
                line, err := reader.ReadString('\n')
                // lose trailing whitespace
                line = strings.TrimRight(line, " \t\r\n")
                if err != nil {
                        break
                }
                // split into command + arg
                strs := strings.SplitN(line, " ", 2)
                // decode user request
                switch strs[0] {
                case uiDir:
                        dirRequest(conn)
                case uiCd:
                        if len(strs) != 2 {
                                fmt.Println("cd <dir>")
                                continue
                        }
                        fmt.Println("CD \"", strs[1], "\"")
                        cdRequest(conn, strs[1])
                case uiPwd:
                        pwdRequest(conn)
                case uiQuit:
                        conn.Close()
                        os.Exit(0)
                default:
                        fmt.Println("Unknown command")
                }
        }
}

func dirRequest(conn net.Conn) {
        conn.Write([]byte(DIR + " "))
        var buf [512]byte
        result := bytes.NewBuffer(nil)
        for {
                // read till we hit a blank line
                n, _ := conn.Read(buf[0:])
                result.Write(buf[0:n])
                length := result.Len()
                contents := result.Bytes()
                if string(contents[length-4:]) == "\r\n\r\n" {
                        fmt.Println(string(contents[0 : length-4]))
                        return
                }
        }
}
```

```go
func cdRequest(conn net.Conn, dir string) {
        conn.Write([]byte(CD + " " + dir))
        var response [512]byte
        n, _ := conn.Read(response[0:])
        s := string(response[0:n])
        if s != "OK" {
                fmt.Println("Failed to change dir")
        }
}

func pwdRequest(conn net.Conn) {
        conn.Write([]byte(PWD))
        var response [512]byte
        n, _ := conn.Read(response[0:])
        s := string(response[0:n])
        fmt.Println("Current dir \"" + s + "\"")
}

func checkError(err error) {
        if err != nil {
                log.Fatalln("Fatal error ", err.Error())
        }
}
```

An example session using our FTP server and client; in one terminal, run the server:

```
ch5$ go run ftpserver.go
```

In another terminal, run the ftp client.

```
ch5$ go run ftpclient.go localhost
pwd
Current dir ".../ch5"
dir
ftpserver.go
ftpclient.go
```

Try other commands such as "cd ..".

Textproto Package

The textproto package contains functions designed to simplify the management of text protocols similar to HTTP and SNMP.

These formats have some little-known rules with regard to a single logical line continued over multiple lines such as the following: "HTTP/1.1 header field values can be folded onto multiple lines if the continuation line begins with a space or horizontal tab" (HTTP1.1 specification). Formats allowing lines like these can be read using the textproto.Reader.ReadContinuedLine() function, in addition to simpler functions like textproto.Reader.ReadLine().

These protocols also signal status values with lines beginning with three-digit codes such as HTTP's 404. These can be read using textproto.Reader.ReadCodeLine(). They also have key: value lines such as Content-Type: image/gif. Such lines can be read into a map by textproto.Reader.ReadMIMEHeader().

Here is an example where we leverage an external tool called netcat (i.e., nc). This tool is often used when scripting TCP, UDP, or Unix-domain sockets. In this example, we create a client that sends an HTTP request message. Listening for the request will be netcat. Once the client executes, you will type the result into the netcat terminal (simulating a response). In the client, we only expect a response starting with a 404, else we will error out. Create the following client, textprotoclient.go.

```
ch5$ vi textprotoclient.go

/* textproto
 */

package main

import (
        "fmt"
        "log"
        "net/textproto"
)

func main() {
        conn, e := textproto.Dial("unix", "/tmp/fakewebserver")
        checkerror(e)
        defer conn.Close()
        fmt.Println("Sending request to retrieve /mypage")
        id, e := conn.Cmd("GET /mypage")
        checkerror(e)
        conn.StartResponse(id)
        defer conn.EndResponse(id)
        // fake sending back a 200 via nc or your own server
        code, stringResult, err := conn.ReadCodeLine(200)
        checkerror(err)
        fmt.Println(code, "\n", stringResult, "\n", err)
}

func checkerror(err error) {
        if err != nil {
                log.Fatalln("error: ", err)
        }
}
```

Here is an example session; in one terminal, run netcat.

```
ch$ nc -lkU /tmp/fakewebserver
```

In another terminal, run our client.

```
ch5$ go run textprotoclient.go

Sending request to retrieve /mypage
```

Our netcat server will show:

```
ch5$ nc -lkU /tmp/fakewebserver

GET /mypage
```

In the netcat server, type the following ("200 This will work"):

```
ch5$ nc -lkU /tmp/fakewebserver

GET /mypage
200 This will work
```

Finally, back in our client, we see:

```
ch5$ go run textprotoclient.go
Sending request to retrieve /mypage
200
This will work
<nil>
```

The preceding code shows a response starting with 200; if we try another run and return 400 from the server, we receive an error. Do not confuse this for HTTP; many protocols (e.g., SMTP) use numeric codes.

State Information

Applications often use state information to simplify what is going on. For example:

- Keeping file pointers to a current file location

- Keeping the current mouse position

- Keeping the current customer value

In a distributed system, such state information may be kept in the client, in the server, or in both.

The important point is to whether one process is keeping state information about *itself* or about the *other* process. One process may keep as much state information about itself as it wants, without causing any problems. If it needs to keep information about the state of the other process, then problems arise. The process' actual knowledge of the state of the other may become incorrect. This can be caused by loss of messages (in UDP), by failure to update, or by software errors.

An example is reading a file. In single process applications, the file-handling code runs as part of the application. It maintains a table of open files and the location in each of them. Each time a read or write is done, this file location is updated. In distributed systems, this simple model does not hold. See Figure 5-4.

DCE File System

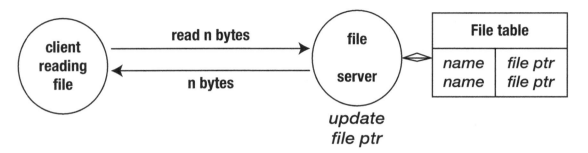

Figure 5-4. *The DCE file system*

In the DCE file system shown in Figure 5-4, the file server keeps track of a client's open files and where the client's file pointer is. If a message could get lost (but DCE uses TCP), these could get out of sync. If the client crashes, the server must eventually time out on the client's file tables and remove them.

NFS File System

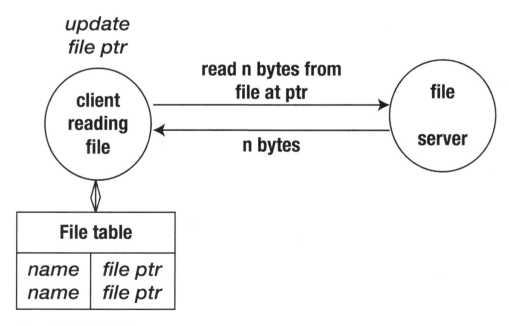

Figure 5-5. *The NFS file system*

In NFS, the server does not maintain this state. The client does. Each file access from the client that reaches the server must open the file at the appropriate point, as given by the client, in order to perform the action. See Figure 5-5.

If the server maintains information about the client, it must be able to recover if the client crashes. If information is not saved, then on each transaction, the client must transfer sufficient information for the server to function.

If the connection is unreliable, additional handling must be in place to ensure that the two do not get out of sync. The classic example is of bank account transactions where the messages get lost. A transaction server may need to be part of the client-server system.

Application State Transition Diagram

A state transition diagram keeps track of the current state of an application and the changes that move it to new states.

The previous example basically only had one state: file transfer. If we add a login mechanism, that would add an extra state called *login*, and the application would need to change states between login and file transfer, as shown in Figure 5-6.

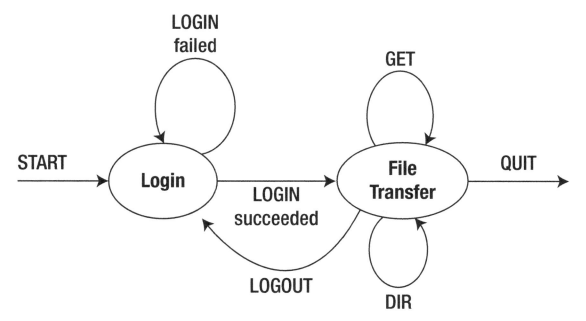

Figure 5-6. *The state-transition diagram*

This state change can also be expressed as a table:

Current State	Transition	Next State
login	login failed	login
	login succeeded	file transfer
file transfer	dir	file transfer
	get	file transfer
	logout	login
	quit	-

Client-State Transition Diagrams

The client state diagram must follow the application diagram. It has more detail though: it *writes* and then *reads*.

Current State	Write	Read	Next State
login	LOGIN name password	FAILED	Login
		OK	file transfer
file transfer	CD dir	OK	file transfer
		FAILED	file transfer
	GET filename	#lines + contents	file transfer
		FAILED	file transfer
	DIR	File names + blank line	file transfer
		blank line (Error)	file transfer
	quit	none	Quit

Server-State Transition Diagrams

The server state diagram must also follow the application diagram. It also has more detail: it *reads* and then *writes*.

Current State	Read	Write	Next State
login	LOGIN name password	FAILED	Login
		OK	file transfer
file transfer	CD dir	SUCCEEDED	file transfer
		FAILED	file transfer
	GET filename	#lines + contents	file transfer
		FAILED	file transfer
	DIR	filenames + blank line	file transfer
		blank line (failed)	file transfer
	quit	none	Login

Server Pseudocode

Here is the server pseudocode:

```
state = login
while true
    read line
    switch (state)
        case login:
            get NAME from line
            get PASSWORD from line
            if NAME and PASSWORD verified
                write SUCCEEDED
                state = file_transfer
            else
                write FAILED
                state = login
        case file_transfer:
            if line.startsWith CD
                get DIR from line
                if chdir DIR okay
                    write SUCCEEDED
                    state = file_transfer
                else
                    write FAILED
                    state = file_transfer
            ...
```

We don't give the actual code for this server or client since it is pretty straightforward.

Conclusion

Building any application requires design decisions before you start writing code. With distributed applications, you have a wider range of decisions to make compared to stand-alone systems. This chapter considered some of those aspects and demonstrated what the resultant code might look like. We only touched on the elements of protocol design. There are many formal and informal models. The IETF (Internet Engineering Task Force) created a standard format for its protocol specifications in its RFCs (Requests for Comments), and sooner or later, every network engineer will need to work with RFCs.

CHAPTER 6

Managing Character Sets and Encodings

Once upon a time, there were EBCDIC and ASCII. Actually, it was never that simple and has just become more complex over time. There is light on the horizon, but some estimates are that it may be 50 years before we all live in the daylight on this!

Early computers were developed in the English-speaking countries of the United States, the UK, and Australia. As a result of this, assumptions were made about the language and character sets in use. Basically, the Latin alphabet was used, plus numerals, punctuation characters, and a few others. These were then encoded into bytes using ASCII or EBCDIC.

The character-handling mechanisms were based on this: text files and I/O consisted of a sequence of bytes, with each byte representing a single character. String comparison could be done by matching corresponding bytes; conversions from upper- to lowercase could be done by mapping individual bytes and so on.

There are about 6,500 spoken languages in the world (850 of them in Papua New Guinea!). A few languages use the "English" characters, but most do not. The Romanic languages such as French have adornments on various characters, so you can write "j'ai arrêté" with two differently accented vowels. Similarly, the Germanic languages have extra characters such as "ß". Even UK English has characters not in the standard ASCII set: the pound symbol "£" and recently the euro "€".

But the world is not restricted to variations on the Latin alphabet. Thailand has its own alphabet, with words looking like this: "ภาษาไทย". There are many other alphabets, and Japan even has two: Hiragana and Katakana.

There are also the hierographic languages such as Chinese where you can write "百度一下，你就知道".

It would be nice from a technical viewpoint if the world just used ASCII. However, the trend is in the opposite direction, with more and more users demanding that software use the language that they are familiar with. If you build an application that can be run in different countries, then users will demand that it uses their own language. In a distributed system, different components of the system may be used by users expecting different languages and characters.

Internationalization (i18n) is how you write your applications so that they can handle the variety of languages and cultures. *Localization* (l10n) is the process of customizing your internationalized application to a particular cultural group.

i18n and l10n are big topics in themselves. For example, they cover issues such as colors: while white means "purity" in Western cultures, it means "death" to the Chinese and "joy" to Egyptians. In this chapter, we just look at issues of character handling.

© Jan Newmarch and Ronald Petty 2022
J. Newmarch and R. Petty, *Network Programming with Go Language*,
https://doi.org/10.1007/978-1-4842-8095-9_6

Definitions

It is important to be careful about exactly what part of a text-handling system you are talking about. Here is a set of definitions that have proven useful.

Character

A *character* is a "unit of information that roughly corresponds to a grapheme (written symbol) of a natural language, such as a letter, numeral, or punctuation mark" (Wikipedia). A character is "the smallest component of written language that has a semantic value" (Unicode). This includes letters such as "a" and "À" (or letters in any other language), digits such as "2", punctuation characters such as "," and various symbols such as the English pound currency symbol "£".

A character is some sort of abstraction of any actual symbol: the character "a" is to any written "a" as a Platonic circle is to any actual circle. The concept of character also includes control characters, which do not correspond to natural language symbols but to other bits of information used to process texts of the language.

A character does not have any particular appearance, although we use the appearance to help recognize the character. However, even the appearance may have to be understood in a context: in mathematics, if you see the symbol π (pi), it is the character for the ratio of circumference to radius of a circle, while if you are reading Greek text, it is the sixteenth letter of the alphabet: "προσ" is the Greek word for "with" and has nothing to do with 3.14159.

Character Repertoire/Character Set

A character repertoire is a set of distinct characters, such as the Latin alphabet. No particular ordering is assumed. In English, although we say that "a" is earlier in the alphabet than "z", we wouldn't say that "a" is less than "z". The "phone book" ordering that puts "McPhee" before "MacRea" shows that "alphabetic ordering" isn't critical to the characters.

A repertoire specifies the names of the characters and often a sample of how the characters might look. For example, the letter "a" might look like "a", "*a*", or "**a**". But it doesn't force them to look like that – they are just samples. The repertoire may make distinctions such as upper- and lowercase so that "a" and "A" are different. But it may regard them as the same, just with different sample appearances (just like some programming languages treat upper- and lowercase as different, Go, but some don't, Basic). On the other hand, a repertoire might contain different characters with the same sample appearance: the repertoire for a Greek mathematician would have two different characters with appearance π. This is also called a noncoded character set.

Character Code

A character code is a mapping from characters to integers. The mapping for a character set is also called a coded character set or code set. The value of each character in this mapping is often called a code point. ASCII is a code set. The code point for "a" is 97, and for "A", it is 65 (decimal).

The character code is still an abstraction. It isn't yet what we will see in text files, or in TCP packets. However, it is getting close, as it supplies the mapping from human-oriented concepts into numerical ones.

Character Encoding

To communicate or store a character, you need to encode it in some way. To transmit a string, you need to encode all characters in the string. There are many possible encodings for any code set.

For example, 7-bit ASCII code points can be encoded as themselves into 8-bit bytes (an octet). So ASCII "A" (with code point 65) is encoded as the 8-bit octet 01000001. However, a different encoding would be to use the top bit for parity checking. For example, with odd parity, ASCII "A" would be the octet 11000001. Some protocols such as Sun's XDR use 32-bit word-length encoding. ASCII "A" would be encoded as 00000000 00000000 0000000 01000001.

The character encoding is where we function at the programming level. Our programs deal with encoded characters. It obviously makes a difference whether we are dealing with 8-bit characters with or without parity checking, or with 32-bit characters.

The encoding extends to strings of characters. A word-length even parity encoding of "ABC" might be 10000000 (parity bit in high byte) 0100000011 (C) 01000010 (B) 01000001 (A in low byte). The comments about the importance of an encoding apply equally strongly to strings, where the rules may be different.

Transport Encoding

A character encoding will suffice for handling characters within a single application. However, once you start sending text *between* applications, then there is the further issue of how the bytes, shorts, or words are put on the wire. An encoding can be based on space- and hence bandwidth-saving techniques such as zipping the text. Or it could be reduced to a 7-bit format to allow a parity checking bit, such as base64.

If we do know the character and transport encoding, then it is a matter of programming to manage characters and strings. If we don't know the character or transport encoding, then it is a matter of guesswork as to what to do with any particular string. There is no convention for files to signal the character encoding.

There *is*, however, a convention for signaling encoding in text transmitted across the Internet. It is simple: the header of a text message contains information about the encoding. For example, an HTTP header can contain lines such as the following:

```
Content-Type: text/html; charset=ISO-8859-4
Content-Encoding: gzip
```

This says that the character set is ISO 8859-4 (corresponding to certain countries in Europe) with the default encoding, but then gziped. The second part – the content encoding – is what we are referring to as "transfer encoding" (IETF RFC 2130).

But how do you read this information? Isn't it encoded? Don't we have a chicken and egg situation? Well, no. The convention is that such information is given in ASCII (to be precise, US ASCII) so that a program can read the headers and then adjust its encoding for the rest of the document.

ASCII

ASCII has the repertoire of the English characters plus digits, punctuation, and some control characters. The code points for ASCII are given by this familiar table:

Oct	Dec	Hex	Char	Oct	Dec	Hex	Char
000	0	00	NUL '¥0'	100	64	40	@
001	1	01	SOH	101	65	41	A
002	2	02	STX	102	66	42	B

003	3	03	ETX	103	67	43	C
004	4	04	EOT	104	68	44	D
005	5	05	ENQ	105	69	45	E
006	6	06	ACK	106	70	46	F
007	7	07	BEL '\a'	107	71	47	G
010	8	08	BS '\b'	110	72	48	H
011	9	09	HT '\t'	111	73	49	I
012	10	0A	LF '\n'	112	74	4A	J
013	11	0B	VT '\v'	113	75	4B	K
014	12	0C	FF '\f'	114	76	4C	L
015	13	0D	CR '\r'	115	77	4D	M
016	14	0E	SO	116	78	4E	N
017	15	0F	SI	117	79	4F	O
020	16	10	DLE	120	80	50	P
021	17	11	DC1	121	81	51	Q
022	18	12	DC2	122	82	52	R
023	19	13	DC3	123	83	53	S
024	20	14	DC4	124	84	54	T
025	21	15	NAK	125	85	55	U
026	22	16	SYN	126	86	56	V
027	23	17	ETB	127	87	57	W
030	24	18	CAN	130	88	58	X
031	25	19	EM	131	89	59	Y
032	26	1A	SUB	132	90	5A	Z
033	27	1B	ESC	133	91	5B	[
034	28	1C	FS	134	92	5C	\
035	29	1D	GS	135	93	5D	]
036	30	1E	RS	136	94	5E	^
037	31	1F	US	137	95	5F	_
040	32	20	SPACE	140	96	60	`
041	33	21	!	141	97	61	a
042	34	22	"	142	98	62	b
043	35	23	#	143	99	63	c
044	36	24	$	144	100	64	d
045	37	25	%	145	101	65	e
046	38	26	&	146	102	66	f
047	39	27	'	147	103	67	g
050	40	28	(	150	104	68	h
051	41	29	)	151	105	69	i
052	42	2A	*	152	106	6A	j
053	43	2B	+	153	107	6B	k
054	44	2C	,	154	108	6C	l
055	45	2D	-	155	109	6D	m
056	46	2E	.	156	110	6E	n
057	47	2F	/	157	111	6F	o
060	48	30	0	160	112	70	p
061	49	31	1	161	113	71	q
062	50	32	2	162	114	72	r
063	51	33	3	163	115	73	s
064	52	34	4	164	116	74	t
065	53	35	5	165	117	75	u

066	54	36	6
067	55	37	7
070	56	38	8
071	57	39	9
072	58	3A	:
073	59	3B	;
074	60	3C	<
075	61	3D	=
076	62	3E	>
077	63	3F	?

166	118	76	v
167	119	77	w
170	120	78	x
171	121	79	y
172	122	7A	z
173	123	7B	{
174	124	7C	|
175	125	7D	}
176	126	7E	~
177	127	7F	DEL

(An interesting four-column version is at Robbie's Garbage, Four Column ASCII at `https://garbagecollected.org/2017/01/31/four-column-ascii/`.)

The most common encoding for ASCII uses the code points as 7-bit bytes, so the encoding of "A", for example, is 65.

This set is actually *US ASCII*. Due to European desires for accented characters, some punctuation characters are omitted to form a minimal set, ISO 646, while there are "national variants" with suitable European characters. The website (`https://jkorpela.fi/chars.html`) by Jukka Korpela has more information for those interested. You don't need these variants for the work in this book, though.

ISO 8859

Octets are now the standard size for bytes. This allows 128 extra code points for extensions to ASCII. A number of different code sets to capture the repertoires of various subsets of European languages are the ISO 8859 series. ISO 8859-1 is also known as Latin-1 and covers many languages in western Europe, while others in this series cover the rest of Europe and even Hebrew, Arabic, and Thai. For example, ISO 8859-5 includes the Cyrillic characters of countries such as Russia, while ISO 8859-8 includes the Hebrew alphabet.

The standard encoding for these character sets is to use their code point as an 8-bit value. For example, the character "Á" in ISO 8859-1 has the code point 193 and is encoded as 193. All of the ISO 8859 series have the bottom 128 values identical to ASCII, so the ASCII characters are the same in all of these sets.

The HTML specifications used to recommend the ISO 8859-1 character set. HTML 3.2 was the last one to do so, and after that, HTML 4.0 recommended Unicode. In 2008, Google made an estimate that of the pages it sees, about 20% were still in ISO 8859 format while 20% were still in ASCII (see "Unicode nearing 50% of the web" at `http://googleblog.blogspot.com/2010/01/unicode-nearing-50-of-web.html`). See also `http://pinyin.info/news/2015/utf-8-unicode-vs-other-encodings-over-time/` and `https://w3techs.com/technologies/history_overview/character_encoding` for more background information.

Unicode

Neither ASCII nor ISO 8859 covers the languages based on hieroglyphs. Chinese is estimated to have about 20,000 separate characters, with about 5,000 in common use. These need more than a byte, and typically, two bytes have been used. There have been many of these two-byte character sets: Big5, EUC-TW, GB2312, and GBK/GBX for Chinese; JIS X 0208 for Japanese; and so on. These encodings are generally not mutually compatible.

Unicode is an embracing standard character set intended to cover all major character sets in use. It includes European, Asian, Indian, and many more. It is now up to version 14.0 and has 144,697 assigned characters. The number of code points is 1,114,112 (65,536 code points across 17 planes). That is more than 2^{16}. This has implications for character encodings.

The first 256 code points correspond to ISO 8859-1, with US ASCII as the first 128. There is thus a backward compatibility with these major character sets, as the code points for ISO 8859-1 and ASCII are exactly the same in Unicode. The same is not true for other character sets: for example, while most of the Big5 characters are also in Unicode, the code points are not the same. The website http://moztw.org/docs/big5/table/unicode1.1-obsolete.txt contains one example of a (large) table mapping from Big5 to Unicode.

To represent Unicode characters in a computer system, an encoding must be used. The encoding UCS is a two-byte encoding using the code point values of the Unicode characters. However, since there are now too many characters in Unicode to fit them all into 2 bytes, this encoding is obsolete and no longer used. Instead, there are the following:

- UTF-32 is a 4-byte encoding but is not commonly used, and HTML5 warns explicitly against using it.

- UTF-16 encodes the most common characters into 2 bytes with a further 2 bytes for the "overflow," with ASCII and ISO 8859-1 having the usual values.

- UTF-8 uses between 1 and 4 bytes per character, with ASCII having the usual values (but not ISO 8859-1).

- Per the Unicode specification, UTF-8, UTF-16, and UTF-32 are fully interoperable with each other.

- UTF-7 is used sometimes but is not common.

Some considerations when selecting a particular UTF encoding[1] include the following:

- Desire fixed width and single code unit access; use UTF-32.

- Space concerns, use UTF-16.

- Serialization is inherent with UTF-8.

UTF-8, Go, and Runes

UTF-8 is the most commonly used encoding. Google estimated that in 2008, 50% of the pages that it sees are encoded in UTF-8 and that proportion is increasing. The ASCII set has the same encoding values in UTF-8, so a UTF-8 reader can read text consisting of just ASCII characters as well as text from the full Unicode set.

Go uses UTF-8 encoded characters in its strings. Each character is of type rune. This is an alias for int32. A Unicode character can be up to 4 bytes in UTF-8 encoding, so 4 bytes are needed to represent all characters. In terms of characters, a string is an array of runes using 1, 2, or 4 bytes per rune.

A string is also an array of bytes, but you have to be careful: only for the ASCII subset is a byte equal to a character. All other characters occupy 2, 3, or 4 bytes. This means that the length of a string in characters (runes) is generally not the same as the length of its byte array. They are equal only when the string consists of ASCII characters only.

The following program fragment illustrates this. If you take a UTF-8 string and test its length, you get the length of the underlying byte array. But if you cast the string to an array of runes [ ]rune, then you get an array of the Unicode code points, which is generally the number of characters:

```
$ mkdir ch6
$ cd ch6
$ vi runeprint.go
```

---

[1] The Unicode Standard – https://www.unicode.org/versions/Unicode14.0.0/UnicodeStandard-14.0.pdf

```
package main

import "fmt"

func main() {
        str := "百度一下，你就知道"
        fmt.Println("String length: ", len([]rune(str)))
        fmt.Println("Byte length: ", len(str))
}

ch6$ go run runeprint.go

String length:  10
Byte length:  26
```

A more detailed explanation of strings and runes is given by The Go Blog (see `https://go.dev/blog/strings`).

UTF-8 Client and Server

Possibly surprisingly, you need to do nothing special to handle UTF-8 text in either the client or the server. The underlying data type for a UTF-8 string in Go is a byte array, and as we just saw, Go looks after encoding the string into 1, 2, 3, or 4 bytes as needed. The length of the string is the length of the byte array, so you write any UTF-8 string by writing the byte array.

Similarly, to read a string, you just read into a byte array and then cast the array to a string using `string([]byte)`. If Go cannot properly decode bytes into Unicode characters, then it gives the Unicode Replacement Character \uFFFD. The length of the resulting byte array is the length of the legal portion of the string.

So the clients and servers given in earlier chapters work perfectly well with UTF-8 encoded text.

ASCII Client and Server

The ASCII characters have the same encoding in ASCII and in UTF-8. So ordinary UTF-8 character handling works fine for ASCII characters. No special handling needs to be done.

UTF-16 and Go

UTF-16 deals with arrays of short 16-bit unsigned integers. The package utf16 is designed to manage such arrays. To convert a normal Go string, which is a UTF-8 string, into UTF-16, you first extract the code points by coercing it into a []rune and then use `utf16.Encode` to produce an array of type uint16.

Similarly, to decode an array of unsigned short UTF-16 values into a Go string, you use `utf16.Decode` to convert it into code points as type []rune and then to a string. The following code fragment illustrates this:

```
ch6$ vi utf16encodedecode.go

package main

import (
        "unicode/utf16"
```

```
        "fmt"
)

func main() {
        str := "百度一下，你就知道"
        fmt.Println("Before encoding:", str)

        runes := utf16.Encode([]rune(str))
        ints := utf16.Decode(runes)

        str = string(ints)
        fmt.Println("After encoding:", str)
}
```

```
ch6$ go run utf16encodedecode.go
Before encoding: 百度一下，你就知道
After encoding: 百度一下，你就知道
```

These type conversions need to be applied by clients or servers as appropriate, to read and write 16-bit short integers, as shown next.

Little-Endian and Big-Endian

Unfortunately, there is a little devil lurking behind UTF-16. It is basically an encoding of characters into 16-bit short integers. The big question is the following: For each short, how is it written as two bytes? The top one first, or the top one second? Either way is fine, as long as the receiver uses the same convention as the sender.

Unicode has addressed this with a special character known as the *BOM* (byte order marker). This is a zero-width nonprinting character, so you never see it in text. But its value (e.g., 0xfffe) is chosen so that you can tell the byte order:

- In a big-endian system, it is FF FE.

- In a little-endian system, it is FE FF.

Text will sometimes place the BOM as the first character in the text. The reader can then examine these two bytes to determine what endian-ness has been used.

UTF-16 Client and Server

Using the BOM convention, you can write a server that prepends a BOM and writes a string in UTF-16 as utf16server.go:

```
ch6$ vi utf16server.go

/* UTF16 Server
 */
package main

import (
    "log"
```

```go
    "net"
    "unicode/utf16"
)

// warning, our server currently only supports big endian
const BOM = '\ufffe'

func main() {
    service := "0.0.0.0:1210"
    tcpAddr, err := net.ResolveTCPAddr("tcp", service)
    checkError(err)
    listener, err := net.ListenTCP("tcp", tcpAddr)
    checkError(err)
    for {
        conn, err := listener.Accept()
        if err != nil {
            continue
        }
        // eg. Ŵ  is 0x0174, Ã is 0x00c3
        str := "Ŵj'ai arrÃªtÃ©"
        shorts := utf16.Encode([]rune(str))
        writeShorts(conn, shorts)
        conn.Close()
    }
}
func writeShorts(conn net.Conn, shorts []uint16) {
    var bytes [2]byte
    // send the BOM as first two bytes
    bytes[0] = BOM >> 8          // taking ff from BOM
    bytes[1] = BOM & 255         // taking fe from BOM
    _, err := conn.Write(bytes[0:]) // send BOM
    checkError(err)
    for _, v := range shorts {
        // breakup the unit16 into two bytes, then send
        bytes[0] = byte(v >> 8)
        bytes[1] = byte(v & 255)
        _, err = conn.Write(bytes[0:])
        if err != nil {
            return
        }
    }
}
func checkError(err error) {
    if err != nil {
        log.Fatalln("Fatal error ", err.Error())
    }
}
```

A client that reads a byte stream, extracts and examines the BOM, and then decodes the rest of the stream is utf16client.go:

```
ch6$ vi utf16client.go

/* UTF16 Client
 */
package main

import (
    "fmt"
    "log"
    "net"
    "os"
    "unicode/utf16"
)

const BOM = '\ufffe'

func main() {
    if len(os.Args) != 2 {
        log.Fatalln("Usage: ", os.Args[0], "host:port")
    }
    service := os.Args[1]
    conn, err := net.Dial("tcp", service)
    checkError(err)
    shorts := readShorts(conn)
    ints := utf16.Decode(shorts)
    str := string(ints)
    fmt.Println(str)
}
func readShorts(conn net.Conn) []uint16 {
    var buf [512]byte
    // read everything into the buffer
    n, err := conn.Read(buf[0:2]) // start with BOM
    for {
        m, err := conn.Read(buf[n:]) // read remaining byte pairs (originally unit16)
        if m == 0 || err != nil {
            break
        }
        n += m
    }
    checkError(err)
    var shorts []uint16
    shorts = make([]uint16, n/2)

    // We are checking for endianess
    // first - big endian 0xfffe
    // second - little endian 0xfeff
    // else - unknown
    // the inner loops are reading one byte per iteration
    // depending on endianess, places in the correct byte order
```

140

```
        // *warning* our server only supports big-endian
        if buf[0] == 0xff && buf[1] == 0xfe {
            for i := 2; i < n; i += 2 {
                shorts[i/2] = uint16(buf[i])<<8 + uint16(buf[i+1])
            }
        } else if buf[0] == 0xfe && buf[1] == 0xff {
            for i := 2; i < n; i += 2 {
                shorts[i/2] = uint16(buf[i+1])<<8 + uint16(buf[i])
            }
        } else {
            // unknown byte order
            fmt.Println("Unknown order")
        }
        return shorts
    }
    func checkError(err error) {
        if err != nil {
            log.Fatalln("Fatal error ", err.Error())
        }
    }
```

Run the server and client in separate terminals:

```
ch6$ go run utf16server.go
```

```
ch6$ go run utf16client.go localhost:1210
Ŵj'ai arrÃªtÃ©
```

We see the client, based on the first two bytes, confirms if the data is big- or little-endian and decodes as necessary.

If you feel adventurous, change the server BOM to little-endian; you will see the following on the client (which does the right thing thinking its little-endian). This is because the server currently only generates as big-endian.

琁楢ə⋖愀椀 愀攀攀쌀诐쌀

Unicode Gotchas

This book is not about i18n issues. In particular, we don't want to delve into the arcane areas of Unicode. But you should know that Unicode is not a simple encoding and there are many complexities. For example, some earlier character sets used *nonspacing* characters, particularly for accents. This was brought into Unicode, so you can produce accented characters in two ways: as a single Unicode character or as a pair of nonspacing accent plus non-accented character. For example, U+04D6, "Cyrillic capital letter ie with breve," is a single character. It is equivalent to U+0415, "Cyrillic capital letter ie" combined with the breve accent U+0306 "combining breve." This makes string comparison difficult on occasions. This could potentially be the cause of some very obscure errors.

There is a package called golang.org/x/text/unicode/norm in the Go experimental tree that can normalize Unicode strings. It can be installed into your Go package tree:

```
go get golang.org/x/text/unicode/norm
```

Note that it is a package in the "subrepositories" Go Project tree and may not be stable.

There are actually four standard Unicode forms. The most common is NFC. A string can be converted to NFC form by norm.NFC.String(str). The following program called norm.go forms strings in two ways, as a single character and as a composed character, and prints the strings, their bytes, and then the normalized form and its bytes. Create the following file, utfnorm.go:

```
ch6$ vi utfnorm.go

/* UTFNorm
 */
package main

import (
        "fmt"
        "golang.org/x/text/unicode/norm"
)

func main() {
        str1 := "\u04d6"
        str2 := "\u0415\u0306"
        norm_str2 := norm.NFC.String(str2)
        bytes1 := []byte(str1)
        bytes2 := []byte(str2)
        norm_bytes2 := []byte(norm_str2)
        fmt.Println("Single char ", str1, " bytes ", bytes1)
        fmt.Println("Composed char ", str2, " bytes ", bytes2)
        fmt.Println("Normalized char", norm_str2, " bytes ",
                norm_bytes2)
}

ch6$ go mod init example.com/user/utfnorm
ch6$ go mod tidy
ch6$ go run utfnorm.go

Single char  Ĕ  bytes  [211 150]
Composed char  Ĕ  bytes  [208 149 204 134]
Normalized char Ĕ  bytes  [211 150]
```

ISO 8859 and Go

The ISO 8859 series are 8-bit character sets for different parts of Europe and some other areas. They all have the ASCII set common in the low part but differ in the top part. According to Google, ISO 8859 codes accounted for about 20% of the web pages it saw, but that has now dropped.

The fourth code, ISO 8859-4 or Latin-4, has the first 256 characters in common with Unicode. The encoded value of the Latin-4 characters is the same in UTF-16 and in the default ISO 8859-4 encoding. But this doesn't really help much, as UTF-16 is a 16-bit encoding and ISO 8859-4 is an 8-bit encoding. UTF-8 is an 8-bit encoding, but it uses the top bit to signal extra bytes, so only the ASCII subset overlaps for UTF-8 and ISO 8859-4. So UTF-8 doesn't help much either. This is true for all 8859-n/Latin-n to Unicode encodings.

But the ISO 8859 series don't have any complex issues. Each character in each set corresponds to a unique Unicode character. For example, in ISO 8859-4, the character "Latin capital letter I with ogonek" has ISO 8859-4 code point 0xc7 (in hexadecimal) and corresponding Unicode code point of U+012E. Transforming either way between an ISO 8859 set and the corresponding Unicode characters is essentially just a table lookup.

A map from ISO 8859 code points to the Unicode code points and could be done as an array of 256 integers. But many of these will have the same value as the index. So we just use a map of the different ones, and those not in the map take the index value. Here is an example program that does that.

```
ch6$ vi isotounicode.go

package main

import (
        "fmt"
        "unicode/utf8"
)

func str2int(str string) []int {
        r := []rune(str)
        b := make([]int, utf8.RuneCountInString(str))
        for i, v := range r {
                b[i] = int(v)
        }
        return b
}


//unicode to 8859-4
var unicodeToISOMap = map[int]uint8{
        // example match ascii 0x0021: 0x21, // !
        0x012e: 0xc7, // Į
        0x010c: 0xc8, // Č
        0x0112: 0xaa, // Ē
        0x0118: 0xca, // Ę
        // example match 0x00c9: 0xc9, // É
        // plus more
}

/* Turn a UTF-8 string into an ISO 8859 encoded byte array
*/
func unicodeStrToISO(str string) []byte {
        // get the unicode code points
        codePoints := str2int(str) //[]int(str)
        // create a byte array of the same length
        bytes := make([]byte, len(codePoints))
        for n, v := range codePoints {
                // see if the point is in the exception map
                iso, ok := unicodeToISOMap[v]
                if !ok {
                        // just use the value
                        iso = uint8(v)
                }
                bytes[n] = iso
```

```go
        }
        return bytes
}

// inverse of unicodeToISOMap
var isoToUnicodeMap = map[uint8]int{
        0xc7: 0x012e,
        0xc8: 0x010c,
        0xaa: 0x0112,
        0xca: 0x0118,
        // and more
}

func isoBytesToUnicode(bytes []byte) string {
        codePoints := make([]int, len(bytes))
        for n, v := range bytes {
                unicode, ok := isoToUnicodeMap[v]
                if !ok {
                        unicode = int(v)
                }
                codePoints[n] = unicode
        }
        return fmt.Sprintf("%q == %U", codePoints, codePoints)
}

func main() {
        x := "ĮĘa!"
        fmt.Printf("UTF-8: %s\n", x)

        fmt.Println("unicode to 8859-4")
        b := unicodeStrToISO(x)
        fmt.Printf("8859-4(hex): %x\n\n", b)

        fmt.Println("8859-4 to Unicode")
        fmt.Printf("Unicode: %v\n", isoBytesToUnicode(b))
}
```

These functions can be used to read and write UTF-8 strings as ISO 8859-4 bytes. By changing the mapping table, you can cover the other ISO 8859 codes. Latin-1, or ISO 8859-1, is a special case – the exception map is empty as the code points for Latin-1 are the same in Unicode. You could also use the same technique for other character sets based on a table mapping, such as Windows 1252.

In the preceding code, we use a sample input, ĮĘa!, where the first two characters are in our exception map and the last two are not (as they are the same values in Unicode and 8859-n). We did use RuneCountInString to help count the correct rune count. Strings in Go are byte arrays; we need to decode properly and use our mappings.

```
ch6$ go run isotounicode.go

UTF-8: ĮĘa!
unicode to 8859-4
8859-4(hex): c7ca6121
```

```
8859-4 to Unicode
Unicode: ['Į' 'Ę' 'a' '!'] == [U+012E U+0118 U+0061 U+0021]
```

Other Character Sets and Go

There are very, very many character set encodings. According to Google, these generally only have a small use in web documents, which will hopefully decrease even further with time. But if your software wants to capture all markets, then you may need to handle them.

In the simplest cases, a lookup table will suffice. But that doesn't always work. The character coding ISO 2022 minimized character set sizes by using a finite state machine to swap code pages in and out. This was borrowed by some of the Japanese encodings and makes things very complex.

Go presently only gives package support for any of these other character sets in the "subrepositories" package tree. For example, the package golang.org/x/text/encoding/japanese handles EUC-JP and Shift JIS.

Conclusion

There hasn't been much code in this chapter. Instead, there have been some of the concepts of a very complex area. It's up to you: if you want to assume everyone speaks US English, then the world is simple. But if you want your applications to be usable by the rest of the world, you need to pay attention to these complexities.

## CHAPTER 7

Security

Although the Internet was originally designed as a system to withstand attacks by hostile agents, it developed into a cooperative environment of relatively trusted entities. Alas, those days are long gone. Spam mail, denial of service (DoS) attacks, phishing attempts, and so on are indicative that anyone using the Internet does so at their own risk.

Applications have to be built to work correctly in hostile situations. "Correctly" no longer means just getting the functional aspects of the program correct but also means ensuring privacy and integrity of data transferred, access only to legitimate users, and other security issues.

This of course makes your programs much more complex. There are *difficult* and *subtle* computing problems involved in making applications secure. Attempts to do it yourself (such as making up your own encryption libraries) are usually doomed to failure. Instead, you need to use the libraries designed by security professionals.

Why should you bother if it makes things harder? Almost every day there are reports of leaked credit card details and of private servers being run by government officials and being hacked and reports of systems being brought down by denial of service attacks. Many of these attacks are possible by coding errors in network-facing applications, such as buffer overflows, cross-site scripting, and SQL injection. But a large number of errors can be traced to poor network handling: passwords passed in plain text, security credentials requested and then not checked, and just trusting the environment you are in. For example, a colleague recently purchased a home IoT (Internet of Things) device. He used Wireshark to see what it was doing on his network and discovered it was sending RTMP messages with authentication token admin. admin. An easy attack vector, without even having to crack passwords! Drones made by one well-known company use encryption with known flaws and can be "stolen" by other drones. An increasingly common method of stealing data is to act as a "rogue" wireless access point, pretending to be a legitimate access point in a local coffee shop, but monitoring everything that passes through, including your bank account details. These are "low hanging fruit." The scope of data breaches is shown by "World's Biggest Data Breaches" at http://www.informationisbeautiful.net/visualizations/worlds-biggest-data-breaches-hacks/.

This chapter addresses the basic cryptographic tools given by Go that you can build into your applications. If you don't and your company loses a million dollars – or worse, your customers lose a million dollars – then the blame comes back to you.

ISO Security Architecture

The ISO OSI (Open Systems Interconnect) seven-layer model of distributed systems is well known and is repeated in Figure 7-1.

© Jan Newmarch and Ronald Petty 2022
J. Newmarch and R. Petty, *Network Programming with Go Language*,
https://doi.org/10.1007/978-1-4842-8095-9_7

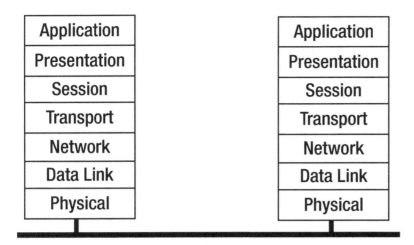

Figure 7-1. *The OSI seven-layer model of distributed systems*

What is less well known is that ISO built a whole series of documents upon this architecture. For our purposes here, the most important is the ISO Security Architecture model, ISO 7498-2. This requires purchase, but the ITU has produced a document technically aligned with this, which is available from ITU at `https://www.itu.int/rec/dologin_pub.asp?lang=e&id=T-REC-X.800-199103-I!!PDF-E&type=items`.

Functions and Levels

The principal functions required of a security system are as follows:

- Authentication: Proof of identity.

- Data integrity: Data is not tampered with.

- Confidentiality: Data is not exposed to others.

- Notarization/signature: Registration of data with a trusted third party for later assurance.

- Access control: Protection against unauthorized access of resources.

- Availability: Accessibility on demand from authorized entity.

These are required at the following levels of the OSI stack:

- Peer entity authentication (3, 4, 7)

- Data origin authentication (3, 4, 7)

- Access control service (3, 4, 7)

- Connection confidentiality (1, 2, 3, 4, 6, 7)

- Connectionless confidentiality (1, 2, 3, 4, 6, 7)

- Selective field confidentiality (6, 7)

- Traffic flow confidentiality (1, 3, 7)

- Connection integrity with recovery (4, 7)

- Connection integrity without recovery (3, 4, 7)

- Connection integrity selective field (7)

- Connectionless integrity selective field (7)

- Nonrepudiation at origin (7)

- Nonrepudiation of delivery (7)

Mechanisms

The mechanisms to achieve this level of security are as follows:

- Peer entity authentication

  - Encryption

  - Digital signature

  - Authentication exchange

- Data origin authentication

  - Encryption

  - Digital signature

- Access control service

  - Access control lists

  - Passwords

  - Capabilities lists

  - Labels

- Connection confidentiality

  - Encryption

  - Routing control

- Connectionless confidentiality

  - Encryption

  - Routing control

- Selective field confidentiality

  - Encryption

- Traffic flow confidentiality

  - Encryption

  - Traffic padding

  - Routing control

.

- Connection integrity with recovery
  - Encryption
  - Data integrity
- Connection integrity without recovery
  - Encryption
  - Data integrity
- Connection integrity selective field
  - Encryption
  - Data integrity
- Connectionless integrity
  - Encryption
  - Digital signature
  - Data integrity
- Connectionless integrity selective field
  - Encryption
  - Digital signature
  - Data integrity
- Nonrepudiation at origin
  - Digital signature
  - Data integrity
  - Notarization
- Nonrepudiation of delivery
  - Digital signature
  - Data integrity
  - Notarization

Data Integrity

Ensuring data integrity means supplying a means of testing that the data has not been tampered with. Usually, this is done by forming a simple number out of the bytes in the data. This process is called *hashing*, and the resulting number is called a *hash* or *hash value*.

A naive hashing algorithm is just to sum up all the bytes in the data. However, this still allows almost any amount of changing the data around and still preserving the hash values. For example, an attacker could just swap two bytes. This preserves the hash value but could end up with you owing someone $65,536 instead of $256.

Hashing algorithms used for security purposes have to be "strong" so that it is very difficult for an attacker to find a different sequence of bytes with the same hash value. This makes it hard to modify the data to the attacker's purposes. Security researchers are constantly testing hash algorithms to see if they can break them – that is, find a simple way of coming up with byte sequences to match a hash value. They have devised a series of *cryptographic* hashing algorithms that are believed to be strong.

Go has support for several hashing algorithms, including MD4, MD5, RIPEMD-160, SHA1, SHA224, SHA256, SHA384, and SHA512. They all follow the same pattern as far as the Go programmer is concerned: a function New (or similar) in the appropriate package returns a Hash object from the hash package. Using the go list command, we can see this and related packages:

```
$ mkdir ch7
$ cd ch7

ch7$ go list crypto/...

crypto
crypto/aes
crypto/cipher
crypto/des
crypto/dsa
crypto/ecdsa
crypto/ed25519
crypto/ed25519/internal/edwards25519
crypto/ed25519/internal/edwards25519/field
crypto/elliptic
crypto/elliptic/internal/fiat
crypto/hmac
crypto/internal/randutil
crypto/internal/subtle
crypto/md5
crypto/rand
crypto/rc4
crypto/rsa
crypto/sha1
crypto/sha256
crypto/sha512
crypto/subtle
crypto/tls
crypto/x509
crypto/x509/internal/macos
crypto/x509/pkix
```

A hash has an io.Writer, and you write the data to be hashed to this writer. You can query the number of bytes in the hash value by Size and the hash value by Sum.

A typical use case is MD5 hashing (warning insecure). This uses the md5 package. The hash value is a 16-byte array. This is typically printed out in ASCII form as four hexadecimal numbers, each made of four bytes. A simple program is md5hash.go:

```
ch7$ vi md5hash.go

/* MD5Hash
 */
package main
```

```go
import (
        "crypto/md5"
        "fmt"
)

func main() {
        hash := md5.New()
        bytes := []byte("hello\n")
        hash.Write(bytes) // add data to running hash
        hashValue := hash.Sum(nil) // retrieve the hashed data
        hashSize := hash.Size() // how many bytes Sum returns
        // for every 4 bytes of hashValue
        // we stuff into an byte of val by shifting
        // val[first_byte] = hashValue[n] after shifting 24
        // second and third byte position after 16 and 8...
        // val[fourth_byte] = hashValue[n+3]
        // in the end, we have unint32 value that we print
        for n := 0; n < hashSize; n += 4 {
                var val uint32
                val = uint32(hashValue[n])<<24 +
                        uint32(hashValue[n+1])<<16 +
                        uint32(hashValue[n+2])<<8 +
                        uint32(hashValue[n+3])
                fmt.Printf("%x ", val)
        }
        fmt.Println()
}
```

```
ch7$ go run md5hash.go

b1946ac9 2492d234 7c6235b4 d2611184
```

If you make a small variation, say, o becomes 0, you will see a new hash.

```
ch$ go run md5hash.go // after changing hello to hell0

cd6fcbf3 8d05a093 9006387 f0446665
```

While md5 provides some protection (i.e., file integrity), it doesn't say who created or provided the file. HMAC provides not only integrity (e.g., via md5) but also authentication. A consumer must have the same key and input in order to reconstruct the HMAC.

The aforementioned focuses on mechanics; md5 is not considered best in class for hashing functions. In general, you should select an improved function such as sha256 instead of md5.

```go
// add "crypto/sha256" to import
hash := hmac.New(sha256.New, []byte("secret"))
```

Changing our prior code to use sha256 (with a hard-coded secret) generates the following output (e.g., using "hello" for the input):

```
171b5670 f7b4037f b90bef77 3b022130 e48100fd d40ea023 730097da 9a68f4ff
```

Considerations beyond hashing algorithm selection include quality of key (e.g., size and randomness). HMAC is not encryption, even though a key is used. Meaning it lives in parallel to the original (i.e., unencrypted data).

md5 provides integrity, but collisions mean another file (preimage) can produce the same hash; hence, authenticity of message is lacking. HMAC provides authenticity with addition of the key; however, maintaining the key authenticity is the source of additional issues.

Symmetric Key Encryption

There are two major mechanisms used for encrypting data. Symmetric key encryption uses a single key that is the same for both encryption and decryption. This key needs to be known to both the encrypting and the decrypting agents. How this key is transmitted between the agents is not discussed (e.g., HMAC).

As with hashing, there are many encryption algorithms. Many are now known to have weaknesses, and in general, algorithms become weaker over time as computers get faster. Go has support for several symmetric key algorithms such as AES and DES.

The algorithms are *block* algorithms. That is, they work on blocks of data. If your data is not aligned to the block size, you will have to pad it with extra blanks at the end.

Each algorithm is represented by a Cipher object. This is created by NewCipher in the appropriate package and takes the symmetric key as parameter.

Once you have a cipher, you can use it to encrypt and decrypt blocks of data. We use AES-128, which has a key size of 128 bits (16 bytes) and a block size of 128 bits. The size of the key determines which version of AES is used. A program to illustrate this is aes.go:

```
ch7$ vi aes.go

/* Aes
 */
package main

import (
        "bytes"
        "crypto/aes"
        "fmt"
)

func main() {
        key := []byte("my key, len 16 b")
        cipher, err := aes.NewCipher(key)
        if err != nil {
                fmt.Println(err.Error())
        }
        src := []byte("hello 16 b block")
        var enc [16]byte
        cipher.Encrypt(enc[0:], src)
        var decrypt [16]byte
```

```
        cipher.Decrypt(decrypt[0:], enc[0:])
        result := bytes.NewBuffer(nil)
        result.Write(decrypt[0:])
        fmt.Println(string(result.Bytes()))
}
```

```
ch7$ go run aes.go
```

```
hello 16 b block
```

This encrypts and decrypts the 16-byte block "hello 16 b block" using the shared 16-byte key "my key, len 16 b".

While we are not detailing how hashing/authenticating works, there are considerations, such as our key must have a length of 16, 24, or 32 bytes, which in turn used to select related AES-128, AES-192, or AES-256 algorithm. If you don't use the correct key size, you will see a crypto.KeySizeError, and upon failure to not deal with that error, a panic will occur during coding operations (e.g., encoding). See go doc crypto/aes. NewCipher and go doc crypto/aes.KeySizeError for more.

Here are some very popular software that uses hashing at their core. In this URL, we see a detailed history on the need to change from sha-1 to sha-256 in Git:

```
https://git-scm.com/docs/hash-function-transition/#_choice_of_hash
```

Bitcoin is also known for leveraging hashing along the blockchain. Here is an example code using hashing:

```
https://github.com/bitcoin/bitcoin/blob/master/src/merkleblock.cpp
```

Furthermore, both are using a technique called Merkle trees, where a Git commit is the tree top and a group of transactions in Bitcoin is represented as the tree top as well. You can learn more about this interesting technique here: https://en.wikipedia.org/wiki/Merkle_tree.

Public Key Encryption

The other major type of encryption is public key encryption. Public key encryption and decryption require *two* keys: one to encrypt and a second one to decrypt. The encryption key is usually made public in some way so that anyone can encrypt messages to you. The decryption key must stay private; otherwise, everyone would be able to decrypt those messages! Public key systems are asymmetric, with different keys for different uses.

Some examples of software systems that leverage PK-related technology include SSH (where you hold a private key and both the client and the server have a public key) and Secure Websites (where a public key is embedded in the cert you download and the server has the private key). These asymmetric public keys are used to generate symmetric key pairs used during a brief session. Keys are just one part of Public Key Infrastructure (e.g., certificate management coupled with keys), which is a large interesting topic.

There are many public key encryption systems supported by Go. A typical one is the RSA scheme.

A program generating RSA private and public keys from a random number is genrsakeys.go:

```
ch7$ vi genrsakeys.go
```

```
/* GenRSAKeys
 */
package main
```

```
import (
        "crypto/rand"
        "crypto/rsa"
        "crypto/x509"
        "encoding/gob"
        "encoding/pem"
        "fmt"
        "log"
        "os"
)

func main() {
        reader := rand.Reader
        bitSize := 2048
        key, err := rsa.GenerateKey(reader, bitSize)
        checkError(err)
        fmt.Printf("Private key primes:\n[0]:%s\n[1]:%s\n", key.Primes[0].String(),
                key.Primes[1].String())
        fmt.Println("Private key exponent:\n", key.D.String())
        publicKey := key.PublicKey
        fmt.Println("Public key modulus:\n", publicKey.N.String())
        fmt.Println("Public key exponent:\n", publicKey.E)
        saveGobKey("private.key", key)
        saveGobKey("public.key", publicKey)
        savePEMKey("private.pem", key)
}
func saveGobKey(fileName string, key interface{}) {
        outFile, err := os.Create(fileName)
        checkError(err)
        encoder := gob.NewEncoder(outFile)
        err = encoder.Encode(key)
        checkError(err)
        outFile.Close()
}
func savePEMKey(fileName string, key *rsa.PrivateKey) {
        outFile, err := os.Create(fileName)
        checkError(err)
        var privateKey = &pem.Block{Type: "RSA PRIVATE KEY",
                Bytes: x509.MarshalPKCS1PrivateKey(key)}
        pem.Encode(outFile, privateKey)
        outFile.Close()
}
func checkError(err error) {
        if err != nil {
                log.Fatalln("Fatal error ", err.Error())
        }
}
```

The program saves the keys and related certificate (via pem) using gob serialization. They can be read back by the loadrsakeys.go program:

```
ch7$ vi loadrsakeys.go
```

```go
/* LoadRSAKeys
 */
package main

import (
        "crypto/rsa"
        "encoding/gob"
        "fmt"
        "log"
        "os"
)

func main() {
        var key rsa.PrivateKey
        loadKey("private.key", &key)
        fmt.Printf("Private key primes:\n[0]:%s\n[1]:%s\n", key.Primes[0].String(),
                key.Primes[1].String())
        fmt.Println("Private key exponent:\n", key.D.String())
        var publicKey rsa.PublicKey
        loadKey("public.key", &publicKey)
        fmt.Println("Public key modulus:\n", publicKey.N.String())
        fmt.Println("Public key exponent:\n", publicKey.E)
}
func loadKey(fileName string, key interface{}) {
        inFile, err := os.Open(fileName)
        checkError(err)
        decoder := gob.NewDecoder(inFile)
        err = decoder.Decode(key)
        checkError(err)
        inFile.Close()
}
func checkError(err error) {
        if err != nil {
                log.Fatalln("Fatal error ", err.Error())
        }
}
```

As we execute the create and load programs, we see the following:

```
ch7$ go run genrsakeys.go

Private key primes:
[0]:1554 ... 3581
[1]:1759 ... 6267
Private key exponent:
 1034 ... 7793
Public key modulus:
 2735 ... 2127
Public key exponent:
 65537
```

```
ch7$ go run loadrsakeys.go

Private key primes:
[0]:1554 ... 3581
[1]:1759 ... 6267
Private key exponent:
 1034 ... 7793
Public key modulus:
 2735 ... 2127
Public key exponent:
 65537
```

The preceding output is abbreviated due to the length. The key thing to note is they generated output (keys) matching the loaded versions after the encoding process. We have not transmitted any encrypted data, just preparing for that eventuality.

X.509 Certificates

A Public Key Infrastructure (PKI) is a framework for a collection of public keys, along with additional information such as owner name and location and links between them giving some sort of approval mechanism.

The principal PKI in use today is based on X.509 certificates. For example, web browsers use them to verify the identity of websites.

An example program to generate a self-signed X.509 certificate for my website and store it in a .cer file is genx509cert.go:

```
ch7$ vi genx509cert.go

/* GenX509Cert
 */
package main

import (
        "crypto/rand"
        "crypto/rsa"
        "crypto/x509"
        "crypto/x509/pkix"
        "encoding/gob"
        "encoding/pem"
        "fmt"
        "math/big"
        "os"
        "time"
)

func main() {
        random := rand.Reader
        var key rsa.PrivateKey
        loadKey("private.key", &key)
        now := time.Now()
```

```go
        then := now.Add(60 * 60 * 24 * 365 * 1000 * 1000 * 1000)
        // one year
        template := x509.Certificate{
                SerialNumber: big.NewInt(1),
                Subject: pkix.Name{
                        CommonName:   "jan.newmarch.name",
                        Organization: []string{"Jan Newmarch"},
                },
                NotBefore:    now,
                NotAfter:     then,
                SubjectKeyId: []byte{1, 2, 3, 4},
                KeyUsage: x509.KeyUsageCertSign |
                        x509.KeyUsageKeyEncipherment | x509.KeyUsageDigitalSignature,
                BasicConstraintsValid: true,
                IsCA:                  true,
                DNSNames: []string{"jan.newmarch.name",
                        "localhost"},
        }
        derBytes, err := x509.CreateCertificate(random, &template,
                &template, &key.PublicKey, &key)
        checkError(err)
        certCerFile, err := os.Create("jan.newmarch.name.cer")
        checkError(err)
        certCerFile.Write(derBytes)
        certCerFile.Close()
        certPEMFile, err := os.Create("jan.newmarch.name.pem")
        checkError(err)
        pem.Encode(certPEMFile, &pem.Block{Type: "CERTIFICATE", Bytes: derBytes})
        certPEMFile.Close()
        keyPEMFile, err := os.Create("private.pem")
        checkError(err)
        pem.Encode(keyPEMFile, &pem.Block{Type: "RSA PRIVATE KEY",
                Bytes: x509.MarshalPKCS1PrivateKey(&key)})
        keyPEMFile.Close()
}
func loadKey(fileName string, key interface{}) {
        inFile, err := os.Open(fileName)
        checkError(err)
        decoder := gob.NewDecoder(inFile)
        err = decoder.Decode(key)
        checkError(err)
        inFile.Close()
}
func checkError(err error) {
        if err != nil {
                fmt.Println("Fatal error ", err.Error())
                os.Exit(1)
        }
}
```

We next load the crypto assests we just generated and provide basic checks for correctness, create loadx509cert.go:

```
ch7$ vi loadx509cert.go

/* LoadX509Cert
 */
package main

import (
    "crypto/rsa"
    "crypto/x509"
    "encoding/gob"
    "fmt"
    "log"
    "os"
)

func main() {
    // load certificate so we can access embedded public key
    certCerFile, err := os.Open("jan.newmarch.name.cer")
    checkError(err)
    derBytes := make([]byte, 1000) // bigger than the file
    count, err := certCerFile.Read(derBytes)
    checkError(err)
    certCerFile.Close()
    // trim the bytes to actual length in call
    cert, err := x509.ParseCertificate(derBytes[0:count])
    checkError(err)
    fmt.Printf("Name %s\n", cert.Subject.CommonName)
    fmt.Printf("Not before %s\n", cert.NotBefore.String())
    fmt.Printf("Not after %s\n", cert.NotAfter.String())

    // load non-emdedded public key
    // should be the same as above embedded key
    pub, err := os.Open("public.key")
    checkError(err)
    dec := gob.NewDecoder(pub)
    publicKey := new(rsa.PrivateKey)
    err = dec.Decode(publicKey)
    checkError(err)
    pub.Close()

    // genx509cert.go created a public key and certificate
    // certificates also embed the public key
    // we are comparing the public key and the embedded public key fields
    // see go doc crypto/rsa.PublicKey for more
    if cert.PublicKey.(*rsa.PublicKey).N.Cmp(publicKey.N) == 0 {
        if publicKey.E == cert.PublicKey.(*rsa.PublicKey).E {
            fmt.Println("Same public key")
            return
        }
    }
```

```
    fmt.Println("Different public key")
}
func checkError(err error) {
    if err != nil {
        log.Fatalln("Fatal error ", err.Error())
    }
}
```

Here, we can see the round trip creation and confirmation of the certificate.

```
ch7$ go run genx509cert.go
```

Note the creation of the certificate and pem files.

```
ch7$ go run loadx509cert.go

Name jan.newmarch.name
Not before 2021-12-26 22:51:42 +0000 UTC
Not after 2022-12-26 22:51:42 +0000 UTC
Same public key
```

TLS

Encryption/decryption schemes are of limited use if you have to do all the heavy lifting yourself. The most popular mechanism on the Internet to give support for encrypted message passing is currently TLS (Transport Layer Security), which was formerly SSL (Secure Sockets Layer).

In TLS, a client and a server negotiate identity using X.509 certificates. Once this is complete, a secret key is invented between them, and all encryption/decryption is done using this key. The negotiation is relatively slow, but once it's complete, the faster secret key mechanism is used. The server is *required* to have a certificate; the client *may* have one if needed.

A Basic Client

We first illustrate connecting to a server that has a certificate signed by a "well-known" certificate authority (CA) such as RSA. The program to get HEAD information from a web server can be adapted to get HEAD information from a TLS web server. The program is tlsgethead.go. We are illustrating TLS.Dial here and will discuss HTTPS in a later chapter.

```
ch7$ vi tlsgethead.go

/* TLSGetHead
 */
package main

import (
        "crypto/tls"
        "fmt"
        "io/ioutil"
```

```
        "log"
        "os"
)

func main() {
        if len(os.Args) != 2 {
                log.Fatalln("Usage: ", os.Args[0], "host:port")
        }
        service := os.Args[1]
        // Dial over secure channel
        conn, err := tls.Dial("tcp", service, nil)
        checkError(err)
        _, err = conn.Write([]byte("HEAD / HTTP/1.0\r\n\r\n"))
        checkError(err)
        result, err := ioutil.ReadAll(conn)
        checkError(err)
        fmt.Println(string(result))
        conn.Close()
        os.Exit(0)
}
func checkError(err error) {
        if err != nil {
                log.Fatalln("Fatal error ", err.Error())
        }
}
```

When we run the tlsgethead.go client against an appropriate site such as google.com we see the HTTP HEAD request results:

```
ch7$ go run tlsgethead.go google.com:443

HTTP/1.0 200 OK
Content-Type: text/html; charset=ISO-8859-1
P3P: CP="This is not a P3P policy! See g.co/p3phelp for more info."
Date: Sun, 26 Dec 2021 23:10:40 GMT
Server: gws
X-XSS-Protection: 0
X-Frame-Options: SAMEORIGIN
Expires: Sun, 26 Dec 2021 23:10:40 GMT
Cache-Control: private
Set-Cookie: 1P_JAR=2021-12-26-23; expires=Tue, 25-Jan-2022 23:10:40 GMT; path=/; domain=.
google.com; Secure
Set-Cookie: NID=511=KAxTu1K-XmrjU5Pml-zPO15rWWWWafskpa1bdm4Kcn96qPutrX_Ezc8-gSprT5Xo3fjkxwR
dBOAm5E7LqAlQJn61VABmytAfahOauqempNg8egIAus5Ch7ypME8dnJ7VRh7HdOF6XSViYsyHAWDcauelaxMCGRtW5R
SU_Nef3UQ; expires=Mon, 27-Jun-2022 23:10:40 GMT; path=/; domain=.google.com; HttpOnly
Alt-Svc: h3=":443"; ma=2592000,h3-29=":443"; ma=2592000,h3-Q050=":443";
ma=2592000,h3-Q046=":443"; ma=2592000,h3-Q043=":443"; ma=2592000,quic=":443"; ma=2592000;
v="46,43"
```

Other sites may produce other responses, but this client is still happy to have set up the TLS session with a properly authenticating server.

It's interesting to run this against the site gooogle.com (note the extra "*o*"!):

```
ch7$ go run tlsgethead.go gooogle.com:443
```

This site actually belongs to Google, as they have probably bought it to reduce fraud risk. The program throws a fatal error, as the site certificate is not for *gooogle* with three "o"s:

```
Fatal error  x509: certificate is valid for www.google.com, not gooogle.com
exit status 1
```

In the past, browsers would error on such types, now they redirect to the proper domain (sometimes).

Server Using a Self-Signed Certificate

If the server uses a self-signed certificate, as might be used internally in an organization or when experimenting, the Go package will generate an error: "x509: certificate signed by unknown authority". Either the certificate must be installed into the client's operating system (which will be O/S dependent), or the client must install the certificate as a root CA. We will show this second way.

An echo server using TLS with *any* certificate is tlsechoserver.go:

```
ch7$ vi tlsechoserver.go

/* TLSEchoServer
 */
package main

import (
        "crypto/tls"
        "fmt"
        "log"
        "net"
)

func main() {
        cert, err := tls.LoadX509KeyPair("jan.newmarch.name.pem",
                "private.pem")
        checkError(err)
        config := tls.Config{Certificates: []tls.Certificate{cert}}
        service := "0.0.0.0:1200"
        listener, err := tls.Listen("tcp", service, &config)
        checkError(err)
        fmt.Println("Listening")
        for {
                conn, err := listener.Accept()
                if err != nil {
                        fmt.Println(err.Error())
                        continue
                }
                fmt.Println("Accepted")
                go handleClient(conn)
```

```
                }
        }
        func handleClient(conn net.Conn) {
                defer conn.Close()
                var buf [512]byte
                for {
                        fmt.Println("Trying to read")
                        n, err := conn.Read(buf[0:])
                        if err != nil {
                                fmt.Println(err)
                                return
                        }
                        fmt.Println(string(buf[0:]))
                        _, err = conn.Write(buf[0:n])
                        if err != nil {
                                return
                        }
                }
        }
        func checkError(err error) {
                if err != nil {
                        log.Fatalln("Fatal error ", err.Error())
                }
        }
```

A simple TLS client won't work with this server if the certificate is self-signed, which it is here. We need to set a configuration as the third parameter to TLS.Dial, which has our certificate installed as a root certificate. Thanks to Josh Bleecher Snyder in "Getting x509: Certificate Signed by Unknown Authority" (https://groups.google.com/forum/#!topic/golang-nuts/v5ShM8R7Tdc) for showing how to do this. The server then works with the tlsechoclient.go client.

ch7$ vi tlsechoclient.go

```
package main

import (
        "crypto/tls"
        "crypto/x509"
        "fmt"
        "os"
)

func main() {
        rootPEM, err := os.ReadFile("jan.newmarch.name.pem")
        // First, create the set of root certificates. For this example we only
        // have one. It's also possible to omit this in order to use the
        // default root set of the current operating system.
        roots := x509.NewCertPool()
        if ok := roots.AppendCertsFromPEM(rootPEM); !ok {
                panic("failed to parse root certificate")
        }
```

```go
    conn, err := tls.Dial("tcp", "localhost:1200", &tls.Config{
        RootCAs: roots,
    })
    if err != nil {
        panic("failed to connect: " + err.Error())
    }

    // Now write and read lots
    for n := 0; n < 10; n++ {
        fmt.Println("Writing...")
        conn.Write([]byte("Hello " + string(n+48)))
        var buf [512]byte
        n, _ := conn.Read(buf[0:])
        fmt.Println(string(buf[0:n]))
    }

    conn.Close()
}
```

Running the server in one terminal.

```
ch7$ go run tlsechoserver.go
```

... listening ...

In another terminal, run the client.

```
ch7$ go run tlsechoclient.go localhost:1200
```

```
Writing...
Hello 0
Writing...
Hello 1
...
Writing...
Hello 9
```

Back on the server, we see the following:

```
Accepted
Trying to read
Hello 0
Trying to read
Hello 1
...
EOF
```

We can also change the client and prevent it from accepting a self-signed certificate. By changing to the following code, the outcome will differ.

```
        conn, err := tls.Dial("tcp", "localhost:1200", &tls.Config{
//              RootCAs: roots,
                InsecureSkipVerify: false,
        })

// assuming the server is running with valid root certificate

ch7$ go run tlsechoclient.go localhost:1200

panic: failed to connect: x509: "jan.newmarch.name" certificate is not trusted

goroutine 1 [running]:
main.main()
        /Users/ronaldpetty/github.com/apress/network-prog-with-go-2e/ch7/tlsechoclient.
        go:25 +0x2bb
exit status 2
```

On the server, we see the following error:

```
Trying to read
remote error: tls: bad certificate
```

Conclusion

Security is a huge area in itself, and this chapter barely touches on it. However, the major concepts have been covered. What has not been stressed is how much security needs to be built into the design phase: security as an afterthought is nearly always a failure.

CHAPTER 8

HTTP

The World Wide Web is a major distributed system, with millions of users. A site may become a web host by running an HTTP server. While web clients are typically users with a browser, there are many other "user agents" such as web spiders, web application clients, and so on.

The Web is built on top of the HTTP (Hypertext Transfer Protocol), which is typically layered on top of a socket (e.g., TCP). HTTP has been through four publicly available versions. Version 1.1 (the third version) is the most recognized (by developers). A behind-the-scene transition to HTTP/2 has captured over 60% of the current HTTP traffic. HTTP/3 is the latest update; a transition to this new version continues to increase due to performance benefits.

This chapter is an overview of HTTP, followed by the Go APIs to manage HTTP connections.

URLs and Resources

URLs specify the location of a *resource*. A resource is often a static file, such as an HTML document, an image, or a sound file. But increasingly, it may be a dynamically generated object, perhaps based on information stored in a database.

When a user agent requests a resource, what is returned is not the resource itself, but some *representation* of that resource. For example, if the resource is a static file, then what is sent to the user agent is a copy of the file.

Multiple URLs may point to the same resource, and an HTTP server will return appropriate representations of the resource for each URL. For example, a company might make product information available both internally and externally using different URLs for the same product. The internal representation of the product might include information such as internal contact officers for the product, while the external representation might include the location of stores selling the product.

This view of resources means that the HTTP protocol can be fairly simple and straightforward, while an HTTP server can be arbitrarily complex. HTTP has to deliver requests from user agents to servers and return a byte stream, while a server might have to do any amount of processing of the request.

i18n

There are complications arising from the increasing internationalization (i18n) of the Internet. Hostnames may be given in an internationalized form known as IDN (Internationalized Domain Name). In order to preserve compatibility with legacy implementations that do not understand Unicode (such as older email servers), non-ASCII domain names are mapped into an ASCII representation known as *punycode*. For example, the domain name 日本語.jp has the punycode value xn--wgv71a119e.jp. For example, we can use telnet to view the translation.

© Jan Newmarch and Ronald Petty 2022
J. Newmarch and R. Petty, *Network Programming with Go Language*,
https://doi.org/10.1007/978-1-4842-8095-9_8

```
$ mkdir ch8
$ ch ch8

ch8$ telnet 日本語.jp 80

Trying 2001:218:3001:7::110...
Connected to xn--wgv71a119e.jp.
Escape character is '^]'.
^]
telnet> quit
Connection closed.
```

The translation from a non-ASCII domain to a punycode value is not performed automatically by the Go net libraries, but there is an extension package called golang.org/x/net/idna that will convert between Unicode and its punycode value. There is an ongoing discussion at "Figure Out IDNA Punycode Story" (https://github.com/golang/go/issues/13835) about this topic.

We can try the IDNs package against the aforementioned domain, 日本語.jp; create the file punycode.go.

```
ch8$ vi punycode.go

package main

import (
        "fmt"
        "golang.org/x/net/idna"
        "net/url"
)

func main() {
        s := "https://日本語.jp:8443"
        r1, _ := idna.ToASCII(s)
        r2, _ := idna.ToUnicode(r1)

        fmt.Println(r1)
        fmt.Println(r2)
        fmt.Println(url.QueryEscape(s))
}

ch8$ go mod init example.com/user/punycode
ch8$ go mod tidy

ch8$ go run punycode.go

xn--https://-5y4qg6h355l.jp:8443
https://日本語.jp:8443
https%3A%2F%2F%E6%97%A5%E6%9C%AC%E8%AA%9E.jp%3A8443
```

Internationalized domain names open up the possibility of what are called *homograph* attacks. Many Unicode characters have a similar appearance, such as the Russian o (U+043E), the Greek o (U+03BF), and the English o (U+006F). A domain name using a homograph such as google.com (with two Russian o's) could cause havoc. A variety of defenses are known, such as always displaying the punycode (here xn–ggle-55da.com, using the Punycode converter).

The path in a URI/URL is more complex to handle, as it refers to a path relative to an HTTP server that may be running in a particular localized environment. The encoding may not be UTF-8, or even Unicode. The IRI (Internationalized Resource Identifier) manages this by first converting any localized string to UTF-8 and then percent-escaping any non-ASCII bytes. The W3C page entitled "An Introduction to Multilingual Web Addresses" (https://www.w3.org/International/articles/idn-and-iri/) has more information. Converting from other encodings to UTF-8 was covered in Chapter 6, while Go has the functions in net/url of QueryEscape/QueryUnescape and in Go 1.8 of PathEscape/PathUnescape to do the percent conversions.

HTTP Characteristics

HTTP is a stateless, connectionless, reliable protocol. In the simplest form, each request from a user agent is handled reliably, and then the connection is broken.

In the earliest version of HTTP, each request involved a separate TCP connection, so if many resources were required (such as images embedded in an HTML page), then many TCP connections had to be set up and torn down in a short space of time.

HTTP 1.1 added many optimizations in HTTP, which added complexity to the simple structure but created a more efficient and reliable protocol. HTTP/2 has adopted a binary form for further efficient gains. HTTP/3 goes one step further by replacing the typical TCP socket with UDP along with other related improvements (e.g., built-in security via TLS).

Versions

There are four versions of HTTP:

- Version 0.9 (1991): Totally obsolete

- Version 1.0 (1996): Almost obsolete

- Version 1.1 (1999): The most popular version at present

- Version 2 (2015): The latest version

- Version 3 (~2022): In final steps of formal approval, already in production use

Each version must understand the requests and responses of earlier versions.

HTTP/0.9

HTTP/0.9 was the original HTTP defined in 1991 by Tim Berners-Lee. You can find the specification here: https://www.w3.org/Protocols/HTTP/AsImplemented.html.

```
Request format:Request = Simple-Request
Simple-Request = "GET" SP Request-URI CRLF
```

Response Format

A response is of the following form:Response = Simple-Response
Simple-Response = [Entity-Body]

The aforementioned only provides a glimpse into HTTP/0.9 (e.g., SP means "space"). Since it is no longer used, we won't spend more time on it.

HTTP/1.0

This version added much more information to the requests and responses. Rather than "growing" the 0.9 format, it was just left alongside the new version. At this point, the W3C and IETF organizations were much more involved. The HTTP/1.0 specification can be found here: `https://datatracker.ietf.org/doc/html/rfc1945`.

Of note, Prof. Roy Fielding during this period became known for his development of REST. His dissertation containing much of REST can be found here: `https://www.ics.uci.edu/~fielding/pubs/dissertation/top.htm`.

Request Format

The format of requests from client to server is

```
Request = Simple-Request | Full-Request
Simple-Request = "GET" SP Request-URI CRLF
Full-Request = Request-Line
                    *(General-Header
                       | Request-Header
                       | Entity-Header)
               CRLF
               [Entity-Body]
```

A Simple-Request is an HTTP/0.9 request and must be replied to by a Simple-Response.
A Request-Line has this format:

```
Request-Line = Method SP Request-URI SP HTTP-Version CRLF
```

where

```
Method = "GET" | "HEAD" | POST |
         extension-method
```

Here's an example:

```
GET http://jan.newmarch.name/index.html HTTP/1.0
```

Response Format

A response is of the following form:

```
Response = Simple-Response | Full-Response
Simple-Response = [Entity-Body]
Full-Response = Status-Line
                *(General-Header
                    | Response-Header
                    | Entity-Header)
                CRLF
                [Entity-Body]
```

The Status-Line gives information about the fate of the request:

```
Status-Line = HTTP-Version SP Status-Code SP Reason-Phrase CRLF
```

Here's an example:

```
HTTP/1.0 200 OK
```

The status codes in the status line are as follows:

```
Status-Code =      "200" ; OK
                | "201" ; Created
                | "202" ; Accepted
                | "204" ; No Content
                | "301" ; Moved permanently
                | "302" ; Moved temporarily
                | "304" ; Not modified
                | "400" ; Bad request
                | "401" ; Unauthorized
                | "403" ; Forbidden
                | "404" ; Not found
                | "500" ; Internal server error
                | "501" ; Not implemented
                | "502" ; Bad gateway
                | "503" | Service unavailable
                | extension-code
```

Some codes were not defined at the time of the HTTP/1.0 standard. For example, 203 "Non-Authoritative Information" and 303 "See Other" are defined in HTTP/1.1.

The General-Header is typically the date, whereas the Response-Header is the location, the server, or an authentication field.

The Entity-Header contains useful information about the Entity-Body to follow:

```
Entity-Header = Allow
                | Content-Encoding
                | Content-Length
                | Content-Type
                | Expires
                | Last-Modified
                | extension-header
```

For example (where the types of field are given after a //):

```
HTTP/1.1 200 OK                          // status line
Date: Fri, 29 Aug 2003 00:59:56 GMT      // general header
Server: Apache/2.0.40 (Unix)             // response header
Content-Length: 1595                     // entity header
Content-Type: text/html; charset=ISO-8859-1 // entity header
```

HTTP 1.1

HTTP 1.1 fixes many problems with HTTP 1.0 but is more complex because of it. This version is done by extending or refining the options available to HTTP 1.0. For example:

- There are more commands such as TRACE and CONNECT.

- HTTP 1.1 tightened up the rules for the request URLs to allow proxy handling. If the request is directed through a proxy, the URL should be an absolute URL, as in

  ```
  GET http://www.w3.org/index.html HTTP/1.1
  ```

  Otherwise, an absolute path should be used and should include a Host header field, as in

  ```
  GET /index.html HTTP/1.1
  Host: www.w3.org
  ```

- There are more attributes such as If-Modified-Since, also for use by proxies.

The changes include

- Hostname identification (which allows virtual hosts)

- Content negotiation (multiple languages)

- Persistent connections (which reduce TCP overheads; this is very complex)

- Chunked transfers

- Byte ranges (request parts of documents)

- Proxy support

Thanks to the popularity of the Web, HTTP continues to be improved. HTTP/1.1 initial development started in 1997 continuing until 2014. You can find more about HTTP/1.1, including the original specification and the later more detailed documents redocumenting it.

- Single document (original format):

  - Original (1997) – https://datatracker.ietf.org/doc/html/rfc2068

  - Update (1999) – https://datatracker.ietf.org/doc/html/rfc2616

- Detailed series (all in 2014):

  - Message Syntax and Routing – https://datatracker.ietf.org/doc/html/rfc7230

- Semantics and Context – `https://datatracker.ietf.org/doc/html/rfc7231`

- Conditional Requests – `https://datatracker.ietf.org/doc/html/rfc7232`

- Range Requests – `https://datatracker.ietf.org/doc/html/rfc7233`

- Caching – `https://datatracker.ietf.org/doc/html/rfc7234`

- Authentication – `https://datatracker.ietf.org/doc/html/rfc7235`

HTTP Major Upgrades

The HTTP/0.9 protocol took one page. The HTTP/1.0 protocol was described in about 20 pages and included the HTTP/0.9 protocol. The HTTP/1.1 protocol takes 120 pages and is a substantial extension to HTTP/1.0, whereas HTTP/2 takes about 96 pages. The HTTP/2 specification just adds to the HTTP/1.1 specification. Nearing completion, the HTTP/3 specification is around 75 pages, adding more features and improvements around transport.

HTTP/2

All the earlier versions of HTTP are text based. The most significant departure for HTTP/2 is that it is a binary format. In order to ensure backward compatibility, this can't be managed by sending a binary message to an older server to see what it does. Instead, an HTTP 1.1 message is sent with extra attributes, essentially asking if the server wants to switch to HTTP/2. If it doesn't understand the extra fields, it replies with a normal HTTP 1.1 response, and the session continues with HTTP 1.1.

Otherwise, the server can respond that it is willing to change, and the session can continue with HTTP/2.

HTTP/3

HTTP/3 further improves upon ideas begun in HTTP/2 including:

- Stream multiplexing

- Per-stream flow control

- Low-latency connection establishment

A new transport mechanism was created to allow HTTP transport to perform even better. To simply compare the various major protocols:

- HTTP/1.1 is used over a variety of transport and session layers.

- HTTP/2 is used primarily with TLS over TCP.

- HTTP/3 uses the same semantics over a new transport protocol called QUIC.

HTTP/2 improved upon HTTP over TCP flaws yet didn't fully integrate with TCP (e.g., no comanagement of congestion controls across connections). HTTP/3 combines much of the HTTP/2 controls with TLS into a new protocol called QUIC. QUIC in a sense merges layers 4 and 5 yet runs on top of UDP (layer 4). Using UDP, allows HTTP/3 to ride on top of existing networks (some concern remains with TCP traffic often optimized and UDP less so on intermediate routers).

Even with the preceding improvements, a web engineer often is still working in the realm of HTTP/1.1. Creators of browsers and servers (e.g., proxies) will need to learn even more, including HTTP/2 and HTTP/3.

You can learn about QUIC transport here: `https://datatracker.ietf.org/doc/html/draft-ietf-quic-transport`.

You can learn about HTTP and QUIC here: `https://datatracker.ietf.org/doc/html/draft-ietf-quic-http`.

Simple User Agents

User agents such as browsers make requests and get responses. Go provides a set of request and response types in the net/http package. First, we take a look at net/http.Response.

The Response Type

The response type is as follows:

```
type Response struct {
    Status     string // e.g. "200 OK"
    StatusCode int    // e.g. 200
    Proto      string // e.g. "HTTP/1.0"
    ProtoMajor int    // e.g. 1
    ProtoMinor int    // e.g. 0
    Header Header
    Body io.ReadCloser
    ContentLength int64
    TransferEncoding []string
    Close bool
    Uncompressed bool
    Trailer Header
    Request *Request
    TLS *tls.ConnectionState
}
```

with the following helper methods:

```
func (r *Response) Cookies() []*Cookie
func (r *Response) Location() (*url.URL, error)
func (r *Response) ProtoAtLeast(major, minor int) bool
func (r *Response) Write(w io.Writer) error
```

Some methods are for convenience such as Cookies and Location; others are to assist with connection management like ProtoAtLeast and Write.

See the documentation for exact details (e.g., go doc -short net/http.Response.Body).

We started with Response because Go provides helper functions to make requests; later, we investigate the Request type.

The HEAD Method

We examine this data structure through examples. Each HTTP request type has its own Go function in the net/http package. The simplest request is from a user agent called HEAD, which asks for information about a resource and its HTTP server. This function can be used to make the query:

```
func Head(url string) (r *Response, err error)
```

The status of the response is in the response field Status, while the field Header is a map of the header fields in the HTTP response. A program called head.go to make this request and display the results is as follows:

```
ch8$ vi head.go

/* Head
 */
package main

import (
        "fmt"
        "log"
        "net/http"
        "os"
)

func main() {
        if len(os.Args) != 2 {
                log.Fatalln("Usage: ", os.Args[0], "host:port")
        }
        url := os.Args[1]
        response, err := http.Head(url)
        if err != nil {
                log.Fatalln(err)
        }
        fmt.Println(response.Status)
        for k, v := range response.Header {
                fmt.Println(k+":", v)
        }
}
```

When run against go.dev, we see

```
ch8$ go run head.go https://go.dev

200 OK
Content-Security-Policy: [connect-src 'self' www.google-analytics.com stats.g.doubleclick.
net ; default-src 'self' ; font-src 'self' fonts.googleapis.com fonts.gstatic.com data: ;
frame-ancestors 'self' ; frame-src 'self' www.google.com feedback.googleusercontent.com www.
googletagmanager.com scone-pa.clients6.google.com www.youtube.com player.vimeo.com ; img-
src 'self' www.google.com www.google-analytics.com ssl.gstatic.com www.gstatic.com gstatic.
com data: * ; object-src 'none' ; script-src 'self' 'sha256-n6OdwTrm52KqKm6aHYgDOTFUdMgww4a
```

```
OGQlIAVrMzck=' 'sha256-4ryYrf7Y5daLOBvOCpYtyBIcJPZkRD2eBPdfqsN3r1M=' 'sha256-sVKXO8+SqOmnWh
iySYk3xC7RDUgKyAkmbXV2GWts4fo=' www.google.com apis.google.com www.gstatic.com gstatic.com
support.google.com www.googletagmanager.com www.google-analytics.com ssl.google-analytics.
com tagmanager.google.com ; style-src 'self' 'unsafe-inline' fonts.googleapis.com feedback.
googleusercontent.com www.gstatic.com gstatic.com tagmanager.google.com ;]
Strict-Transport-Security: [max-age=31536000; includeSubDomains; preload]
X-Cloud-Trace-Context: [7ba1cc2dfaeebe50e11befbb48523327]
Date: [Thu, 31 Mar 2022 23:19:03 GMT]
Server: [Google Frontend]
Content-Type: [text/html; charset=utf-8]
Vary: [Accept-Encoding]
```

The response comes from a server out of our control, and it may pass through other servers on the way. The fields displayed may be different, and certainly, the values of the fields will differ. Here is a brief description of some of the response headers:

- Vary: Tells an origin server which fields to use aside from "method", "Host", and request target when selecting a representation of a resource

  - Vary is part of HTTP/1.1 – https://datatracker.ietf.org/doc/html/rfc7231#section-7.1.4

- Strict-Transport-Security: Used by the server to tell a browser (client) to use HTTPS instead of HTTP

  - Also known as HSTS, an added policy to HTTP – https://www.rfc-editor.org/rfc/rfc6797

- X-Cloud-Trace-Context: Is a tracing header used by Google Cloud Platform

- Date: When the origin server generated the response

- Server: Used to identify the response generating software

  - Server is part of HTTP/1.1 – https://datatracker.ietf.org/doc/html/rfc2616#section-14.38

- Alt-Svc: Stands for Alternative Services, allows origin's resources to be authoritatively available at a separate location and even different protocol

  - The proposal can be found here: https://datatracker.ietf.org/doc/html/rfc7838

  - The proposal explains that Alt-Svc was added to clarify the location of a resource vs. the identification of the resource. Here, we see it used to explain we can modify our request to h3 (HTTP/3) and even QUIC!

    - "ma" stands for max-age for availability of resource at this location/protocol.

    - "v" is used to indicate the version of protocol used, part of earlier QUIC-HTTP drafts still used by some.

- Content-Type: Used to parse response body

While this book is not focused on any particular aspect of networking and its main focus is Go's network abilities; we find it instructive to explain related items such as the aforementioned headers.

These convenience functions such as Head have unspoken complexity behind them. Take a peek at Head's documentation.

```
ch8$ go doc net/http.Head

package http // import "net/http"

func Head(url string) (resp *Response, err error)
    Head issues a HEAD to the specified URL. If the response is one of the
    following redirect codes, Head follows the redirect, up to a maximum of 10
    redirects:

        301 (Moved Permanently)
        302 (Found)
        303 (See Other)
        307 (Temporary Redirect)
        308 (Permanent Redirect)

    Head is a wrapper around DefaultClient.Head

    To make a request with a specified context.Context, use
    NewRequestWithContext and DefaultClient.Do.
```

The following are a couple of critical items to consider:

- 30z causes a redirect (a.k.a. another request).

- A default client exists:

```
ch8$ go doc net/http.DefaultClient

package http // import "net/http"

var DefaultClient = &Client{}
    DefaultClient is the default Client and is used by Get, Head, and Post.
```

We will learn more about this client including its related Do method.

The GET Method

Usually, we want to retrieve a representation of a resource rather than just getting information about it. The GET request will do this and can be done using the following:

```
func Get(url string) (r *Response, finalURL string, err error)
```

The content of the response is in the response field Body, which is of type io.ReadCloser. We can print the content to the screen with the program get.go:

```
ch8$ vi get.go

/* Get
 */
package main
```

```go
import (
        "fmt"
        "io"
        "log"
        "net/http"
        "net/http/httputil"
        "os"
        "strings"
)

func main() {
        if len(os.Args) != 2 {
                log.Fatalln("Usage: ", os.Args[0], "host:port")
        }
        url := os.Args[1]
        response, err := http.Get(url)
        checkError(err)
        if response.StatusCode != http.StatusOK {
                log.Fatalln(response.StatusCode)
        }
        fmt.Println("The response header is")
        b, _ := httputil.DumpResponse(response, false)
        fmt.Print(string(b))
        contentTypes := response.Header["Content-Type"]
        if !acceptableCharset(contentTypes) {
                log.Fatalln("Cannot handle", contentTypes)
        }
        fmt.Println("The response body is")
        var buf [512]byte
        reader := response.Body
        for {
                n, err := reader.Read(buf[0:])
                if err != nil {
                        if err == io.EOF {
                                fmt.Print(string(buf[0:n]))
                                reader.Close()
                                break
                        }
                        checkError(err)
                }
                fmt.Print(string(buf[0:n]))
        }
}
func acceptableCharset(contentTypes []string) bool {
        // each type is like [text/html; charset=utf-8]
        // we want the UTF-8 only
        for _, cType := range contentTypes {
                if strings.Index(cType, "utf-8") != -1 {
```

```
                        return true
                }
        }
        return false
}

func checkError(err error) {
        if err != nil {
                log.Fatalln(err)
        }
}
```

When the get.go client run against the Go website we see the following.

```
ch8$ go run get.go https://go.dev

The response header is
HTTP/2.0 200 OK
Cache-Control: private
Content-Security-Policy: connect-src 'self' www.google-analytics.com stats.g.doubleclick.
net ; default-src 'self' ; font-src 'self' fonts.googleapis.com fonts.gstatic.com data: ;
frame-ancestors 'self' ; frame-src 'self' www.google.com feedback.googleusercontent.com www.
googletagmanager.com scone-pa.clients6.google.com www.youtube.com player.vimeo.com ; img-
src 'self' www.google.com www.google-analytics.com ssl.gstatic.com www.gstatic.com gstatic.
com data: * ; object-src 'none' ; script-src 'self' 'sha256-n6OdwTrm52KqKm6aHYgDOTFUdMgww4a
OGQlIAVrMzck=' 'sha256-4ryYrf7Y5daLOBvOCpYtyBIcJPZkRD2eBPdfqsN3r1M=' 'sha256-sVKXO8+SqOmnWh
iySYk3xC7RDUgKyAkmbXV2GWts4fo=' www.google.com apis.google.com www.gstatic.com gstatic.com
support.google.com www.googletagmanager.com www.google-analytics.com ssl.google-analytics.
com tagmanager.google.com ; style-src 'self' 'unsafe-inline' fonts.googleapis.com feedback.
googleusercontent.com www.gstatic.com gstatic.com tagmanager.google.com ;
Content-Type: text/html; charset=utf-8
Date: Thu, 31 Mar 2022 23:33:22 GMT
Server: Google Frontend
Strict-Transport-Security: max-age=31536000; includeSubDomains; preload
Vary: Accept-Encoding
X-Cloud-Trace-Context: d6e6efc338f0723fe7550203794db95c

The response body is
<!DOCTYPE html>
<html lang="en" data-theme="light">
<head>

<link rel="preconnect" href="https://www.googletagmanager.com">
<script >(function(w,d,s,l,i){w[l]=w[l]||[];w[l].push({'gtm.start':
  new Date().getTime(),event:'gtm.js'});var f=d.getElementsByTagName(s)[0],
  j=d.createElement(s),dl=l!='dataLayer'?'&l='+l:'';j.async=true;j.src=
  'https://www.googletagmanager.com/gtm.js?id='+i+dl;f.parentNode.insertBefore(j,f);
  })(window,document,'script','dataLayer','GTM-W8MVQXG');</script>

<meta charset="utf-8">
```

```
<meta name="description" content="Go is an open source programming language that makes it
easy to build simple, reliable, and efficient software.">
<meta name="viewport" content="width=device-width, initial-scale=1">
<meta name="theme-color" content="#00add8">
<link rel="stylesheet" href="https://fonts.googleapis.com/css?family=Material+Icons">
<link rel="stylesheet" href="/css/styles.css">

  <script>(function(w,d,s,l,i){w[l]=w[l]||[];w[l].push({'gtm.start':
  new Date().getTime(),event:'gtm.js'});var f=d.getElementsByTagName(s)[0],
  j=d.createElement(s),dl=l!='dataLayer'?'&l='+l:'';j.async=true;j.src=
  'https://www.googletagmanager.com/gtm.js?id='+i+dl;f.parentNode.insertBefore(j,f);
  })(window,document,'script','dataLayer','GTM-W8MVQXG');</script>

<script src="/js/site.js"></script>
<title>The Go Programming Language</title>
</head>
<body class="Site">
...
```

This request been sent with HTTP/2. The Go library has performed the version negotiation for you. Based on TLS handshake and other information, Go upgrades to HTTP/2. Again, these convenience functions and related client make it easy to start using HTTP with Go. If you want to keep with HTTP/1.1, you can try the following override:

```
GODEBUG=http2client=0 go run get.go https://go.dev
```

The related code is documented as follows:

```
ch8$ go doc -u net/http onceSetNextProtoDefaults

package http // import "net/http"

func (srv *Server) onceSetNextProtoDefaults()
    onceSetNextProtoDefaults configures HTTP/2, if the user hasn't configured
    otherwise. (by setting srv.TLSNextProto non-nil) It must only be called via
    srv.nextProtoOnce (use srv.setupHTTP2_*).

func (t *Transport) onceSetNextProtoDefaults()
    onceSetNextProtoDefaults initializes TLSNextProto. It must be called via
    t.nextProtoOnce.Do.
```

Later, we look at customizing the client behavior.

There are important character set issues of the type discussed in the previous chapter. The server will deliver the content using some character set encoding and possibly some transfer encoding. Usually, this is a matter of negotiation between user agent and server, but the simple GET command that we used does not include the user agent component of the negotiation. So the server can send whatever character encoding it wants.

At the time of first writing, I (Jan) was in China (and Google could be accessed). When I tried this program on www.google.com, Google's server tried to be helpful by guessing my location and sending me the text in the Chinese character set Big5! How to tell the server what character encoding is okay for me is discussed later.

Configuring HTTP Requests

Go also supplies a lower-level interface for user agents to communicate with HTTP servers. As you might expect, not only does it give you more control over the client requests, but it also requires you to spend more effort in building the requests. However, there is only a small increase in complexity.

The data type used to build requests is the type Request; have a look at the documentation.

```go
type Request struct {
    Method string
    URL *url.URL
    Proto      string // "HTTP/1.0"
    ProtoMajor int    // 1
    ProtoMinor int    // 0
    Header Header
    Body io.ReadCloser
    GetBody func() (io.ReadCloser, error)
    ContentLength int64
    TransferEncoding []string
    Close bool
    Host string
    Form url.Values
    PostForm url.Values
    MultipartForm *multipart.Form
    Trailer Header
    RemoteAddr string
    RequestURI string
    TLS *tls.ConnectionState
    Cancel <-chan struct{}
    Response *Response
}
```

Here are the related methods:

```go
func (r *Request) AddCookie(c *Cookie)
func (r *Request) BasicAuth() (username, password string, ok bool)
func (r *Request) Clone(ctx context.Context) *Request
func (r *Request) Context() context.Context
func (r *Request) Cookie(name string) (*Cookie, error)
func (r *Request) Cookies() []*Cookie
func (r *Request) FormFile(key string) (multipart.File, *multipart.FileHeader, error)
func (r *Request) FormValue(key string) string
func (r *Request) MultipartReader() (*multipart.Reader, error)
func (r *Request) ParseForm() error
func (r *Request) ParseMultipartForm(maxMemory int64) error
func (r *Request) PostFormValue(key string) string
func (r *Request) ProtoAtLeast(major, minor int) bool
func (r *Request) Referer() string
func (r *Request) SetBasicAuth(username, password string)
func (r *Request) UserAgent() string
func (r *Request) WithContext(ctx context.Context) *Request
func (r *Request) Write(w io.Writer) error
func (r *Request) WriteProxy(w io.Writer) error
```

Some methods of Request are used during client setup; others are used by the server to retrieve information.

There is a lot of information that can be stored in a request. You do not need to fill in all the fields, only those of interest. The simplest way to create a request with default values is using this, for example:

```
request, err := http.NewRequest("GET", url.String(), nil)
```

Once a request has been created, you can modify the fields. For example, to specify that you want to receive only UTF-8, add an Accept-Charset field to a request as follows:

```
request.Header.Add("Accept-Charset", "UTF-8;q=1, ISO-8859-1;q=0")
```

(Note that the default set ISO-8859-1 always gets a value of 1 unless mentioned explicitly in the list, as we do. The HTTP 1.1 specification dates back to 1999!)

A client setting a charset request is simple. But there is some confusion about what happens with the server's return value of a charset. The returned resource *should* have a Content-Type that will specify the media type of the content such as text/html. If appropriate, the media type should state the charset, such as text/html; charset=UTF-8. If there is no charset specification, then according to the HTTP specification, it should be treated as the default ISO-8859-1 charset. But the HTML4 specification states that since many servers don't conform to this, you can't make any assumptions.

If there is a charset specified in the server's Content-Type, then assume it is correct. If there is none specified, since more than 50% of pages are in UTF-8 and some are in ASCII, it is safe to assume UTF-8. Fewer than 10% of pages may be wrong :-(.

The Client Object

To send a request to a server and get a reply, the convenience object Client is the easiest way. This object can manage multiple requests and will look after issues such as whether the server keeps the TCP connection alive and so on.

This is illustrated in the following program: clientget.go.

The program shows how to add HTTP headers, as we add the header Accept-Charset to only accept UTF-8. There is a little hiccup here, caused by a bug in Go, which has only been fixed in Go 1.8. The Client. Do function will automatically do a redirect if it gets a 301, 302, 303, or 307 response. Prior to Go 1.8, it didn't copy across the HTTP headers in this redirect.

If you try against a site such as http://www.google.com, then it will redirect to a site such as http://www.google.com.au but will lose the Accept-Charset header and return ISO-8859-1 (as it should do according to the 1999 HTTP 1.1 specification). With that proviso – that the program may not give correct results on versions prior to Go 1.8 – the program is as follows:

```
ch8$ vi clientget.go

/* ClientGet
 */
package main

import (
        "io"
        "fmt"
        "log"
        "net/http"
```

```go
                "net/http/httputil"
        "net/url"
        "os"
        "strings"
)

func main() {
        if len(os.Args) != 2 {
                log.Fatalln("Usage: ", os.Args[0], "http://host:port/page")
        }
        url, err := url.Parse(os.Args[1])
        checkError(err)
        client := &http.Client{}
        request, err := http.NewRequest("HEAD", url.String(), nil)
        // only accept UTF-8
        request.Header.Add("Accept-Charset", "utf-8;q=1,ISO-8859-1;q=0")
        checkError(err)
        response, err := client.Do(request)
        checkError(err)
        if response.StatusCode != http.StatusOK {
                log.Fatalln(response.Status)
        }
        fmt.Println("The response header is")
        b, _ := httputil.DumpResponse(response, false)
        fmt.Print(string(b))
        chSet := getCharset(response)
        if chSet != "utf-8" {
                log.Fatalln("Cannot handle", chSet)
        }
        var buf [512]byte
        reader := response.Body
        fmt.Println("got body")
        for {
                n, err := reader.Read(buf[0:])
                if err != nil {
                        if err == io.EOF {
                                fmt.Print(string(buf[0:n]))
                                break
                        }
                        checkError(err)
                }
                fmt.Print(string(buf[0:n]))
        }
}
func getCharset(response *http.Response) string {
        contentType := response.Header.Get("Content-Type")
        if contentType == "" {
                // guess
                return "utf-8"
        }
        idx := strings.Index(contentType, "charset=")
```

```
        if idx == -1 {
                // guess
                return "utf-8"
        }
        // we found charset now remove it
        chSet := strings.Trim(contentType[idx+8:], " ")
        return strings.ToLower(chSet)
}
func checkError(err error) {
        if err != nil {
                log.Fatalln("Fatal error ", err.Error())
        }
}
```

The program is run as follows, for example:

```
ch8$ go run clientget.go https://go.dev

The response header is
HTTP/2.0 200 OK
Connection: close
Content-Security-Policy: connect-src 'self' www.google-analytics.com stats.g.doubleclick.
net ; default-src 'self' ; font-src 'self' fonts.googleapis.com fonts.gstatic.com data: ;
frame-ancestors 'self' ; frame-src 'self' www.google.com feedback.googleusercontent.com www.
googletagmanager.com scone-pa.clients6.google.com www.youtube.com player.vimeo.com ; img-
src 'self' www.google.com www.google-analytics.com ssl.gstatic.com www.gstatic.com gstatic.
com data: * ; object-src 'none' ; script-src 'self' 'sha256-n6OdwTrm52KqKm6aHYgDOTFUdMgww4a
OGQlIAVrMzck=' 'sha256-4ryYrf7Y5daLOBvOCpYtyBIcJPZkRD2eBPdfqsN3r1M=' 'sha256-sVKXO8+SqOmnWh
iySYk3xC7RDUgKyAkmbXV2GWts4fo=' www.google.com apis.google.com www.gstatic.com gstatic.com
support.google.com www.googletagmanager.com www.google-analytics.com ssl.google-analytics.
com tagmanager.google.com ; style-src 'self' 'unsafe-inline' fonts.googleapis.com feedback.
googleusercontent.com www.gstatic.com gstatic.com tagmanager.google.com ;
Content-Type: text/html; charset=utf-8
Date: Thu, 31 Mar 2022 23:45:09 GMT
Server: Google Frontend
Strict-Transport-Security: max-age=31536000; includeSubDomains; preload
Vary: Accept-Encoding
X-Cloud-Trace-Context: 9caa17c0647c300f6e52d795661bf512

got body
```

Proxy Handling

It is very common now for HTTP requests to pass through specific HTTP proxies. This is in addition to the servers that form the TCP connection and act at the application layer. Companies use proxies to limit what their own staff can see, while many organizations use proxy services such as Cloudflare to act as caches, reducing the load on the organization's own servers. Accessing websites through proxies requires additional handling by the client.

Simple Proxy

HTTP 1.1 laid out how HTTP should work through a proxy. A GET request should be made to a proxy. However, the URL requested should be the full URL of the destination. In addition, the HTTP header should contain a Host field, set to the proxy. As long as the proxy is configured to pass such requests through, then that is all that needs to be done.

Go considers this to be part of the HTTP transport layer. To manage this, it has a class Transport. This contains a field that can be set to a *function* that returns a URL for a proxy. If we have a URL as a string for the proxy, the appropriate transport object is created and then given to a client object as follows:

```
// prepare for transport
proxyURL, err := url.Parse(proxyString)

// RoundTripper implementation that supports HTTP proxies
// see go doc net/http.RoundTripper
transport := &http.Transport{Proxy: http.ProxyURL(proxyURL)}

// used to send our HTTP quest
client := &http.Client{Transport: transport}
```

The client can then continue as before.

The following program proxyget.go illustrates this.

```
ch8$ vi proxyget.go

/* ProxyGet
 */
package main

import (
        "fmt"
        "io"
        "log"
        "net/http"
        "net/url"
        "os"
)

func main() {
        if len(os.Args) != 2 {
                log.Fatalln("Usage: ", os.Args[0], "http://host:port/page")
        }
        rawURL := os.Args[1]
        url, err := url.Parse(rawURL)
        checkError(err)

        response, err := http.Get(url.String())

        checkError(err)
        fmt.Println("Read ok")

        if response.StatusCode != http.StatusOK {
```

```
                log.Fatalln(response.StatusCode)
        }
        fmt.Println("Response ok")

        var buf [512]byte
        reader := response.Body
        for {
                n, err := reader.Read(buf[0:])
                if err != nil {
                        if err == io.EOF {
                                fmt.Print(string(buf[0:n]))
                                reader.Close()
                                break
                        }
                        checkError(err)
                }
                fmt.Print(string(buf[0:n]))
        }
}
func checkError(err error) {
        if err != nil {
                log.Fatalln("Fatal error ", err.Error())
        }
}
```

If you have a proxy at, say, XYZ.com on port 8080, you can test this as follows:

```
ch8$ go run proxyget.go http://XYZ.com:8080 https://www.google.com
```

If you don't have a suitable proxy to test this, then download and install the Squid proxy (http://www.squid-cache.org/) to your own computer. For example, on a Mac with Homebrew installed:

```
ch8$ brew install squid        // install via Homebrew
ch8$ brew service start squid // run Squid on port 3128
```

You can now run the client against this locally running proxy.

```
ch8$ HTTP_PROXY=localhost:3128 go run proxyget.go https://www.google.com
```

```
Read ok
Response ok
<!doctype html><html itemscope=""...
```

This program used our proxy passed (via HTTP_PROXY) as an environment variable to the program. There are many ways that proxies can be made known to applications. Most browsers have a configuration menu in which you can enter proxy information; such information is not available to a Go application. Some applications may get proxy information using the Web Proxy Autodiscovery Protocol (WPAD – https://en.wikipedia.org/wiki/Web_Proxy_Autodiscovery_Protocol) via a file often known as proxy.pac somewhere in your network. Go does not (yet) know how to parse these JavaScript files and so cannot use them. Particular operating systems may have system-specific means of specifying proxies. Go cannot access these. But it can find proxy information if it is set in operating system environment variables such as HTTP_ PROXY or http_proxy using this function:

```
func ProxyFromEnvironment(req *Request) (*url.URL, error)
```

If your programs are running in such an environment, you can use this function instead of having to explicitly know the proxy parameters. See go doc net/http ProxyFromEnvironment for more.

Authenticating Proxy

Some proxies will require authentication by a username and password in order to pass requests. A common scheme is "basic authentication" in which the username and password are concatenated into a string "user:password" and then Base64 encoded. This is then given to the proxy by the HTTP request header "Proxy-Authorization" with the flag that it is the basic authentication.

The following program proxyauthget.go illustrates this, adding the Proxy-Authentication header to the previous proxy program:

```
ch8$ vi proxyauthget.go

/* ProxyAuthGet
 */
package main

import (
        "encoding/base64"
        "fmt"
        "io"
        "net/http"
        "net/http/httputil"
        "net/url"
        "os"
)

const auth = "jannewmarch:mypassword"

func main() {
        if len(os.Args) != 3 {

                fmt.Println("Usage: ", os.Args[0], "http://proxy-host:port http://
                host:port/page")
                os.Exit(1)
        }
        proxy := os.Args[1]
        proxyURL, err := url.Parse(proxy)
        checkError(err)
        rawURL := os.Args[2]
        url, err := url.Parse(rawURL)
        checkError(err)

        // encode the auth
```

```
        basic := "Basic " +
                base64.StdEncoding.EncodeToString([]byte(auth))

        transport := &http.Transport{Proxy: http.ProxyURL(proxyURL)}
        client := &http.Client{Transport: transport}

        request, err := http.NewRequest("GET", url.String(), nil)

        request.Header.Add("Proxy-Authorization", basic)
        dump, _ := httputil.DumpRequest(request, false)
        fmt.Println(string(dump))

        // send the request
        response, err := client.Do(request)

        checkError(err)
        fmt.Println("Read ok")
        if response.Status != "200 OK" {
                fmt.Println(response.Status)
                os.Exit(2)
        }
        fmt.Println("Response ok")

        var buf [512]byte
        reader := response.Body
        for {
                n, err := reader.Read(buf[0:])
                if err != nil {
                        os.Exit(0)
                }
                fmt.Print(string(buf[0:n]))
        }
        os.Exit(0)
}
func checkError(err error) {
        if err != nil {
                if err == io.EOF {
                        return
                }
                fmt.Println("Fatal error ", err.Error())
                os.Exit(1)
        }
}
```

There doesn't seem to be a publicly available test site for this type of program. I tested it at work where an authenticating proxy is used. Setting up such a proxy is beyond the scope of this book. There is a discussion on how to do this called "How to Set Up a Squid Proxy with Basic Username and Password Authentication" (see http://stackoverflow.com/questions/3297196/how-to-set-up-a-squid-proxy-with-basic-username-and-password-authentication).

The code currently hard-codes the username and password. If you fail to use the correct login, you may get an error such as

```
ch8$ go run proxyauthget.go http://localhost:3128/ http://www.google.com

GET / HTTP/1.1
Host: www.google.com
Proxy-Authorization: Basic amphbm5ld21hcmNoOm15cGFzc3dvcmQ=

Read ok
407 Proxy Authentication Required
exit status 2
```

If it works, you will receive similar results as with the unauthenticated proxy.

```
ch8$ go run proxyauthget.go http://localhost:3128/ http://www.google.com

GET / HTTP/1.1
Host: www.google.com
Proxy-Authorization: Basic amFubmV3bWFyY2g6bXlwYXNzd29yZA==

Read ok
Response ok
<!doctype html><html...
```

HTTPS Connections by Clients

For secure, encrypted connections, HTTP uses TLS, which is described in Chapter 7. The protocol of HTTP+TLS is called HTTPS and uses https:// URLs instead of http:// URLs.

Servers are required to return valid X.509 certificates before a client will accept data from them. If the certificate is valid, then Go handles everything under the hood, and the clients given previously run okay with https URLs. That is, programs such as the earlier clientget.go run unchanged – you just give them an HTTPS URL.

Many sites have invalid certificates. They may have expired, they may be self-signed instead of by a recognized certificate authority, or they may just have errors (such as having an incorrect server name). Browsers such as Firefox put a big warning notice with a "Get me out of here!" button, but you can carry on at your risk, which many people do.

Go presently bails out when it encounters certificate errors. However, you can configure a client to ignore certificate errors. This is, of course, not advisable – sites with misconfigured certificates may have other problems.

In Chapter 7, we generated self-signed X.509 certificates. Later in this chapter, we will give an HTTPS server using X.509 certificates, and if the self-signed certificates are used, then clientget.go will generate this error:

```
x509: certificate signed by unknown authority
```

A client that removes these errors and continues does so by turning on the Transport configuration flag InsecureSkipVerify. The unsafe program is tlsunsafeclientget.go:

```
ch8$ vi tlsunsafeclientget.go
```

```
/* TLSUnsafeClientGet
 */
package main

import (
        "crypto/tls"
        "fmt"
        "log"
        "net/http"
        "net/url"
        "os"
        "strings"
)

func main() {
        if len(os.Args) != 2 {
                log.Fatalln("Usage: ", os.Args[0], "https://host:port/page")
        }
        url, err := url.Parse(os.Args[1])
        checkError(err)
        if url.Scheme != "https" {
                log.Fatalln("Not https scheme ", url.Scheme)
        }

        transport := &http.Transport{}
        transport.TLSClientConfig = &tls.Config{InsecureSkipVerify: false}
        client := &http.Client{Transport: transport}

        request, err := http.NewRequest("GET", url.String(), nil)
        // only accept UTF-8
        checkError(err)

        response, err := client.Do(request)
        checkError(err)

        if response.StatusCode != http.StatusOK {
                log.Fatalln(response.Status)
        }
        fmt.Println("get a response")

        chSet := getCharset(response)
        fmt.Printf("got charset %s\n", chSet)
        if chSet != "UTF-8" {
                log.Fatalln("Cannot handle", chSet)
        }

        var buf [512]byte
        reader := response.Body
        fmt.Println("got body")
        for {
                n, err := reader.Read(buf[0:])
```

```
                checkError(err)
                fmt.Print(string(buf[0:n]))
        }
}
func getCharset(response *http.Response) string {
        contentType := response.Header.Get("Content-Type")
        if contentType == "" {
                // guess
                return "UTF-8"
        }
        idx := strings.Index(contentType, "charset:")
        if idx == -1 {
                // guess
                return "UTF-8"
        }
        return strings.Trim(contentType[idx:], " ")
}
func checkError(err error) {
        if err != nil {
                log.Fatalln("Fatal error ", err.Error())
        }
}
```

Until we create the server side, let's try against https://gooogle.com (notice three "o"s), probably not valid.

```
ch8$ go run tlsunsafeclientget.go https://gooogle.com

Fatal error  Get "https://gooogle.com": x509: certificate is valid for www.google.com, not
gooogle.com
exit status 1
```

Servers

The other side to building a client is a web server handling HTTP requests. The simplest – and earliest – servers just returned copies of files. However, any URL can now trigger an arbitrary computation in current servers.

File Server

We start with a basic file server. Go supplies a *multiplexer*, that is, an object that will read and interpret requests. It hands out requests to handlers, which run in their own thread. Thus, much of the work of reading HTTP requests, decoding them, and branching to suitable functions in their own thread is done for us.

For a file server, Go also gives a FileServer object, which knows how to deliver files from the local file system. It takes a "root" directory, which is the top of a file tree in the local system, and a pattern to match URLs against. The simplest pattern is /, which is the top of any URL. This will match all URLs.

An HTTP server delivering files from the local file system is almost embarrassingly trivial given these objects. It is fileserver.go:

```
ch8$ vi fileserver.go

/* File Server
 */
package main

import (
        "log"
        "net/http"
)

func main() {
        // deliver files from the directory /tmp/www
        fileServer := http.FileServer(http.Dir("/tmp/www"))

        // register the handler and deliver requests to it
        err := http.ListenAndServe(":8000", fileServer)
        if err != nil {
                log.Fatalln(err)
        }
        // That's it!
}
```

This server even delivers "404 not found" messages for requests for file resources that don't exist! If the file requested is a directory, it returns a list wrapped in <pre> ... </pre> tags with no other HTML headers or markup. If Wireshark or a simple telnet client is used, directories are sent as text/html, HTML files as text/html, Perl files as text/x-perl, Java files as text/x-java, and so on. The FileServer employs some type recognition and includes that in the HTTP request, but it does not give the control over markup that a server such as Apache does.

The server and a curl client run as follows:

```
ch8$ go run FileServer.go

ch8$ curl localhost:8000

404 page not found

ch8$ mkdir -p /tmp/www/

ch8$ echo hi > /tmp/www/hi.txt

ch8$ curl localhost:8000/

<pre>
<a href="hi.txt">hi.txt</a>
</pre>
```

```
ch8$ curl localhost:8000/hi.txt

hi
```

Handler Functions

In this last program, the handler was given in the second argument to ListenAndServe. Any number of handlers can be registered first by calls to Handle or HandleFunc, with these signatures:

```
func Handle(pattern string, handler Handler)
func HandleFunc(pattern string, handler func(ResponseWriter, *Request))
```

The second argument to ListenAndServe could be nil, and then calls are dispatched to all registered handlers. Each handler should have a different URL pattern. For example, the file handler might have URL pattern /, while a function handler might have URL pattern /cgi-bin (we used /tmp/www). A more specific pattern takes precedence over a more general pattern.

Common CGI programs are test-cgi (written in the shell) and printenv (written in Perl), which print the values of the environment variables. A handler can be written to work in a similar manner as printenv.go.

```
ch8$ vi printenv.go

/* Print Env
 */
package main

import (
        "fmt"
        "net/http"
        "os"
)

func main() {
        // file handler for most files
        fileServer := http.FileServer(http.Dir("/tmp/www"))
        http.Handle("/", fileServer)
        // function handler for /cgi-bin/printenv
        http.HandleFunc("/cgi-bin/printenv", printEnv)

        // deliver requests to the handlers
        err := http.ListenAndServe(":8000", nil)
        checkError(err)
        // That's it!
}
func printEnv(writer http.ResponseWriter, req *http.Request) {
        env := os.Environ()
        writer.Write([]byte("<h1>Environment</h1><pre>"))
        for _, v := range env {
                writer.Write([]byte(v + "\n"))
        }
```

```
        writer.Write([]byte("</pre>"))
}
func checkError(err error) {
        if err != nil {
                fmt.Println("Fatal error ", err.Error())
                os.Exit(1)
        }
}
```

Run the server as follows:

```
ch8$ go run printenv.go
```

Now we run a curl client as follows:

```
ch8$ curl localhost:8000/cgi-bin/printenv
```

```
<h1>Environment</h1><pre>TERM_PROGRAM=Apple_Terminal
SHELL=/bin/zsh
TERM=xterm-256color
TMPDIR=/var/folders/c5/l52zshy12q1bsfhp_sbdtg5r0000gn/T/
TERM_PROGRAM_VERSION=444
TERM_SESSION_ID=803B4A5C-F403-40E8-97CC-0EC807C35D77
USER=ronaldpetty
SSH_AUTH_SOCK=/private/tmp/com.apple.launchd.vj8cVxhj0c/Listeners
```

Using the `cgi-bin` directory in this program is a bit cheeky: it doesn't call an external program like CGI scripts do. It just calls the Go function `printEnv`. Go does have the ability to call external programs using `os.ForkExec` but does not yet have support for dynamically linkable modules like Apache's `mod_perl`. You most likely want to wrap the results as proper HTML in this case.

Bypassing the Default Multiplexer

HTTP requests received by a Go server are usually handled by a multiplexer, which examines the path in the HTTP request and calls the appropriate file handler, etc. You can define your own handlers. These can be registered with the default multiplexer by calling `http.HandleFunc`, which takes a pattern and a function. The functions such as `ListenAndServe` then take a `nil` handler function. This was done in the last example.

However, if you want to take over the multiplexer role, then you can give a non-`nil` function as the handler function to `ListenAndServe`. This function will then be responsible for managing the requests and responses.

The following example is trivial but illustrates the use of this. The multiplexer function simply returns a `"204 No content"` for *all* requests to `serverhandler.go`:

```
ch8$ vi serverhandler.go
```

```
/* ServerHandler
 */

package main
```

```
import (
        "net/http"
)

func main() {
        myHandler := http.HandlerFunc(func(rw http.ResponseWriter,
                request *http.Request) {

                // Just return no content - arbitrary headers can be set, arbitrary body
                rw.WriteHeader(http.StatusNoContent)
        })

        http.ListenAndServe(":8080", myHandler)
}
```

The server may be tested by running telnet against it to give output such as this:

```
ch8$ curl -v localhost:8080

*   Trying 127.0.0.1:8080...
* Connected to localhost (127.0.0.1) port 8080 (#0)
> GET / HTTP/1.1
> Host: localhost:8080
> User-Agent: curl/7.79.1
> Accept: */*
>
* Mark bundle as not supporting multiuse
< HTTP/1.1 204 No Content
< Date: Fri, 01 Apr 2022 03:21:41 GMT
<
* Connection #0 to host localhost left intact
```

HTTPS

For secure, encrypted connections, HTTP uses TLS, which is described in Chapter 7. The protocol of HTTP+TLS is called HTTPS and uses https:// URLs instead of http:// URLs.

For a server to use HTTPS, it needs an X.509 certificate and a private key file for that certificate. Go at present requires that these be PEM-encoded as used in Chapter 7. Then the HTTP function ListenAndServe is replaced with the HTTPS (HTTP+TLS) function ListenAndServeTLS.

The file server program given earlier can be written as an HTTPS server as httpsfileserver.go:

```
ch8$ vi httpsfileserver.go

/* HTTPSFileServer
 */
package main
```

```
import (
        "net/http"
        "log"
)

func main() {
        // deliver files from the directory /tmp/www
        fileServer := http.FileServer(http.Dir("/tmp/www"))
        // register the handler and deliver requests to it
        err := http.ListenAndServeTLS(":8000", "jan.newmarch.name.pem",
                "private.pem", fileServer)
        if err != nil {
                log.Fatalln(err)
        }
}
```

This server is accessed by https://localhost:8000/index.html, for example. If the certificate is a self-signed certificate, an unsafe client will be needed to access the server contents. For example:

```
ch8$ go run httpsfileserver.go

ch8$ curl -i https://localhost:8000

curl: (60) SSL certificate problem: self signed certificate
More details here: https://curl.se/docs/sslcerts.html

curl failed to verify the legitimacy of the server and therefore could not
establish a secure connection to it. To learn more about this situation and
how to fix it, please visit the web page mentioned above.
```

We can instruct the curl client to be insecure via the "-k" flag.

```
ch8$ curl -ik https://localhost:8000

HTTP/2 200
content-type: text/html; charset=utf-8
last-modified: Mon, 27 Dec 2021 04:30:01 GMT
content-length: 41
date: Mon, 27 Dec 2021 04:46:56 GMT

<pre>
<a href="hi.txt">hi.txt</a>
</pre>
```

We can also do that with our Go client code (tlsunsafeclientget.go).
With InsecureSkipVerify set to **true**:

```
ch8$ go run tlsunsafeclientget.go https://localhost:8000

get a response
got charset UTF-8
got body
```

With InsecureSkipVerify set to **false**:

```
ch8$ go run tlsunsafeclientget.go https://localhost:8000

Fatal error  Get "https://localhost:8000": x509: certificate signed by unknown authority
exit status 1
```

If you want a server that supports both HTTP and HTTPs, run each listener in its own go routine.

Conclusion

Go has extensive support for HTTP. This is not surprising, since Go was partly invented to fill a need by Google for their own servers. This chapter discussed the various levels of support given by Go for HTTP and HTTPS. In the chapter about Gorilla, we will talk in more detail about Go multiplex requests (path -> code).

CHAPTER 9

Templates

Most server-side languages have a mechanism for taking predominantly static pages and inserting a dynamically generated component, such as a list of items. Typical examples are scripts in Java Server Pages, PHP scripting, and many others. Go has adopted a relatively simple scripting language in the `template` package.

The package is designed to take text as input and output different text, based on transforming the original text using the values of an object. Unlike JSP or similar, it is not restricted to HTML files, but it is likely to find greatest use there. We first describe the `text/template` package and later the `html/template` package.

The original source is called a *template* and will consist of text that is transmitted unchanged and embedded commands that can act on and change text. The commands are delimited by {{ ... }}, similar to the JSP commands <%= ... =%> and PHP's <?php ... ?>. In Go's template module, commands are also known as actions.

Inserting Object Values

A template is applied to a Go object. Fields from that Go object can be inserted into the template, and you can "dig" into the object to find subfields, etc. The current object is represented as the *cursor*, so to insert the value of the current object as a string, you use {{.}}. The package uses the `fmt` package by default to work out the string used as inserted values.

To insert the value of a field of the current cursor object, you use the field name prefixed by .. For example, if the current cursor object is of type

```
type Person struct {
        Name      string
        Age       int
        Emails    []string
        Jobs      []*Job
}
```

you insert the values of Name and Age as follows:

```
The name is {{.Name}}.
The age is {{.Age}}.
```

© Jan Newmarch and Ronald Petty 2022
J. Newmarch and R. Petty, *Network Programming with Go Language*,
https://doi.org/10.1007/978-1-4842-8095-9_9

You can loop over the elements of an array or other lists using the range command. So to access the contents of the Emails array, you use this:

```
{{range .Emails}}
        The email is {{.}}
{{end}}
```

During the loop over emails, the cursor . is set to each email in turn. On conclusion of the loop, the cursor reverts to the person. If Job is defined as follows:

```
type Job struct {
    Employer string
    Role     string
}
```

and we want to access the fields of a person's jobs, we can do it as before with a {{range .Jobs}}. An alternative is to switch the current object to the Jobs field. This is done using the {{with ...}} ... {{end}} construction, where now {{.}} is the Jobs field, which is an array:

```
{{with .Jobs}}
    {{range .}}
        An employer is {{.Employer}}
        and the role is {{.Role}}
    {{end}}
{{end}}
```

You can use this with any field, not just an array.

Using Templates

Once you have a template, you can apply it to an object to generate a new string using the object to fill in the template values. This is a two-step process that involves parsing the template and then applying it to an object. The result is output to a Writer, as in

```
t := template.New("Person template")
t, err := t.Parse(templ)
if err == nil {
        buff := bytes.NewBufferString("")
        t.Execute(buff, person)
}
```

An example program to apply a template to an object and print to standard output is printperson.go:

```
$ mkdir ch9
ch9$ cd ch9

ch9$ vi printperson.go

/* PrintPerson
 */
package main
```

```go
import (
        "log"
        "os"
        "text/template"
)

type Person struct {
        Name    string
        Age     int
        Emails  []string
        Jobs    []Job
}
type Job struct {
        Employer string
        Role     string
}

const templ = `The name is {{.Name}}.
The age is {{.Age}}.
{{range .Emails}}
        An email is {{.}}
{{end}}
{{with .Jobs}}
    {{range .}}
        An employer is {{.Employer}}
        and the role is {{.Role}}
    {{end}}
{{end}}
`

func main() {
        job1 := Job{Employer: "Box Hill Institute", Role: "Director, Commerce and ICT"}
        job2 := Job{Employer: "Canberra University", Role: "Adjunct Professor"}
        person := Person{
                Name: "jan",
                Age:  66,
                Emails: []string{"jan@newmarch.name",
                        "jan.newmarch@gmail.com"},
                Jobs: []Job{job1, job2},
        }
        t := template.New("Person template")
        t, err := t.Parse(templ)
        checkError(err)
        err = t.Execute(os.Stdout, person)
        checkError(err)
}
func checkError(err error) {
        if err != nil {
                log.Fatalln("Fatal error ", err.Error())
        }
}
```

The output from this is as follows:

```
ch9$ go run printperson.go

The name is jan.
The age is 66.

        An email is jan@newmarch.name

        An email is jan.newmarch@gmail.com

        An employer is Box Hill Institute
        and the role is Director, Commerce and ICT

        An employer is Canberra University
        and the role is Adjunct Professor
```

Note that there is plenty of whitespace as newlines in this printout. This is due to the whitespace we have in our template. If you want to reduce this whitespace, eliminate the newlines in the template as follows:

```
{{range .Emails}} An email is {{.}} {{end}}
```

An alternative is to use the command delimiters "{{- " and " -}}" to eliminate all trailing whitespace from the immediately preceding text and all leading whitespace from the immediately following text, respectively.

In the example, we used a string in the program as the template. You can also load templates from a file using the `template.ParseFiles()` function. For some reason that I don't understand (and which wasn't required in earlier versions), the name assigned to the template must be the same as the basename of the first file in the list of files. Is this a bug?

Pipelines

The preceding transformations insert pieces of text into a template. Those pieces of text are essentially arbitrary, whatever the string values of the fields are. If we want them to appear as part of an HTML document (or other specialized form), we will have to escape particular sequences of characters. For example, to display arbitrary text in an HTML document, we have to change < to <. The Go templates have a number of built-in functions, and one of these is html(). These functions act in a similar manner to UNIX pipelines, reading from standard input and writing to standard output.

To take the value of the current object . and apply HTML escapes to it, you write a "pipeline" in the template:

```
{{. | html}}
```

Here is another example, where we add a pipelined formatted message stating how many jobs a person has.

```
const templ = `The name is {{.Name}}.
The age is {{.Age}}.
{{range .Emails}}
```

```
        An email is {{.}}
{{end}}
{{with .Jobs}}
    {{range .}}
        An employer is {{.Employer}}
        and the role is {{.Role}}
    {{end}}
    {{ . | len | printf "%d jobs total" }}
{{end}}
`
```

Running the modified prior example, we now see a new line of output:

```
go run printperson.go

...
2 jobs total
```

And do similarly for other functions. There are additional considerations when pipelining including how arguments are passed in. You can learn more about pipelining in your templates here: https://pkg. go.dev/text/template#hdr-Pipelines.

Defining Functions

The templates use the string representation of an object to insert values using the fmt package to convert the object to a string. Sometimes, this isn't what is needed. For example, to avoid spammers getting hold of email addresses, it is quite common to see the symbol @ replaced by the word "at," as in "jan at newmarch. name". If we want to use a template to display email addresses in that form, we have to build a custom function to do this transformation.

Each template function has a name that is used in the templates themselves and an associated Go function. These are linked by this type:

```
type FuncMap map[string]interface{}
```

For example, if we want our template function to be emailExpand, which is linked to the Go function EmailExpander, we add this to the functions in a template as follows:

```
t = t.Funcs(template.FuncMap{"emailExpand": EmailExpander})
```

The signature for EmailExpander is typically this:

```
func EmailExpander(args ...interface{}) string
```

For the use we are interested in, there should be only one argument to the function, which will be a string. Existing functions in the Go template library have some initial code to handle nonconforming cases, so we just copy that. Then it is just simple string manipulation to change the format of the email address. A program is printemails.go:

```
ch9$ vi printemails.go

/* PrintEmails
 */
package main

import (
        "log"
        "os"
        "strings"
        "text/template"
)

type Person struct {
        Name    string
        Emails []string
}

const templ = `The name is {{.Name}}.
{{range .Emails}}
An email is "{{. | emailExpand}}"
{{end}}`

func main() {
        person := Person{
                Name: "jan",
                Emails: []string{"jan@newmarch.name",
                        "jan.newmarch@gmail.com"},
        }
        t, err := template.New("Person template").Funcs(
                template.FuncMap{
                        "emailExpand": func(emailAddress string) string {
                                return strings.Replace(emailAddress, "@", " at ", -1)
                        },
                },
        ).Parse(templ)

        err = t.Execute(os.Stdout, person)
        checkError(err)
}

func checkError(err error) {
        if err != nil {
                log.Fatalln("Fatal error ", err.Error())
        }
}
```

The output is as follows:

```
ch9$ go run printemails.go

The name is jan.

An email is "jan at newmarch.name"

An email is "jan.newmarch at gmail.com"
```

Variables

The template package allows you to define and use variables. As motivation for this, consider how we might print each person's email address *prefixed* by their name. The type we use is again this one:

```
type Person struct {
        Name        string
        Emails      []string
}
```

To access the email strings, we use a range statement such as this:

```
{{range .Emails}}
    {{.}}
{{end}}
```

But at that point, we cannot access the Name field, as . is now traversing the array elements and Name is outside of this scope. The solution is to save the value of the Name field in a variable that can be accessed anywhere in its scope. We also apply the same idea with loop variables. Variables in templates are prefixed by $. So we write this:

```
{{$name := .Name}}
{{range $idx, $email := .Emails}}
    Name is {{$name}}, email is {{$email}}
{{end}}
```

The program is printnameemails.go:

```
ch9$ vi printnameemails.go

/**
 * PrintNameEmails
 */
package main

import (
        "log"
        "os"
        "text/template"
)
```

```
type Person struct {
        Name    string
        Emails  []string
}

const templ = `{{$name := .Name}}
{{ $numEmails := .Emails | len -}}
{{range $idx, $email := .Emails -}}
Name is {{$name}}, email {{$email}} is {{ $idx | increment }} of {{ $numEmails }}
{{end}}
`

func main() {
        person := Person{
                Name: "jan",
                Emails: []string{"jan@newmarch.name",
                        "jan.newmarch@gmail.com"},
        }
        t, err := template.New("Person template").Funcs(
                template.FuncMap{
                        "increment": func(val int) int {
                                return val + 1
                        },
                },
        ).Parse(templ)
        checkError(err)
        err = t.Execute(os.Stdout, person)
        checkError(err)
}
func checkError(err error) {
        if err != nil {
                log.Fatalln("Fatal error ", err.Error())
        }
}
```

Here is the output:

```
ch9$ go run printnameemails.go

Name is jan, email jan@newmarch.name is 1 of 2
Name is jan, email jan.newmarch@gmail.com is 2 of 2
```

Conditional Statements

Continuing with the Person example, suppose you just want to print out the list of emails, without digging into it. You can do that with a template:

```
Name is {{.Name}}
Emails are {{.Emails}}
```

This will print the following:

```
Name is jan
Emails are [jan@newmarch.name jan.newmarch@gmail.com]
```

because this is how the fmt package will display a list.

In many circumstances, that may be fine, if that is what you want. Let's consider a case where it is *almost* right, but not quite. There is a JSON package to serialize objects, which we looked at in Chapter 4. This would produce the following:

```
{"Name": "jan",
 "Emails": ["jan@newmarch.name", "jan.newmarch@gmail.com"]
}
```

The JSON package is the one you use in practice, but let's see if we can produce JSON output using templates. We can do something similar just by the templates we have. This is *almost* right as a JSON serializer:

```
{"Name": "{{.Name}}",
 "Emails": {{.Emails}}
}
```

It will produce this:{"Name": "jan",
```
 "Emails": [jan@newmarch.name jan.newmarch@gmail.com]
}
```

This has two problems: the addresses aren't in quotes, and the list elements should be , separated. How about this – look at the array elements, put them in quotes, and add commas?

```
{"Name": {{.Name}},
  "Emails": [
    {{range .Emails}}
      "{{.}}",
    {{end}}
  ]
}
```

This will produce{"Name": "jan",
```
 "Emails": ["jan@newmarch.name", "jan.newmarch@gmail.com",]
}
```

(plus some whitespace).

Again, it's almost correct, but if you look carefully, you will see a trailing , after the last list element. According to the JSON syntax (see http://www.json.org/), this trailing , is not allowed. Implementations may vary in how they deal with this.

What we want is to print every element followed by a , except for the last one. This is actually a bit hard to do, so a better way is to print every element *preceded* by a , except for the *first* one (I got this tip from "brianb" at Stack Overflow – http://stackoverflow.com/questions/201782/can-you-use-a-trailing-comma-in-a-json-object). This is easier because the first element has index zero and many programming languages, including the Go template language, treat zero as a Boolean false.

One form of the conditional statement is {{if pipeline}} T1 {{else}} T0 {{end}}. We need the pipeline to be the index into the array of emails. Fortunately, a variation on the range statement gives us this. There are two forms that introduce variables:

```
{{range $elmt := array}}
{{range $index, $elmt := array}}
```

So we set up a loop through the array, and if the index is false (0), we just print the element. Otherwise, we print it preceded by a ,. The template is as follows:

```
{"Name": "{{.Name}}",
 "Emails": [
 {{range $index, $elmt := .Emails}}
    {{if $index}}
        , "{{$elmt}}"
    {{else}}
          "{{$elmt}}"
    {{end}}
 {{end}}
 ]
}
```

The full program is printjsonemails.go:

```
ch9$ vi printjsonemails.go

/**
 * PrintJSONEmails
 */
package main

import (
        "bytes"
        "encoding/json"
        "fmt"
        "log"
        "os"
        "text/template"
)

type Person struct {
        Name    string
        Emails  []string
}

const templ = `{"Name": "{{- .Name -}}", "Emails": [
{{- range $index, $elmt := .Emails -}}
    {{- if $index -}}
        , "{{- $elmt -}}"
    {{- else -}}
          "{{- $elmt -}}"
```

```
      {{- end -}}
   {{- end -}}
   ] }`

   func main() {
         person := Person{
                 Name: "jan",
                 Emails: []string{"jan@newmarch.name",
                         "jan.newmarch@gmail.com"},
         }
         t := template.New("Person template")
         t, err := t.Parse(templ)
         checkError(err)
         err = t.Execute(os.Stdout, person)
         checkError(err)

         // check via validity json package
         var b bytes.Buffer
         err = t.Execute(&b, person)
         checkError(err)
         if json.Valid(b.Bytes()) {
                 fmt.Println("\nvalid json")
         }
   }
   func checkError(err error) {
         if err != nil {
                 log.Fatalln("Fatal error ", err.Error())
         }
   }
```

This gives the correct JSON output, it also runs json.Valid() checker function to validate for proper JSON.

```
ch9$
go run printjsonemails.go

{"Name": "jan", "Emails": ["jan@newmarch.name", "jan.newmarch@gmail.com"] }
valid json
```

Before leaving this section, note that the problem of formatting a list with comma separators can be approached by defining suitable functions in Go that are made available as template functions. To reuse a well-known saying from another programming language, "There's more than one way to do it!" The following program was sent to me by Roger Peppe as sequence.go:

```
ch9$ vi sequence.go

/* Sequence.go
 * Copyright Roger Peppe
 */
package main

import (
```

```
            "errors"
            "fmt"
            "os"
            "text/template"
)

var tmpl = `{{$comma := sequence "" ", "}}
{{range $}}{{$comma.Next}}{{.}}{{end}}
{{$comma := sequence "" ", "}}
{{$colour := cycle "black" "white" "red"}}
{{range $}}{{$comma.Next}}{{.}} in {{$colour.Next}}{{end}}
`
var fmap = template.FuncMap{
            "sequence": sequenceFunc,
            "cycle":    cycleFunc,
}

func main() {
            t, err := template.New("").Funcs(fmap).Parse(tmpl)
            if err != nil {
                    fmt.Printf("parse error: %vn", err)
                    return
            }
            err = t.Execute(os.Stdout, []string{"a", "b", "c",
                    "d", "e", "f"})
            if err != nil {
                    fmt.Printf("exec error: %vn", err)
            }
}

type generator struct {
            ss []string
            i  int
            f  func(s []string, i int) string
}

func (seq *generator) Next() string {
            s := seq.f(seq.ss, seq.i)
            seq.i++
            return s
}
func sequenceGen(ss []string, i int) string {
            if i >= len(ss) {
                    return ss[len(ss)-1]
            }
            return ss[i]
}
func cycleGen(ss []string, i int) string {
            return ss[i%len(ss)]
}
func sequenceFunc(ss ...string) (*generator, error) {
```

```
        if len(ss) == 0 {
                return nil, errors.New("sequence must have at least one element")
        }
        return &generator{ss, 0, sequenceGen}, nil
}
func cycleFunc(ss ...string) (*generator, error) {
        if len(ss) == 0 {
                return nil, errors.New("cycle must have at least one element")
        }
        return &generator{ss, 0, cycleGen}, nil
}
```

Here is the output:

```
ch9$ go run sequence.go

a, b, c, d, e, f

a in black, b in white, c in red, d in black, e in white, f in red
```

The html/template Package

The preceding programs all dealt with the text/template package. This applies transformations without regard to any context in which the text might be used. For example, if the text in PrintPerson.go changes to

```
job1 := Job{Employer: "<script>alert('Could be nasty!')</script>", Role: "Director, Commerce and ICT"}
```

the program will generate this text:

```
An employer is <script>alert('Could be nasty!')</script>
```

This will cause an unexpected effect if downloaded to a browser.

The use of the html command in a pipeline can reduce this, as in {{. | html}}, and will produce the following:

```
An employer is &lt;script&gt;alert(&#39;Could be nasty!&#39;)&lt;/script&gt
```

Applying this filter to all expressions will become tedious. In addition, it may not catch potentially dangerous JavaScript, CSS, or URI expressions.

The html/template package is designed to overcome these issues. By the simple step of replacing text/template with html/template, the appropriate transformations will be applied to the resultant text, sanitizing it so that it is suitable for web contexts.

When using "go doc" for either template package, be sure to note which one you are looking at. "go doc template" is actually "go doc html/template" and "go doc text/template" for the non-HTML package.

Conclusion

The Go template package is useful for certain kinds of text transformations involving inserting values of objects. It does not have the power of regular expressions, for example, but it is faster and, in many cases, will be easier to use than regular expressions.

211

CHAPTER 10

A Complete Web Server

This chapter is principally an illustration of the HTTP chapter, building a complete website hosted via standard Go. It also shows how to use templates in order to use expressions in text files to insert variable values and to generate repeated sections. It deals with serialized data and Unicode character sets. The programs in this chapter are sufficiently long and complex, so they are not always given in their entirety but can be downloaded from the book's GitHub website, which is https://github.com/Apress/network-prog-with-go-2e.

Jan is learning Chinese. Rather, after many years of trying, he is still *attempting* to learn Chinese. Of course, rather than buckling down and getting on with it, he has tried all sorts of technical aids. He tried textbooks, videos, and many other teaching aids. Eventually he realized that the reason for his poor progress was that there *wasn't a good computer program for Chinese flashcards*, and so in the interests of learning, he needed to build one.

He found a program in Python to do some of the task. But sad to say, it wasn't well written, and after a few attempts at turning it upside down and inside out, he came to the conclusion that it was better to start from scratch. Of course, a web solution would be far better than a stand-alone one because then all the other people in his Chinese class could share it, as well as any other learners out there. And of course, the server would be written in Go.

He used the vocabulary from the lessons in the book *Intensive Spoken Chinese* by Zhang Pengpeng (Sinolingua, 2007, ISBN 978-7-80052577-3), but the program is applicable to any vocabulary sets.

Browser Site Diagram

The resultant program as viewed in the browser has three types of pages, illustrated in Figure 10-1.

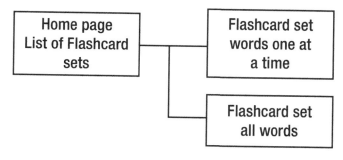

Figure 10-1. *Browser pages*

© Jan Newmarch and Ronald Petty 2022
J. Newmarch and R. Petty, *Network Programming with Go Language*,
https://doi.org/10.1007/978-1-4842-8095-9_10

The home page shows a list of flashcard sets (see Figure 10-2). It consists of a list of flashcard sets currently available, how you want a set displayed (random card order, Chinese or English shown first, or random), and whether to display a set of cards or just the words in a set.

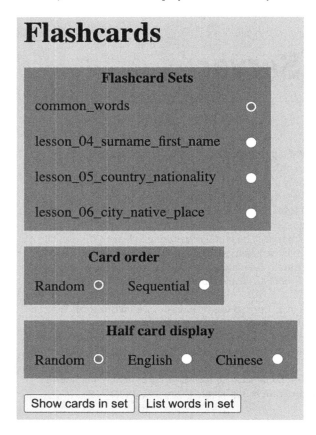

Figure 10-2. *The home page of the website*

The flashcard set shows a flashcard, one at a time. One looks like Figure 10-3.

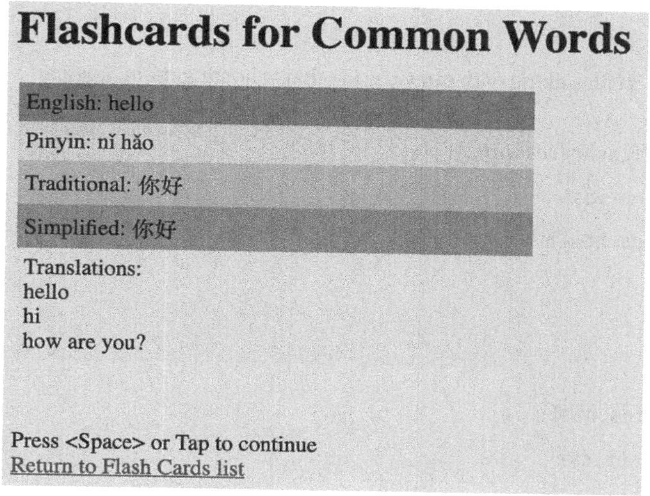

Flashcards for Common Words

English: hello

Pinyin: nǐ hǎo

Traditional: 你好

Simplified: 你好

Translations:
hello
hi
how are you?

Press <Space> or Tap to continue
Return to Flash Cards list

Figure 10-3. *Typical flashcard showing all the components*

The set of words for a flashcard set looks like Figure 10-4.

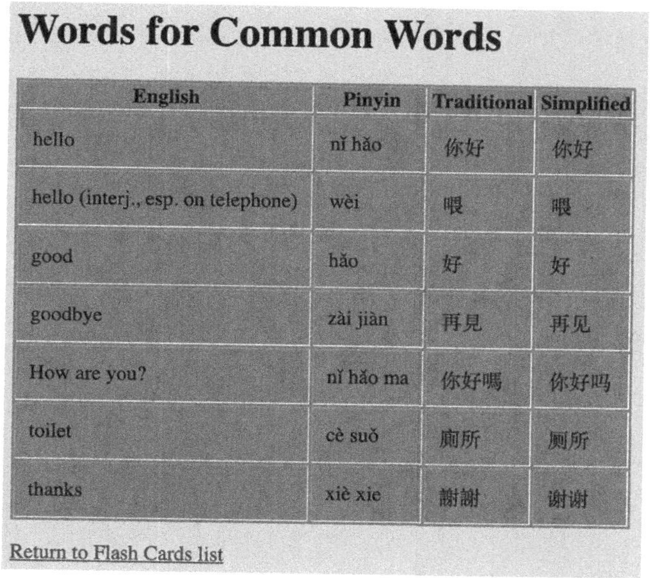

Words for Common Words

English	Pinyin	Traditional	Simplified
hello	nǐ hǎo	你好	你好
hello (interj., esp. on telephone)	wèi	喂	喂
good	hǎo	好	好
goodbye	zài jiàn	再見	再见
How are you?	nǐ hǎo ma	你好嗎	你好吗
toilet	cè suǒ	廁所	厕所
thanks	xiè xie	謝謝	谢谢

Return to Flash Cards list

Figure 10-4. *The list of words in a flashcard set*

Browser Files

The browser side has HTML, CSS, and JavaScript files along with our Go code that is hosting them. Logical paths and related files are as follows:

- Home page paths include (/ and /flashcards.html):
  - css/listflashcardsstylesheet.css
- Flashcard set path (showflashcards.html):
  - css/cardstylesheet.css
  - jscript/jquery.js
  - jscript/slideviewer.js
- Flashcard set words path (listwords.html):
  - css/listflashcardsstylesheet.css
  - jscript/sortable.js

The overall project looks as follows:

```
$ mkdir ch10
$ cd ch10
ch10$ tree .
.
├──── cedict_ts.u8
├──── css
│     ├──── cardstylesheet.css
│     └──── listflashcardsstylesheet.css
├──── dictionary.go
├──── flashcards.go
├──── flashcardsets
│     ├──── common_words
│     ├──── lesson_04_surname_first_name
│     ├──── lesson_05_country_nationality
│     └──── lesson_06_city_native_place
├──── html
│     ├──── listflashcards.html
│     ├──── listwords.html
│     └──── showflashcards.html
├──── jscript
│     ├──── jquery.js
│     ├──── slideviewer.js
│     └──── sorttable.js
├──── pinyinformatter.go
└──── server.go
4 directories, 17 files
```

Basic Server

The server is an HTTP server as discussed in the previous chapter. It has a number of functions to handle different URLs. The functions are outlined here:

Path	Function	HTML Delivered
/	listFlashCards	html/listflashcards.html
/flashcards.html	listFlashCards	html/listflashcards.html
/flashcardSets	manageFlashCards	html/showflashcards.html
/flashcardSets	manageFlashCards	html/listwords.html
/jscript/*	fileServer	Files from directory /jscript
/html/*	fileserver	Files from directory /html
/css/*	fileserver	Files from directory /css

The server is server.go under ch10 of https://github.com/Apress/network-prog-with-go-2e.

```
ch10$ cat server.go

/* Server
 */

package main

import (
        "fmt"
        "html/template"
        "log"
        "net/http"
        "os"
)

const (
        DefaultSet           = "common_words"
        DefaultAmount        = "Random"
        ActionShow           = "Show cards in set"
        ActionList           = "List words in set"
        ActionUnknown        = "Unknown action"
        URLFlashCardSetsPath = "flashcardSets"
        FlashCardPage        = "flashcards.html"
        ListFlashCardPage    = "list" + FlashCardPage
        ShowFlashCardPage    = "show" + FlashCardPage
        ListWordsPage        = "listwords.html"
        CardOrderSequential  = "Sequential"
        CardOrderRandom      = "Random"
)
```

```go
var showHalf = map[string]string{
        "Random":   "RANDOM_HALF",
        "English":  "ENGLISH_HALF",
        "Chinese":  "CHINESE_HALF",
}

func main() {
        if len(os.Args) != 2 {
                log.Fatalln("Usage: ", os.Args[0], ":port")
        }
        port := os.Args[1]

        http.HandleFunc("/", listFlashCards)
        fileServer := http.StripPrefix("/jscript/", http.FileServer(http.Dir("jscript")))
        http.Handle("/jscript/", fileServer)
        fileServer = http.StripPrefix("/html/", http.FileServer(http.Dir("html")))
        http.Handle("/html/", fileServer)
        fileServer = http.StripPrefix("/css/", http.FileServer(http.Dir("css")))
        http.Handle("/css/", fileServer)

        http.HandleFunc("/"+FlashCardPage, listFlashCards)
        http.HandleFunc("/"+URLFlashCardSetsPath, manageFlashCards)

        // deliver requests to the handlers
        err := http.ListenAndServe(port, nil)
        checkError(err)
}

func listFlashCards(rw http.ResponseWriter, req *http.Request) {

...

}

/*
 * Called from listflashcards.html on form submission
 */
func manageFlashCards(rw http.ResponseWriter, req *http.Request) {

...

}

func showFlashCards(rw http.ResponseWriter, cardname, order, half string) {

...

}

func listWords(rw http.ResponseWriter, cardname string) {

...

}
```

```
func httpErrorHandler(rw http.ResponseWriter, err error) {
        http.Error(rw, err.Error(), http.StatusInternalServerError)
}

func checkError(err error) {
        if err != nil {
                log.Fatalln("Fatal error ", err.Error())
        }
}
```

We now turn to the discussion of the individual functions.

The listFlashCards Function

The listFlashCards function is called to create HTML for the top-level page. The list of flashcard names is extensible and is the set of file entries in the directory flashcardSets. This list is used to create the table in the top-level page and is best done using the template package:

```
<table id="sets">
        <tr>
                <th colspan="2">
                        Flashcard Sets
                </th>
        </tr>
        {{range $i, $e := .}}
        <tr>
                <td>
                        {{$e}}
                </td>
                <td>
<input type="radio" name="flashcardSets" value="{{$e}}" {{if eq $i 0}}checked{{end}} />
                </td>
        </tr>
        {{end}}
</table>
```

where the range is over the list of names. The file html/listflashcards.html contains this template as well as the HTML for the side lists of card order, half card display, and the form buttons at the bottom. Omitting the side lists and the submit buttons, the HTML is as follows:

```
ch10$ cat html/listflashcards.html

<html>

<head>
    <title>
        Flashcards
    </title>
```

```
        <link type="text/css" rel="stylesheet" href="/css/listflashcardsstylesheet.css">
        </link>

</head>

<body>
    <h1>
        Flashcards
    </h1>
    <p>

    <div id="choose">
        <form method="GET" action="http:flashcardSets">

            <table id="sets">
                <tr>
                    <th colspan="2">
                        Flashcard Sets
                    </th>
                </tr>
                {{range $i, $e := .}}
                <tr>
                    <td>
                        {{$e}}
                    </td>
                    <td>
                        <input type="radio" name="flashcardSets" value="{{$e}}" {{if eq $i
                        0}}checked{{end}} />
                    </td>
                </tr>
                {{end}}
            </table>
            <br />
            <div id="options">
                <table id="order">
                    <tr>
                        <th colspan="3">
                            Card order
                        </th>
                    </tr>
                    <tr>
                        <td>
                            Random <input type="radio" name="order" value="Random"
                            checked="true" />
                        </td>
                        <td>
                            Sequential <input type="radio" name="order"
                            value="Sequential" />
                        </td>
                    </tr>
                </table>
```

```
                <br />
                <table id="half">
                    <tr>
                        <th colspan="3">
                            Half card display
                        </th>
                    </tr>
                    <tr>
                        <td>
                            Random <input type="radio" name="half" value="Random"
                            checked="true" />
                        </td>
                        <td>
                            English <input type="radio" name="half" value="English" />
                        </td>
                        <td>
                            Chinese <input type="radio" name="half" value="Chinese" />
                        </td>
                    </tr>
                </table>
            </div>

            <br />
            <div id="submit">
                <button type="submit" name="submit" value="Show cards in set">
                    Show cards in set
                </button>
                <button type="submit" name="submit" value="List words in set">
                    List words in set
                </button>
            </div>
        </form>
    </div>
    </p>

</body>

</html>
```

From server.go, the function listFlashCards, which applies the template to this, is as follows:

```
func listFlashCards(rw http.ResponseWriter, req *http.Request) {
        flashCardsNames := ListFlashCardsNames()
        t, err := template.ParseFiles("html/" + ListFlashCardPage)

        if err != nil {
                httpErrorHandler(rw, err)
                return
        }

        t.Execute(rw, flashCardsNames)
}
```

From `flashcards.go`, the function `ListFlashCardsNames()` just iterates through the flashcards directory, returning an array of strings (the file names of each flashcard set):

```
func ListFlashCardsNames() []string {
    flashcardsDir, err := os.Open("flashcardsets")
    if err != nil {
        return nil
    }
    files, err := flashcardsDir.Readdir(-1)

    fileNames := make([]string, len(files))
    for n, f := range files {
        fileNames[n] = f.Name()
    }
    sort.Strings(fileNames)
    return fileNames
}
```

The manageFlashCards Function

From `server.go`, the `manageFlashCards` function is called to manage the form submission on pressing the "Show Cards in Set" button or the "List Words in Set" button. It extracts values from the form request and then chooses between `showFlashCards` and `listWords`:

```
/*
 * Called from listflashcards.html on form submission
 */
func manageFlashCards(rw http.ResponseWriter, req *http.Request) {
        set := req.FormValue("flashcardSets")
        order := req.FormValue("order")
        action := req.FormValue("submit")
        half := req.FormValue("half")

        //if unset
        //http://localhost:8000/flashcardSets?flashcardSets=common_words&order=Random&half=
Random&submit=Show+cards+in+set
        if len(set) == 0 {
                set = DefaultSet
                order = DefaultAmount
                action = ActionShow
                half = DefaultAmount
        }

        cardname := URLFlashCardSetsPath + "/" + set

        fmt.Printf("Set %s, order %s, action %s, half %s, cardname %s\n", set, order,
action, half, cardname)
```

```
switch action {
case ActionShow:
        showFlashCards(rw, cardname, order, half)
case ActionList:
        listWords(rw, cardname)
default:
        fmt.Println(ActionUnknown)
}
}
```

The Chinese Dictionary

The previous code was fairly generic: it delivers static files using a FileServer, creates HTML tables using templates based on a listing of files in a directory, and processes information from an HTML form. To proceed further by looking at what is displayed in each card, we have to get into the application-specific detail, and that means looking at the source of words (a dictionary), how to represent it and the cards, and how to send flashcard data to the browser. First, the dictionary.

Chinese is a complex language – aren't they all :-(. The written form is hieroglyphic, that is, "pictograms," instead of using an alphabet. But this written form has evolved over time and even recently split into two forms: "traditional" Chinese as used in Taiwan and Hong Kong and "simplified" Chinese as used in mainland China. While most of the characters are the same, about 1,000 are different. Thus, a Chinese dictionary will often have two written forms of the same character.

Most Westerners like me can't understand these characters. So there is a "Latinized" form called Pinyin, which writes the characters in a phonetic alphabet based on the Latin alphabet. It isn't quite the Latin alphabet because Chinese is a tonal language, and the Pinyin form has to show the tones (much like accents in French and other European languages). So a typical dictionary has to show four things: the traditional form, the simplified form, the Pinyin, and the English. In addition (just like in English), a word may have multiple meanings. For example, there is a free Chinese/English dictionary at http://www.mandarintools. com/worddict.html, and even better, you can download it as a UTF-8 file. In it, the word 好 has this entry:

Traditional	Simplified	Pinyin	English	Meanings
好	好	hǎo	good	/good/well/proper/good to/easy to/very/so/ (suffix indicating completion or readiness)/

There is a little complication in this dictionary. Most keyboards are not good at representing accents such as the caron in ǎ. So while the Chinese characters are written in Unicode, the Pinyin characters are not. Although there are Unicode characters for letters such as ǎ, many dictionaries including this one use the Latin a and place the tone at the end of the word. Here, it is the third tone, so hǎo is written as hao3. This makes it easier for those who only have US keyboards and no Unicode editor to still communicate in Pinyin. A copy of the dictionary as used by the web server is cedict_ts.u8.

This data format mismatch is not a big deal. Just that somewhere along the line, between the original text dictionary and the display in the browser, a data massage has to be performed. Go templates allow this to be done by defining a custom template, so I chose that route. Alternative approaches include doing this as the dictionary is read in, or in the JavaScript to display the final characters.

The Dictionary Type

From dictionary.go, we use a DictionaryEntry to hold the basic information about one word:

```
type DictionaryEntry struct {
        Traditional  string
        Simplified   string
        Pinyin       string
        Translations []string
}
```

The preceding word would be represented by the following:

```
DictionaryEntry {Traditional: 好,
        Simplified: 好,
        Pinyin: `hao3`
        Translations: []string{`good`, `well`,`proper`,
                               `good to`, `easy to`, `very`, `so`,
                               `(suffix indicating completion or readiness)`}
}
```

The dictionary itself is just an array of these entries:

```
type Dictionary struct {
        Entries []*DictionaryEntry
}
```

Flashcard Sets

A single flashcard is meant to represent a Chinese word and the English translation of that word. We have already seen that a single Chinese word can have many possible English meanings. But this dictionary also sometimes has multiple occurrences of a Chinese word. For example, 好 occurs at least twice, once with the meaning we have already seen, but also with another meaning, "to be fond of." It turned out to be overkill, but to allow for this, each flashcard is given a full dictionary of words. Typically, there is only one entry in the dictionary! The rest of a flashcard is just the simplified and English words to act as possible keys, from flashcards.go:

```
type FlashCard struct {
        Simplified string
        English    string
        Dictionary *Dictionary
}
```

The *set* of flashcards is an array of these, plus the name of the set and information that will be sent to the browser for presentation of the set: random or fixed order, showing the top or bottom of each card first, or random, from flashcards.go.

```
type FlashCards struct {
        Name       string
```

```
        CardOrder  string
        ShowHalf   string
        Cards      []*FlashCard
}
```

We have shown one function for this type already, ListFlashCardsNames(). There is one other function of interest for this type to load a JSON file for a flashcard set. This uses the techniques mentioned in Chapter 4, in *flashcards.go*.

```
func LoadJSON(r io.Reader, key any) {
        decoder := json.NewDecoder(r)
        err := decoder.Decode(key)
        checkError(err)
}
```

A typical flashcard set is of common words. When the JSON file is pretty printed (e.g., jq), part of it looks like this:

```
{
    "ShowHalf":"",
    "Cards":[
        {
            "Simplified":"\u4f60\u597d",
            "Dictionary":{
                "Entries":[
                    {
                        "Traditional":"\u4f60\u597d",
                        "Pinyin":"ni3 hao3",
                        "Translations":[
                            "hello",
                            "hi",
                            "how are you?"
                        ],
                        "Simplified":"\u4f60\u597d"
                    }
                ]
            },
            "English":"hello"
        },
        {
            "Simplified":"\u5582",
            "Dictionary":{
                "Entries":[
                    {
                        "Traditional":"\u5582",
                        "Pinyin":"wei4",
                        "Translations":[
                            "hello (interj., esp. on telephone)",
                            "hey",
                            "to feed (sb or some animal)"
                        ],
```

```
                    "Simplified":"\u5582"
                }
            ]
        },
        "English":"hello (interj., esp. on telephone)"
    },
  ],
  "CardOrder":"",
  "Name":"Common Words"
}
```

Fixing Accents

There is one last major task before we can complete the code for the server. The accents as given in the dictionaries place the accent at the end of the Pinyin word, as in hao3 for hǎo. The translation to Unicode can be performed by a custom template, as discussed in Chapter 9.

The code for the Pinyin formatter is given here. Don't bother reading it unless you are *really* interested in knowing the rules for Pinyin formatting. The program is pinyinformatter.go:

```
ch10$ cat pinyinformatter.go

package main

import (
        "fmt"
        "strings"
)

func PinyinFormatter(args ...interface{}) string {
        ok := false
        var s string
        if len(args) == 1 {
                s, ok = args[0].(string)
        }
        if !ok {
                s = fmt.Sprint(args...)
        }
        fmt.Println("Formatting func " + s)
        // the string may consist of several pinyin words
        // each one needs to be changed separately and then
        // added back together
        words := strings.Fields(s)

        for n, word := range words {
                // convert "u:" to "ü" if present
                uColon := strings.Index(word, "u:")
                if uColon != -1 {
                        parts := strings.SplitN(word, "u:", 2)
                        word = parts[0] + "ü" + parts[1]
                }
```

```
                println(word)
                // get last character, will be the tone if present
                chars := []rune(word)
                tone := chars[len(chars)-1]
                if tone == '5' {
                        // there is no accent for tone 5
                        words[n] = string(chars[0 : len(chars)-1])
                        println("lost accent on", words[n])
                        continue
                }
                if tone < '1' || tone > '4' {
                        // not a tone value
                        continue
                }
                words[n] = addAccent(word, int(tone))
        }
        s = strings.Join(words, ` `)
        return s
}

var (
        // maps 'a1' to '\u0101' etc
        aAccent = map[int]rune{
                '1': '\u0101',
                '2': '\u00e1',
                '3': '\u01ce',
                '4': '\u00e0'}
        eAccent = map[int]rune{
                '1': '\u0113',
                '2': '\u00e9',
                '3': '\u011b',
                '4': '\u00e8'}
        iAccent = map[int]rune{
                '1': '\u012b',
                '2': '\u00ed',
                '3': '\u01d0',
                '4': '\u00ec'}
        oAccent = map[int]rune{
                '1': '\u014d',
                '2': '\u00f3',
                '3': '\u01d2',
                '4': '\u00f2'}
        uAccent = map[int]rune{
                '1': '\u016b',
                '2': '\u00fa',
                '3': '\u01d4',
                '4': '\u00f9'}
        üAccent = map[int]rune{
                '1': 'ǖ',
                '2': 'ǘ',
                '3': 'ǚ',
```

```go
                    '4': 'ǜ'}
)

func addAccent(word string, tone int) string {
        /*
         * Based on "Where do the tone marks go?"
         * at http://www.pinyin.info/rules/where.html
         */

        n := strings.Index(word, "a")
        if n != -1 {
                aAcc := aAccent[tone]
                // replace 'a' with its tone version
                word = word[0:n] + string(aAcc) + word[(n+1):len(word)-1]
        } else {
                n := strings.Index(word, "e")
                if n != -1 {
                        eAcc := eAccent[tone]
                        word = word[0:n] + string(eAcc) +
                                word[(n+1):len(word)-1]
                } else {
                        n = strings.Index(word, "ou")
                        if n != -1 {
                                oAcc := oAccent[tone]
                                word = word[0:n] + string(oAcc) + "u" +
                                        word[(n+2):len(word)-1]
                        } else {
                                chars := []rune(word)
                                length := len(chars)
                                // put tone onthe last vowel
                        L:
                                for n, _ := range chars {
                                        m := length - n - 1
                                        switch chars[m] {
                                        case 'i':
                                                chars[m] = iAccent[tone]
                                                break L
                                        case 'o':
                                                chars[m] = oAccent[tone]
                                                break L
                                        case 'u':
                                                chars[m] = uAccent[tone]
                                                break L
                                        case 'ü':
                                                chars[m] = üAccent[tone]
                                                break L
                                        default:
                                        }
                                }
                                word = string(chars[0 : len(chars)-1])
                        }
```

```
            }
    }
    return word
}
```

The ListWords Function

We can now return to the outstanding functions of the server. One was to list the words in a flashcard set. This populates an HTML table using a template for a flashcard set. The HTML for this uses the template package to walk over a FlashCards struct and insert the fields from that struct:

```
ch10$ cat html/listwords.html

<html>

<head>
        <title>
                Words for {{.Name}}
        </title>

        <script type="text/javascript" language="JavaScript1.2" src="/jscript/sorttable.js">
                < !--empty -->
        </script>

        <link type="text/css" rel="stylesheet" href="/css/listflashcardsstylesheet.css">
        </link>
</head>

<body>
        <h1>
                Words for {{.Name}}
        </h1>
        <p>
        <table border="1" class="sortable">
                <tr>
                        <th> English </th>
                        <th> Pinyin </th>
                        <th> Traditional </th>
                        <th> Simplified </th>
                </tr>
                {{range .Cards}}
                <div class="card">
                        <tr>
                                <div class="english">
                                        <div class="vcenter">
                                                <td>
                                                        {{.English}}
                                                </td>
                                        </div>
                                </div>
```

```
                                    {{with .Dictionary}}
                                    {{range .Entries}}
                                    <div class="pinyin">
                                            <div class="vcenter">
                                                    <td>
                                                            {{.Pinyin|pinyin}}
                                                    </td>
                                            </div>
                                    </div>

                                    <div class="traditional">
                                            <div class="vcenter">
                                                    <td>
                                                            {{.Traditional}}
                                                    </td>
                                            </div>
                                    </div>

                                    <div class="simplified">
                                            <div class="vcenter">
                                                    <td>
                                                            {{.Simplified}}
                                                    </td>
                                            </div>
                                    </div>

                                    {{end}}
                                    {{end}}
                            </tr>
                    </div>
                    {{end}}
            </table>
            </p>
            <p class="return">
                    <a href="http:/flashcards.html"> Return to Flash Cards list</a>
            </p>
</body>

</html>
```

The Go function in server.go to do this uses the PinyinFormatter discussed in the last section:

```go
func listWords(rw http.ResponseWriter, cardname string) {
    fmt.Println("Loading card name", cardname)
    cards := new(FlashCards)
    LoadJSON(cardname, cards)
    fmt.Println("loaded cards", len(cards.Cards))
    fmt.Println("Card name", cards.Name)

    t := template.New("listwords.html")
```

```
    t = t.Funcs(template.FuncMap{"pinyin": PinyinFormatter})
    t, err := t.ParseFiles("html/listwords.html")

    if err != nil {
        fmt.Println("Parse error " + err.Error())
        http.Error(rw, err.Error(), http.StatusInternalServerError)
        return
    }
    err = t.Execute(rw, cards)
    if err != nil {
        fmt.Println("Execute error " + err.Error())
        http.Error(rw, err.Error(), http.StatusInternalServerError)
        return
    }
}
```

This sends the populated table to the browser, as shown in Figure 10-4.

The showFlashCards Function

The final function to complete the server is showFlashCards. This changes the default values of CardOrder and ShowHalf in the flashcard set based on the form submitted from the browser. It then applies the PinyinFormatter and sends the resulting document to the browser. I captured the output of a command-line session using the UNIX command script and then ran the command:

```
GET /flashcardSets?flashcardSets=Common+Words&order=Random&half=Chinese&submit=Show+cards+
in+set HTTP/1.0
```

Part of the result is as follows:

```
ch10$ cat ./html/showflashcards.html

<html>

<head>
  <title>
    Flashcards for {{.Name}}
  </title>

  <link type="text/css" rel="stylesheet" href="/css/cardstylesheet.css">
  </link>

  <script type="text/javascript" language="JavaScript1.2" src="/jscript/jquery.js">
      < !--empty -->
  </script>

  <script type="text/javascript" language="JavaScript1.2" src="/jscript/slideviewer.js">
      < !--empty -->
  </script>
```

```html
  <script type="text/javascript" language="JavaScript1.2">
      cardOrder = {{- .CardOrder }};
    showHalfCard = {{- .ShowHalf }};
  </script>
</head>

<body onload="showSlides();">
  <!-- <body> -->
  <h1>
    Flashcards for {{.Name}}
  </h1>
  <p>

    {{range .Cards}}
  <div class="card">
    <div class="english">
      <div class="vcenter">
        English: {{.English}}
      </div>
    </div>

    {{with .Dictionary}}
    {{range .Entries}}
    <div class="pinyin">
      <div class="vcenter">
        Pinyin: {{.Pinyin|pinyin}}
      </div>
    </div>

    <div class="traditional">
      <div class="vcenter">
        Traditional: {{.Traditional}}
      </div>
    </div>

    <div class="simplified">
      <div class="vcenter">
        Simplified: {{.Simplified}}
      </div>
    </div>

    <div class="translations">
      <div class="vcenter">
        Translations:<br />
        {{range .Translations}}
        {{.}} <br />
        {{end}}
      </div>
    </div>
    {{end}}
    {{end}}
  </div>
```

```
        {{end}}
        </p>
        <div style="position: absolute; bottom: 0px">
          <p class="return">
            Press &lt;Space&gt; or Tap to continue
            <br />
            <a href="http:/flashcards.html"> Return to Flash Cards list</a>
          </p>
        </div>

</body>

</html>
```

The actual function is shown in the following. We see the card set, presentation order, and rendering, very similar to prior functions.

```go
func showFlashCards(rw http.ResponseWriter, cardname, order, half string) {
        cards := new(FlashCards)
        content, err := os.Open(cardname)
        checkError(err)
        LoadJSON(content, &cards)

        switch order {
        case CardOrderSequential:
                cards.CardOrder = "SEQUENTIAL"
        default:
                cards.CardOrder = "RANDOM"
        }

        if v, ok := showHalf[half]; ok {
                cards.ShowHalf = v
        } else {
                cards.ShowHalf = showHalf["Chinese"]
        }

        fmt.Printf("Loading card %s, half %s, loaded # of %d, card name %s\n", cardname,
half, len(cards.Cards), cards.Name)

        t, err := template.New(ShowFlashCardPage).Funcs(template.FuncMap{"pinyin":
PinyinFormatter}).ParseFiles("html/" + ShowFlashCardPage)

        if err != nil {
                httpErrorHandler(rw, err)
                return
        }

        err = t.Execute(rw, cards)
```

```
        if err != nil {
                httpErrorHandler(rw, err)
                return
        }
}
```

Aside rendering, we have basic error handling: "checkError" for exceptional errors (enough to shut down) and httpErrorHandler used when we wish to indicate an HTTP 500 status.

Presentation on the Browser

The final part of this system is how this HTML is shown in the browser. Figure 10-3 shows a screen of four parts displaying the English, the simplified Chinese, the alternative translations, and the traditional/simplified pair. How this is done is by the JavaScript program downloaded to the server (this takes place using the FileServer Go object). The JavaScript slideviewer.js file is actually pretty long and is omitted from the text. It is included in the program files at https://github.com/Apress/network-prog-with-go-2e.

Running the Server

The server can then be run on port 8000 (or other port) using a command such as this:

```
ch10$ go run *.go :8000
```

or

```
ch10$ go run server.go pinyinformatter.go flashCards.go dictionary.go :8000
```

Conclusion

This chapter has considered a relatively simple but complete web server using static and dynamic web pages with form handling and using templates for simplifying coding.

CHAPTER 11

HTML

The Web was originally created to serve HTML documents. Now it is used to serve all sorts of documents as well as data of different kinds. Nevertheless, HTML is still the main document type delivered over the Web.

HTML has been through a large number of versions, with the current version being HTML5. There have also been many "vendor" versions of HTML, introducing tags that never made it into the standards.

HTML is simple enough to be edited by hand. Consequently, many HTML documents are "ill formed," which means they don't follow the syntax of the language. HTML parsers generally are not very strict and will accept many "illegal" documents.

The HTML package itself only has two functions: EscapeString and UnescapeString. These properly handle characters such as <, converting them to < and back again.

A principal use of this might be to escape the markup in an HTML document so that if it is displayed in a browser, it will show all the markup (much like Ctrl+U in Chrome on Linux or Option+Cmd+U on Mac Chrome).

I'm more likely to use this to show the text of a program as a web page. Most programming languages have the < symbol, and many have &. These mess up an HTML viewer unless escaped properly. I like to show program text directly out of the file system rather than copying and pasting it into a document, to avoid getting out of sync.

The following program escapestring.go is a web server that shows its URL in preformatted code, having escaped the troublesome characters:

```
$ mkdir ch11
$ cd ch11
ch11$ vi escapestring.go

/*
 * This program serves a file in preformatted, code layout
 * Useful for showing program text, properly escaping special
 * characters like '<', '>' and '&'
 */

package main

import (
        "fmt"
        "html"
        "log"
        "net/http"
        "os"
)
```

© Jan Newmarch and Ronald Petty 2022
J. Newmarch and R. Petty, *Network Programming with Go Language*,
https://doi.org/10.1007/978-1-4842-8095-9_11

```go
func main() {
        http.HandleFunc("/", escapeString)
        err := http.ListenAndServe(":8080", nil)
        checkError(err)
}
func escapeString(rw http.ResponseWriter, req *http.Request) {
        fmt.Println(req.URL.Path)
        bytes, err := os.ReadFile("." + req.URL.Path)
        if err != nil {
                rw.WriteHeader(http.StatusNotFound)
                return
        }
        escapedStr := html.EscapeString(string(bytes))
        htmlText := "<html><body><pre><code>" +
                escapedStr +
                " </code></pre></body></html>"
        rw.Write([]byte(htmlText))
}
func checkError(err error) {
        if err != nil {
                log.Fatalln("Error ", err.Error())
        }
}
```

When it runs, serving files from the directory including the escapestring.go program, a browser will display it correctly using the URL localhost:8080/escapestring.go.

Run the server with this command:

```
ch11$ go run escapestring.go
```

Run a client with this command, as an example (or in a browser):

```
ch11$ curl localhost:8080/escapestring.go
<html><body><pre><code>/*
 * This program serves a file in preformatted, code layout
...
}
 </code></pre></body></html>
```

In both cases, the result is our original code (wrapped in a pre/code block)! If you typo the name, you will receive an HTTP 404.

The html/template Package

There are many attacks that can be made on web servers, the most notable being SQL injection, where a user-agent enters data into a web form deliberately designed to be passed into a database and wreaks havoc there. Go does not have any particular support to avoid this, since there are many variances among databases as to the SQL injection techniques that can succeed. The SQL Injection Prevention Cheat Sheet (see https://cheatsheetseries.owasp.org/cheatsheets/SQL_Injection_Prevention_Cheat_Sheet. html) summarizes the defenses against such attacks. The principal one is to avoid such attacks by using SQL *prepared statements,* which can be done using the Prepare function in the database/sql package.

More subtle attacks are based on XSS – cross-site scripting. This is where an attacker is not trying to attack the website itself but stores malicious code on the server to attack any of the clients of that website.

These attacks are based on inserting data into the database strings that, when delivered to a browser, for example, will attack the browser and, through it, attack the client of the website. (There are several variants of this, discussed at "OWASP: Types of XSS" – https://owasp.org/www-community/Types_of_Cross-Site_Scripting.)

For example, JavaScript may be inserted where a blog comment was requested to redirect a browser to an attacker's site:

```
<script>
  window.location='http://attacker/'
</script>
```

The Go html/template package is designed on top of the text/template package. The assumption is made that whereas the template will be trusted, the data that it deals with may not. What html/template adds is suitable escaping of the data to try to eliminate the possibility of XSS. It is based on the document called "Using Type Inference to Make Web Templates Robust Against XSS" by Mike Samuel and Prateek Saxena. Read that paper at https://rawgit.com/mikesamuel/sanitized-jquery-templates/trunk/safetemplate.html#problem_definition for the theory behind the package and the package documentation itself.

In short, prepare templates as per the text/template package and use the html/template package if the resultant text is delivered to an HTML agent.

Tokenizing HTML

The package golang.org/x/net/html in the Go subrepositories contains a tokenizer for HTML. This allows you to build a parse tree of HTML tokens. It is compliant with HTML5.

Here is an example program using this package in readhtml.go.

```
ch11$ vi readhtml.go

/* Read HTML
 */
package main

import (
        "fmt"
        "golang.org/x/net/html"
        "io"
        "log"
        "os"
        "strings"
)

func main() {
        if len(os.Args) != 2 {
                log.Fatalln("Usage: ", os.Args[0], "file")
        }
        file := os.Args[1]
        bytes, err := os.ReadFile(file)
```

```
            checkError(err)
            r := strings.NewReader(string(bytes))
            z := html.NewTokenizer(r)
            depth := 0
            for {
                    tt := z.Next()
                    for n := 0; n < depth; n++ {
                            fmt.Print(" ")
                    }
                    switch tt {
                    case html.ErrorToken:
                            if z.Err() == io.EOF {
                                    fmt.Println("EOF")
                            } else {
                                    fmt.Println("Error ", z.Err().Error())
                            }
                            os.Exit(0)
                    case html.TextToken:
                            fmt.Println("Text: \"" + z.Token().String() + "\"")
                    case html.StartTagToken, html.EndTagToken:
                            fmt.Println("Tag: \"" + z.Token().String() + "\"")
                            if tt == html.StartTagToken {
                                    depth++
                            } else {
                                    depth--
                            }
                    }
            }
}
func checkError(err error) {
        if err != nil {
                log.Fatalln("Fatal error ", err.Error())
        }
}
```

When we run readhtml.go on a simple HTML document such as this, sample.html:

```
ch11$ vi sample.html

<html>
  <head>
    <title> Test HTML </title>
  </head>
  <body>
    <h1> Header one </h1>
    <p>
      Test para
    </p>
  </body>
</html>
```

After setting up the dependencies, it produces the following output:

```
$ go mod init example.com/user/readhtml
$ go mod tidy
$ go run readhtml.go sample.html

Tag: "<html>"
 Text: "
  "
 Tag: "<head>"
  Text: "
   "
 Tag: "<title>"
  Text: " Test HTML "
  Tag: "</title>"
 Text: "
  "
 Tag: "</head>"
Text: "
  "
Tag: "<body>"
 Text: "
  "
 Tag: "<h1>"
  Text: " Header one "
  Tag: "</h1>"
 Text: "
  "
 Tag: "<p>"
  Text: "
    Test para
   "
 Tag: "</p>"
 Text: "
  "
 Tag: "</body>"
 Text: "
"
 Tag: "</html>"
Text: "
 "
EOF
```

(All the whitespace it produces is correct.)

XHTML/HTML

There is also limited support for XHTML/HTML in the XML package, discussed in the next chapter.

JSON

There is good support for JSON, as discussed in Chapter 4.

Conclusion

There isn't much to this package. The subpackage `html/template` was discussed in Chapter 9 on templates.

CHAPTER 12

XML

XML is a significant markup language mainly intended as a means of representing structured data using a text format. In the language we used in Chapter 4, it can be considered as a means of serializing data structures as a text document. It is used to describe documents such as DocBook and XHTML. It is used in specialized markup languages such as MathML and CML (Chemical Markup Language). It is used to encode data as SOAP messages for Web Services, and the Web Service can be specified using WSDL (Web Services Description Language).

At the simplest level, XML allows you to define your own tags for use in text documents. Tags can be nested and can be interspersed with text. Each tag can also contain attributes with values. For example, the file person.xml may contain

```
$ mkdir ch12
$ cd ch12
ch12$ vi person.xml

<person>
  <name>
    <family> Newmarch </family>
    <personal> Jan </personal>
  </name>
  <email type="personal">
    jan@newmarch.name
  </email>
  <email type="work">
    j.newmarch@boxhill.edu.au
  </email>
</person>
```

The structure of any XML document can be described in a number of ways:

- A document type definition (DTD) is good for describing structure.

- XML schema are good for describing the data types used by an XML document.

- RELAX NG is proposed as an alternative to both.

There is argument over the relative value of each way of defining the structure of an XML document. We won't buy into that, as Go does not support any of them. Go cannot check for validity of any document against a schema, but only for well-formedness. Even well-formedness is an important characteristic of XML documents and is often a problem with HTML documents in practice. That makes XML suitable for representation of even very complex data, while HTML is not.

© Jan Newmarch and Ronald Petty 2022
J. Newmarch and R. Petty, *Network Programming with Go Language*,
https://doi.org/10.1007/978-1-4842-8095-9_12

Four topics are discussed in this chapter: marshalling and unmarshalling Go data into XML, parsing an XML stream, and XHTML.

Unmarshalling XML

Go provides a function called Unmarshal to unmarshal XML into Go data structures. The unmarshalling is not perfect: Go and XML are different languages.

We consider a simple example before looking at the details. First, consider the XML document given earlier (person.xml):

```
<person>
  <name>
    <family> Newmarch </family>
    <personal> Jan </personal>
  </name>
  <email type="personal">
    jan@newmarch.name
  </email>
  <email type="work">
    j.newmarch@boxhill.edu.au
  </email>
</person>
```

We would like to map this onto the Go structures:

```
type Person struct {
        Name Name
        Email []Email
}
type Name struct {
        Family string
        Personal string
}
type Email struct {
        Type string
        Address string
}
```

This requires several comments:

- Unmarshalling uses the Go reflection package. This requires that all fields be exported; that is, start with a capital letter. Earlier versions of Go used case-insensitive matching to match fields such as the XML string "name" to the field Name. Now, though, *case-sensitive* matching is used. To perform a match, the structure fields must be tagged to show the XML string that will be matched against. This changes Person to the following:

```
type Person struct {
        Name Name `xml:"name"`
        Email []Email `xml:"email"`
}
```

- While tagging of fields can attach XML strings to fields, it can't do so with the names of the structures. An additional field is required, with the field name XMLName. This only affects the top-level struct, Person:

```
type Person struct {
            XMLName Name `xml:"person"`
            Name Name `xml:"name"`
            Email []Email `xml:"email"`
}
```

- Repeated tags map to a slice in Go.

- Attributes within tags will match to fields in a structure only if the Go field has the tag ,attr. This occurs with the field Type of Email, where matching the attribute type of the email tag requires xml:"type,attr".

- If an XML tag has no attributes and only has character data, then it matches a string field by the same name (case-sensitive, though). So the tag xml:"family" with character data Newmarch maps to the string field Family.

- But if the tag has attributes, then it must map to a structure. Go assigns the character data to the field with tag ,chardata. This occurs with the email data and the field Address with tag ,chardata.

A program to unmarshal the preceding document is unmarshal.go:

```
ch12$ vi unmarshal.go

/* Unmarshal
 */
package main

import (
        "encoding/xml"
        "fmt"
        "log"
)

type Person struct {
        XMLName Name    `xml:"person"`
        Name    Name    `xml:"name"`
        Email   []Email `xml:"email"`
}

type Name struct {
        Family   string `xml:"family"`
        Personal string `xml:"personal"`
}

type Email struct {
        Type    string `xml:"type,attr"`
        Address string `xml:",chardata"`
}
```

```go
func main() {
        str := `<?xml version="1.0" encoding="utf-8"?>
<person>
  <name>
    <family> Newmarch </family>
    <personal> Jan </personal>
  </name>
  <email type="personal">
    jan@newmarch.name
  </email>
  <email type="work">
    j.newmarch@boxhill.edu.au
  </email>
</person>`
        var person Person
        err := xml.Unmarshal([]byte(str), &person)
        checkError(err)
        // now use the person structure e.g.
        fmt.Println("Family name: \"" + person.Name.Family + "\"")
        for _, email := range person.Email {
                fmt.Println(email)
        }
}
func checkError(err error) {
        if err != nil {
                log.Fatalln("Fatal error ", err.Error())
        }
}
```

```
ch12$ go run unmarshal.go

Family name: " Newmarch "
{personal
    jan@newmarch.name
  }
{work
    j.newmarch@boxhill.edu.au
  }
```

(Note that the spaces are correct.) The strict rules are given in the package specification; see go doc -all encoding/xml.

Marshalling XML

Go also has support for marshalling data structures into an XML document. The function is

```go
func Marshal(v interface}{) ([]byte, error)
```

A program to marshal a simple structure is marshal.go:

```
ch12$ vi marshal.go

/* Marshal
 */
package main

import (
        "encoding/xml"
        "fmt"
)

type Person struct {
        XMLName xml.Name `xml:"person"`
        Name    Name     `xml:"name"`
        Email   []Email  `xml:"email"`
}
type Name struct {
        Family   string `xml:"family"`
        Personal string `xml:"personal"`
}
type Email struct {
        Kind    string "attr"
        Address string "chardata"
}

func main() {
        person := Person{
                Name: Name{Family: "Newmarch", Personal: "Jan"},
                Email: []Email{Email{Kind: "home", Address: "jan"},
                        Email{Kind: "work", Address: "jan"}}}
        buff, _ := xml.Marshal(person)
        fmt.Println(string(buff))
}
```

It produces the text with no whitespace.

```
ch12$ go run marshal.go

<Person><Name><Family>Newmarch</Family><Personal>Jan</Personal></Name><Email><Kind>home
</Kind><Address>jan</Address></Email><Email><Kind>work</Kind><Address>jan</Address>
</Email></Person>
```

Parsing XML

Go has an XML parser that's created using NewDecoder from the encoding/xml package. This takes an io.
Reader as a parameter and returns a pointer to Decoder. The main method of this type is Token, which
returns the next token in the input stream. The token is one of these types: StartElement, EndElement,
CharData, Comment, ProcInst, or Directive.

The XML types are `StartElement`, `EndElement`, `CharData`, `Comment`, `ProcInst`, and `Directive`. They are described next.

The StartElement Type

The type `StartElement` is a structure with two field types:

```
type StartElement struct {
    Name Name
    Attr []Attr
}

wheretype Attr struct {
    Name  Name
    Value string
}
```

The EndElement Type

This is also a structure as follows:

```
type EndElement struct {
    Name Name
}
```

The CharData Type

This type represents the text content enclosed by a tag and is a simple type:

```
type CharData []byte
```

The Comment Type

Similarly, for comments this type is similar to CharData's type:

```
type Comment []byte
```

The ProcInst Type

A `ProcInst` represents an XML processing instruction of the form `<?target inst?>`:

```
type ProcInst struct {
    Target string
    Inst   []byte
}
```

The Directive Type

A Directive represents an XML directive of the form <!text>. The bytes do not include the <! and > markers.

```
type Directive []byte
```

A program to print out the tree structure of an XML document is parsexml.go:

```
ch12$ vi parsexml.go

/* Parse XML
 */
package main

import (
        "encoding/xml"
        "fmt"
        "io/ioutil"
        "log"
        "os"
        "strings"
)

func main() {
        if len(os.Args) != 2 {
                log.Fatalln("Usage: ", os.Args[0], "file")
        }
        file := os.Args[1]
        bytes, err := ioutil.ReadFile(file)
        checkError(err)
        r := strings.NewReader(string(bytes))
        parser := xml.NewDecoder(r)
        depth := 0
        for {
                token, err := parser.Token()
                if err != nil {
                        break
                }
                switch elmt := token.(type) {
                case xml.StartElement:
                        name := elmt.Name.Local
                        printElmt(name+":start", depth)
                        depth++
                case xml.EndElement:
                        depth--
                        name := elmt.Name.Local
                        printElmt(name+":end", depth)
                case xml.CharData:
                        printElmt(string([]byte(elmt)), depth)
                case xml.Comment:
```

```
                        printElmt("Comment", depth)
                case xml.ProcInst:
                        printElmt("ProcInst", depth)
                case xml.Directive:
                        printElmt("Directive", depth)
                default:
                        fmt.Println("Unknown")
                }
        }
}
func printElmt(s string, depth int) {
        slimS := strings.TrimSpace(s)
        if len(slimS) == 0 {
                return
        }
        for n := 0; n < depth; n++ {
                fmt.Print("  ")
        }
        fmt.Println(slimS)
}
func checkError(err error) {
        if err != nil {
                log.Fatalln("Fatal error ", err.Error())
        }
}
```

Note that the parser includes all CharData, including the whitespace between the tags.

If we run the parsexml.go program against the person data structure given earlier, as follows:

```
ch12$ go run parsexml.go person.xml

person:start
  name:start
    family:start
      Newmarch
    family:end
    personal:start
      Jan
    personal:end
  name:end
  email:start
    jan@newmarch.name
  email:end
  email:start
    j.newmarch@boxhill.edu.au
  email:end
person:end
```

Note that as no DTD or other XML specification has been used, the tokenizer correctly prints out all the whitespace (a DTD may specify that the whitespace can be ignored, but without it, that assumption cannot be made). To make things prettier, we removed extra space via Trim.

There is a potential trap in using this parser. It reuses space for strings, so once you see a token, you need to copy its value if you want to refer to it later. Go has methods such as func (c CharData) Copy() CharData to make a copy of data; see go doc encoding.xml.Copy.

XHTML

HTML does not conform to XML syntax. It has unterminated tags such as <br>. XHTML is a cleanup of HTML to make it compliant with XML. Documents in XHTML can be managed using the techniques mentioned before for XML. XHTML does not appear to be as widely used as originally expected. My own suspicion is that an HTML parser is usually tolerant of errors and, when used in a browser, generally makes a reasonable job of rendering a document; XHTML parsers even in a browser tend to be more strict and often fail to render anything upon encountering even a single XML error. This is not a generally appropriate behavior for user-facing software.

HTML

There is some support in the XML package to handle HTML documents even though they may not be XML compliant. The XML parser discussed earlier can handle many HTML documents if it is modified by turning off strict parse checking.

```
parser := xml.NewDecoder(r)
parser.Strict = false
parser.AutoClose = xml.HTMLAutoClose
parser.Entity = xml.HTMLEntity
```

Conclusion

Go has basic support for dealing with XML strings. It does not as yet have mechanisms for dealing with XML specification languages such as XML Schema or Relax NG.

CHAPTER 13

Remote Procedure Call

Socket and HTTP programming both use a message-passing paradigm. A client sends a message to a server, which usually sends a message back. Both sides are responsible for creating messages in a format understood by both sides and reading the data out of those messages.

However, most stand-alone applications do not use message-passing techniques much. Generally, the preferred mechanism is that of the *function* (or method or procedure) call. In this style, a program will call a function with a list of parameters and, on completion of the function call, will have a set of return values. These values may be the function value, or if addresses have been passed as parameters, then the contents of those addresses might have been changed.

The remote procedure call is an attempt to bring this style of programming into the network world. Thus, a client will make what looks to it like a normal procedure call. The client side will package this into a network message and transfer it to the server. The server will unpack this and turn it back into a procedure call on the server side. The results of this call will be packaged up for return to the client.

Diagrammatically, it looks like Figure 13-1.

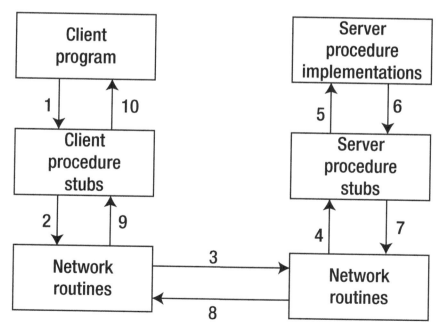

Figure 13-1. *The remote procedure call steps*

© Jan Newmarch and Ronald Petty 2022
J. Newmarch and R. Petty, *Network Programming with Go Language*,
https://doi.org/10.1007/978-1-4842-8095-9_13

The steps are as follows:

1. The client calls the client procedure stubs. The stub packages the parameters into a network message. This is called *marshalling*.

2. Networking routines in the O/S kernel are called by the stub to send the message.

3. The kernel sends the message(s) to the remote system. This may be connection oriented or connectionless.

4. The server procedure stubs unmarshal the arguments from the network message.

5. The server procedure stubs execute server procedure implementations.

6. The procedures complete, returning execution to the server procedure stubs.

7. The server stubs marshal the return values into a network message.

8. The return messages are sent back.

9. The client procedure stubs read the messages using the network routines.

10. The message is unmarshalled, and the return values are set on the stack for the client program.

There are two common styles for implementing RPC. The first is typified by Sun's ONC/RPC and by CORBA. In this, a specification of the service is given in some abstract language such as CORBA IDL (interface definition language). This is then compiled into code for the client and for the server. The client then writes a normal program containing calls to a procedure/function/method, which is linked to the generated client-side code. The server-side code is actually a server itself, which is linked to the procedure implementation that you write.

In this first way, the client-side code is almost identical in appearance to a normal procedure call. Generally, there is a little extra code to locate the server. In Sun's ONC, the address of the server must be known; in CORBA, a naming service is called to find the address of the server; in Java RMI, the IDL is Java itself, and a naming service is used to find the address of the service.

In the second style, you have to use a special client API. You hand the function name and its parameters to this library on the client side. On the server side, you have to explicitly write the server yourself, as well as the remote procedure implementation.

This second approach is used by many RPC systems, such as Web Services. It is also the approach used by Go's RPC.

Go's RPC

Go's RPC is so far unique to Go. It is different than the other RPC systems, so a Go client will only talk to a Go server. It uses the Gob serialization system discussed in Chapter 4, which defines the data types that can be used.

RPC systems generally make some restrictions on the functions that can be called across the network. This is so that the RPC system can properly determine which value arguments are sent, which reference arguments receive answers, and how to signal errors.

In Go, the restriction is that

- The method's type is exported (it begins with a capital letter).

- The method is exported.

- The method has two arguments, both exported (or built-in) types. The first is for data passed into the method; the second is for returned results.

- The method's second argument is a pointer.

- It has a return value of type error.

For example, here is a valid function:

```
F(T1, &T2) error
```

The restriction on arguments means that you typically have to define a structure type. Go's RPC uses the gob package for marshalling and unmarshalling data, so the argument types have to follow the rules of Gob as discussed in an earlier chapter.

We will follow the example given in the Go documentation, as it illustrates the important points. The server performs two trivial operations – they do not require the "grunt" of RPC but are simple to understand. The two operations are to multiply two integers and to find the quotient and remainder after dividing the first by the second.

The two values to be manipulated are given in a structure:

```
type Values struct {
    A, B int
}
```

The product is just an int, while the quotient/remainder is another structure:

```
type Quotient struct {
    Quo, Rem int
}
```

We will have two functions, multiply and divide, to be callable on the RPC server. These functions need to be registered with the RPC system. The Register function takes a single parameter, which is an interface. So we need a type with these two functions:

```
type Arith int

func (t *Arith) Multiply(args *Args, reply *int) error {
        *reply = args.A * args.B
        return nil
}

func (t *Arith) Divide(args *Args, quo *Quotient) error {
        if args.B == 0 {
                return errors.New("divide by zero")
        }
        quo.Quo = args.A / args.B
        quo.Rem = args.A % args.B
        return nil
}
```

The underlying type of Arith is given as int. That doesn't matter – any type will suffice.

An object of this type can now be registered using Register, and then it's methods can be called by the RPC system.

HTTP RPC Server

Any RPC needs a transport mechanism to get messages across the network. Go can use HTTP or TCP. The advantage of the HTTP mechanism is that it can leverage the HTTP support library. You need to add an RPC handler to the HTTP layer, which is done using HandleHTTP, and then start an HTTP server. The complete code is arithserver.go:

```
$ mkdir ch13
$ cd ch13
ch13$ vi arithserver.go

/* ArithServer
 */
package main

import (
        "errors"
        "fmt"
        "net/http"
        "net/rpc"
)

type Values struct {
        A, B int
}
type Quotient struct {
        Quo, Rem int
}
type Arith int

func (t *Arith) Multiply(args *Values, reply *int) error {
        *reply = args.A * args.B
        return nil
}
func (t *Arith) Divide(args *Values, quo *Quotient) error {
        if args.B == 0 {
                return errors.New("divide by zero")
        }
        quo.Quo = args.A / args.B
        quo.Rem = args.A % args.B
        return nil
}
func main() {
        arith := new(Arith)
        rpc.Register(arith)
        rpc.HandleHTTP()
        err := http.ListenAndServe(":1234", nil)
        if err != nil {
                fmt.Println(err.Error())
        }
}
```

and it is run by

```
ch13$ go run arithserver.go
```

Let the server run. Next, we look at the user of the RPC service, the RPC client.

HTTP RPC Client

The client needs to set up an HTTP connection to the RPC server. It needs to prepare a structure with the values to be sent and the address of a variable in which to store the results. Then it can make a `Call` with these arguments:

- The name of the remote function to execute

- The values to be sent

- The address of a variable in which to store the result

A client that calls both functions of the arithmetic server is `arithclient.go`:

```
ch13$ vi arithclient.go

/* ArithClient
 */
package main

import (
        "fmt"
        "log"
        "net/rpc"
        "os"
)

type Args struct {
        A, B int
}
type Quotient struct {
        Quo, Rem int
}

func main() {
        if len(os.Args) != 2 {
                fmt.Println("Usage: ", os.Args[0], "server")
                os.Exit(1)
        }
        serverAddress := os.Args[1]
        client, err := rpc.DialHTTP("tcp", serverAddress+":1234")
        if err != nil {
                log.Fatal("dialing:", err)
        }
        // Synchronous call
        args := Args{17, 8}
        var reply int
```

```
        err = client.Call("Arith.Multiply", args, &reply)
        if err != nil {
                log.Fatal("arith error:", err)
        }
        fmt.Printf("Arith: %d*%d=%d\n", args.A, args.B, reply)
        var quot Quotient
        err = client.Call("Arith.Divide", args, &quot)
        if err != nil {
                log.Fatal("arith error:", err)
        }
        fmt.Printf("Arith: %d/%d=%d remainder %d\n", args.A, args.B,
                quot.Quo, quot.Rem)
}
```

When it runs, we see the following output:

```
ch13$ go run arithclient.go localhost

Arith: 17*8=136
Arith: 17/8=2 remainder 1
```

TCP RPC Server

A version of the server that uses TCP sockets is tcparithserver.go:

```
ch13$ vi tcparithserver.go

/* TCPArithServer
 */
package main

import (
        "errors"
        "log"
        "net"
        "net/rpc"
)

type Args struct {
        A, B int
}
type Quotient struct {
        Quo, Rem int
}
type Arith int

func (t *Arith) Multiply(args *Args, reply *int) error {
        *reply = args.A * args.B
        return nil
}
```

```go
func (t *Arith) Divide(args *Args, quo *Quotient) error {
        if args.B == 0 {
                return errors.New("divide by zero")
        }
        quo.Quo = args.A / args.B
        quo.Rem = args.A % args.B
        return nil
}
func main() {
        arith := new(Arith)
        rpc.Register(arith)
        tcpAddr, err := net.ResolveTCPAddr("tcp", ":1234")
        checkError(err)
        listener, err := net.ListenTCP("tcp", tcpAddr)
        checkError(err)
        /* This works:
           rpc.Accept(listener)
        */
        /* and so does this:
         */
        for {
                conn, err := listener.Accept()
                if err != nil {
                        continue
                }
                rpc.ServeConn(conn)
        }
}
func checkError(err error) {
        if err != nil {
                log.Fatalln("Fatal error ", err.Error())
        }
}
```

Note that the call to Accept is blocking and just handles client connections. If the server wants to do other work as well, it should call this in a go routine.

Launch the server as follows:

```
ch13$ go run tcparithserver.go
```

As before, we now look at the related client.

TCP RPC Client

A client that uses the TCP server and calls both functions of the arithmetic server is tcparithclient.go:

```
ch13$ vi tcparithclient.go
```

```go
/* TCPArithClient
 */
package main
```

```go
import (
        "fmt"
        "log"
        "net/rpc"
        "os"
)

type Args struct {
        A, B int
}
type Quotient struct {
        Quo, Rem int
}

func main() {
        if len(os.Args) != 2 {
                log.Fatalln("Usage: ", os.Args[0], "server:port")
        }
        service := os.Args[1]
        client, err := rpc.Dial("tcp", service)
        if err != nil {
                log.Fatalln("dialing:", err)
        }
        // Synchronous call
        args := Args{17, 8}
        var reply int
        err = client.Call("Arith.Multiply", args, &reply)
        if err != nil {
                log.Fatalln("arith error:", err)
        }
        fmt.Printf("Arith: %d*%d=%d\n", args.A, args.B, reply)
        var quot Quotient
        err = client.Call("Arith.Divide", args, &quot)
        if err != nil {
                log.Fatalln("arith error:", err)
        }
        fmt.Printf("Arith: %d/%d=%d remainder %d\n", args.A, args.B,
                quot.Quo, quot.Rem)
}
```

When it's run, we see the following:

```
ch13$ go run tcparithclient.go localhost:1234

Arith: 17*8=136
Arith: 17/8=2 remainder 1
```

When choosing to use rpc.HandleHTTP vs. rpc.ServeConn, it's more about control and speed. The TCP server gives us more control as it sits below HTTP. If that is unimportant, then the former arithserver.go may be the way.

Matching Values

You may have noticed that the types of the value arguments are not the same on the HTTP client and HTTP server. In the server, we used Values, while in the client, we used Args. That doesn't matter, as we are following the rules of Gob serialization, and the names and types of the two structures' fields match. Better programming practice would say that the names should be the same, of course!

However, this does point out a possible trap in using Go RPC. If we change the structure in the server to be this:

```go
type Values struct {
        C, B int
}
```

then Gob has no problems. On the client side, the unmarshalling will ignore the value of C given by the server and use the default zero value for A. This could cause problems if, say, a divide by A (zero) was done.

Using Go RPC will require a rigid enforcement of the stability of field names and types by the programmer. We note that there is no version control mechanism to do this and no mechanism in Gob to signal any possible mismatches. There is also no required external representation to act as a reference. If you are just adding fields, then it may be okay, but it will still need control. Perhaps adding a version field to the data structure would help.

JSON

This section adds nothing new to the earlier concepts. It just uses a different "wire" format for the data, JSON instead of Gob. As such, clients or servers could be written in other languages that understand sockets and JSON.

JSON RPC Server

A version of the server that uses JSON encoding is jsonarithserver.go:

```
ch13$ vi jsonarithserver.go

/* JSONArithServer
 */
package main

import (
        "errors"
        "log"
        "net"
        "net/rpc"
        "net/rpc/jsonrpc"
)

type Args struct {
        A, B int
}
```

```go
type Quotient struct {
        Quo, Rem int
}
type Arith int

func (t *Arith) Multiply(args *Args, reply *int) error {
        *reply = args.A * args.B
        return nil
}
func (t *Arith) Divide(args *Args, quo *Quotient) error {
        if args.B == 0 {
                return errors.New("divide by zero")
        }
        quo.Quo = args.A / args.B
        quo.Rem = args.A % args.B
        return nil
}
func main() {
        arith := new(Arith)
        rpc.Register(arith)
        tcpAddr, err := net.ResolveTCPAddr("tcp", ":1234")
        checkError(err)
        listener, err := net.ListenTCP("tcp", tcpAddr)
        checkError(err)
        /* This works:
           rpc.Accept(listener)
        */
        /* and so does this:
         */
        for {
                conn, err := listener.Accept()
                if err != nil {
                        continue
                }
                jsonrpc.ServeConn(conn)
        }
}
func checkError(err error) {
        if err != nil {
                log.Fatalln("Fatal error ", err.Error())
        }
}
```

running as follows:

```
ch13$ go run jsonarithserver.go
```

Again, we look at the related client next.

260

JSON RPC Client

A client that calls both functions of the arithmetic server is jsonarithclient.go:

ch13$ vi jsonarithclient.go

```
/* JSONArithCLient
 */
package main

import (
        "fmt"
        "log"
        "net/rpc/jsonrpc"
        "os"
)

type Args struct {
        A, B int
}
type Quotient struct {
        Quo, Rem int
}
func main() {
        if len(os.Args) != 2 {
                log.Fatalln("Usage: ", os.Args[0], "server:port")
        }
        service := os.Args[1]
        client, err := jsonrpc.Dial("tcp", service)
        if err != nil {
                log.Fatalln("dialing:", err)
        }
        // Synchronous call
        args := Args{17, 8}
        var reply int
        err = client.Call("Arith.Multiply", args, &reply)
        if err != nil {
                log.Fatalln("arith error:", err)
        }
        fmt.Printf("Arith: %d*%d=%d\n", args.A, args.B, reply)
        var quot Quotient
        err = client.Call("Arith.Divide", args, &quot)
        if err != nil {
                log.Fatalln("arith error:", err)
        }
        fmt.Printf("Arith: %d/%d=%d remainder %d\n", args.A, args.B,
                quot.Quo, quot.Rem)
}
```

It's run as follows:

```
ch13$ go run jsonarithclient.go localhost:1234

Arith: 17*8=136
Arith: 17/8=2 remainder 1
```

While not obvious (aside from the jsonrpc.Dial), the request and response are encoded and decoded via the encoding/json package. Take a look at related docs such as go doc -u jsonrpc.WriteRequest or the source itself here: /usr/local/go/src/net/rpc/jsonrpc/client.go.

Conclusion

RPC is a popular means of distributing applications. Several ways of doing it have been presented here, based on the Gob or JSON serialization techniques and using HTTP and TCP for transport.

CHAPTER 14

REST

In previous chapters, we looked at HTTP and gave an example of a web system. However, we didn't give any particular structure to the system, just what was simple enough for the problem. There is an architectural style developed by one of the key authors of HTTP 1.1 (Roy Fielding) called *REST* (REpresentational State Transfer). In this chapter, we look at the REST style and what it means for building web applications. We have to go back to fundamentals for this.

REST has many components that have to be followed if the term REST can be properly applied. Unfortunately, it has become a buzzword, and many applications have "bits" of REST but not the full thing. We discuss the Richardson Maturity Model, which says how far along the path to RESTful-ness an API has gone.

In the last chapter, we looked at RPCs (remote procedure calls). This is a completely different style than REST. We also compare the two styles, looking at when it is appropriate to use each style.

URIs and Resources

Resources are the "things" that we want to interact with on a network or the Internet. I like to think of them as objects, but there is no requirement that their implementation should be object based – they should just "look like" a thing, possibly with components.

Each resource has one or more addresses known as URIs (uniform resource identifiers).

Note The internationalized form is IRIs – internationalized resource identifiers.

These have this generic form:

```
scheme:[//[user:password@]host[:port]][/]path[?query][#fragment]
```

Typical examples are URLs (uniform resource locator), where the scheme is `http` or `https`, and the host refers to a computer by its IP address or DNS name, as follows:

```
https://jan.newmarch.name/IoT/index.html
```

There are non-HTTP URL schemes such as telnet, news, and IPP (Internet Printing Protocol). These also contain a location component. There are also others, such as URNs (uniform resource names), which are often wrappers around other identification systems, and they do not contain location information. For example, the IETF has a standard URN scheme for books identified by their ISBN, such as the ISBN for this book:

```
urn:ISBN:978-1-4842-2692-6
```

© Jan Newmarch and Ronald Petty 2022
J. Newmarch and R. Petty, *Network Programming with Go Language*,
https://doi.org/10.1007/978-1-4842-8095-9_14

These URNs tend not to be widely used but still exist. A list is given by IANA Uniform Resource Names (URN) Namespaces at `https://www.iana.org/assignments/urn-namespaces/urn-namespaces.xhtml`. The original schemes, such as ISBN, are still in wider use.

A formal definition of a resource may be hard to pin down. For example, `http://www.google.com` represents Google in some sense (it is the scheme and the host part of a URL), but the host certainly isn't some fixed computer somewhere. Similarly, the ISBN for this book represents something about this book, but certainly not any extant copies (at the time this chapter was written, no copies existed even though the ISBN did).

Nevertheless, we take the concept of resource as primitive, and URIs are identifiers for these resources. The IETF at Uniform Resource Identifier (URI): Generic Syntax (`https://www.ietf.org/rfc/rfc3986.txt`) is similarly vague: "the term "resource" is used in a general sense for whatever might be identified by a URI."

A resource may have more than one URI. As a person, I have a number of different identifiers: my tax file number refers to one aspect of me, my financial affairs; my Medicare number refers to me as a recipient of health treatments; my name (fairly unique) is often used to refer to different aspects of me. My URL of `https://jan.newmarch.name` refers to those aspects of me that I chose to reveal on my website. And Google, LinkedIn, Facebook, Twitter, etc., also presumably have URIs of some kind that label those aspects of me that they have chosen to save.

What is agreed upon is that resources are *nouns* and not *verbs* or *adjectives*. A URL for a bank account that says `http://mybank/myaccount/withdraw` is not counted as a resource as it contains the verb `withdraw`. Similarly, `http://amazon.com/buy/book-id` would not label a resource as it contains the verb `buy` (Amazon does not have such a URL).

This is the first key to REST for HTTP: identify the resources in your information system and assign URLs to them. There are conventions in this, the most common one being that if there is a hierarchical structure, then that should be reflected in the URL path. However, that isn't necessary as the information should be given in other ways as well.

The REST approach to designing URIs is still a bit of an art form. Legal (and perfectly legitimate) URIs are not necessarily "good" REST URIs, and many examples of so-called RESTful APIs have URIs that are not very RESTful at all. 2PartsMagic in RESTful URI design (`http://blog.2partsmagic.com/restful-uri-design/`) offers good advice on designing appropriate URIs.

The REST approach to designing URIs is still a bit of an art form. Legal (and perfectly legitimate) URIs are not necessarily "good" REST URIs, and many examples of so-called RESTful APIS have URIs that are not very RESTful at all. The Golang developers blog provides a brief overview of some of the concepts of REST: `https://go.dev/doc/tutorial/web-service-gin`. Beyond examples, OpenAPI is a standard to help us with design and tooling around "http apis": `https://spec.openapis.org/oas/latest.html`.

Representations

A representation of a resource is something that captures some information about a resource in some form. For example, a representation of me from my Tax Office URI might be my tax returns in Australia. A representation of me from my local pizza cafe would be a record of pizza purchases. A representation of me from my website would be an HTML document.

This is one of the keys to REST: URIs identify resources, and requests for that resource return a representation of that resource. The resource itself remains on the server and is not sent to the client at all. In fact, the resource might not even exist at all in any concrete form. For example, a representation might be generated from the results of an SQL query that's triggered by making a request to that URI.

REST does not particularly talk about possibilities for negotiating the representation of a resource. HTTP 1.1 has an extensive section on how to do this, considering *server*, *client*, and *transparent* negotiation. The `Accept` headers can be used by a client to specify, for example:

```
Accept: application/xml; q=1.0, application/json; q=0.5
Accept-Language: fr
Accept-Charset: utf8
```

This states that it would prefer the application/xml format but will accept application/json. The server can either accept one of these or reply with the formats it will accept.

REST Verbs

You can make certain requests to a URI. If you are making an HTTP request to a URL, HTTP defines the requests that can be made: GET, PUT, POST, DELETE, HEAD, OPTIONS, TRACE, and CONNECT, as well as extensions such as PATCH. There is only a limited number of these! This is very different than what we have come to expect from O/O programming. For example, the Java JLabel has about 250 methods, such as getText and setHorizontalAlignment. To some degree, we could map these OO to/from REST/HTTP; an instance of a JLabel is a resource, and we can "get" it via "getText". While that is easy in some minor cases, it's not so clear how to map all 250 methods, or should we.

REST is now commonly interpreted as taking just four verbs from HTTP: GET, PUT, POST, and DELETE. GET roughly corresponds to the getter-methods of OO languages, while PUT roughly corresponds to the setter methods of OOP languages. If a JLabel were a REST resource (which it isn't), how would one single GET verb make up for the hundred or so getter methods of JLabel?

The answer lies in the PATH component of URIs. A label has the properties of text, alignment, and so on. These are really subresources of the label and could be written as sub-URIs of the label. So if the label had a URI of http://jan.newmarch.name/my_label, then the subresources could have (example) URIs:

```
http://jan.newmarch.name/my_label/text
http://jan.newmarch.name/my_label/horizontalAlignment
```

If you want to manipulate just the text of the label, you can use the URI of the text resource, not getter/setter methods on the label itself.

The GET Verb

To retrieve a representation of a resource, you GET the resource. This will return some representation of the resource. There may be innumerable possibilities to this choice. For example, a request for this book's index might return a representation of the index in French, using the UTF-8 character set, as an XML document, or many other possibilities. The client and the server can negotiate these possibilities.

The GET verb is required to be *idempotent*. That is, repeated requests should return the same results (to within representation type). For example, multiple requests for the temperature of a sensor should return the same result (unless of course the temperature has changed).

Idempotency by default allows for caching. This is useful for reducing traffic on the Web and may save battery power for sensors. Caching cannot always be guaranteed: a resource that returns the number of times it has been accessed will give a different result each time it is accessed. This is an unusual behavior and would be signaled using the HTTP Cache-Control header.

The PUT Verb

If you want to change the state of a resource, you can PUT new values. There are two principal limitations to PUT:

- You can only change the state of a resource whose URI you know.
- The representation you send must cover all components of the resource.

For example, if you only want to change the text in a label, you send the PUT message to the URL http://jan.newmarch.name/my_label/text, *not* to http://jan.newmarch.name/my_label. Sending to the label would require all of the hundred or so fields to be sent.

PUT is idempotent but is not *safe*. That is, it changes the state of the resource, but repeated calls change it to the same state.

PUT and DELETE are not part of HTML, and most browsers do not support them directly. They can be called in browsers with Ajax support. There are several discussions as to why they are not included. See, for example, "Why are there no PUT and DELETE methods on HTML forms?" at http://softwareengineering.stackexchange.com/questions/114156/why-are-there-are-no-put-and-delete-methods-on-html-forms.

The DELETE Verb

This deletes the resource. It is idempotent but not safe.

Safe methods (e.g., GET) are ones that have no unexpected side effects. Unsafe methods (e.g., PUT) can be potentially unsafe. Not having the ability to undo a change is something that is unsafe. Ideally, GET returns a version of a resource, and that's all. PUT will overlay a resource, and if you didn't retrieve the prior version, it may be gone for good.

Idempotent methods are ones that produce the same side effect for the same request no matter how many times you run it. DELETE will remove a resource, and if you call it the second time, the "outcome" is the same; the resource is either deleted (if it is created again) or remains nonexisting.

For more on the concepts of "idempotent" and "safe," see https://www.w3.org/Protocols/rfc2616/rfc2616-sec9.html.

The POST Verb

POST is the do-everything-else verb to deal with situations not covered by the other verbs. There is agreement about two uses of POST:

- If you want to create a new resource and you don't know its URI, then POST a representation of the resource to a URI that knows how to create the resource. The returned representation should contain the URI of the new resource. *This is important*. To interact with a new resource, you must know its URI, and the return from POST tells you that.

- If a resource has many attributes and you only want to change one or a few of them, then POST a representation with the changed values only.

There is intense argument about the respective roles of PUT and POST in edge cases. If you want to create a new resource and *do* know the URI it will have, then you could use either PUT or POST. Which one you choose seems to depend on other factors.

SOAP was designed as an RPC system on top of HTTP. It uses POST for *everything*. HTML continues to use POST in forms when it should have the option of using PUT. For these reasons, I do not use POST unless I absolutely have to. I suppose others have their own principled reasons for using POST instead of PUT, but I have no idea what they might be :-).

Due to its open-ended scope, POST could be used for almost anything. Many of these uses could be against the REST model, as is amply illustrated by SOAP. But some of these uses could be legitimate. POST is usually non-idempotent and not safe, although particular cases could be either. The following Stack Overflow post contains a thoughtful discussion on PUT vs. PATCH vs. POST: https://stackoverflow.com/questions/28459418/use-of-put-vs-patch-methods-in-rest-api-real-life-scenarios.

No Maintained State (That Is, Stateless)

Let's establish this up front: cookies are out. Cookies are often used to track the state of a user through an interaction with a server, with a typical example being a shopping cart. A structure is created on the server side, and a cookie is returned to be used to signal that this is the shopping cart to be used.

REST made the decision not to maintain any client state on the server. This simplifies interactions and also sidesteps the tricky issues of how to restore consistency after the client or server has crashed. If the server doesn't need to maintain any state, then it leads to a more robust server model. Often, security-related items are set in a cookie. A REST endpoint should return representations of those resources. An authentication-related cookie often transcends those resources, hence not RESTful. More on this topic can be found here: https://www.ics.uci.edu/~fielding/pubs/dissertation/evaluation.htm#sec_6_3_4_2.

If you can't use cookies, what do you do? It's actually trivial: a cart is created on the server. Under REST, that can only happen in response to a POST request, which returns a new URI for the new resource. So that is what you use – the new URI. You can GET, PUT, POST, and DELETE to this URI, to do all things you want to do directly on the resource without having to do workarounds with cookies.

HATEOAS

HATEOAS stands for "Hypermedia as the Engine of Application State." It is generally recognized as an awful acronym, but it has stuck. The basic principle is that navigating from one URI to another, which is related in some way, should not be done by any out-of-band mechanism but that the new link must be embedded in some way as a hyperlink within the representation of the first URI. This is a key feature of REST, often not done.

REST does not state the format of the links. They could be given using the HTML link tag, by URLs embedded in a PDF document, or by links given in an XML document. Formats that do not have simple representations for URLs are not considered as hypermedia languages and are not contained in REST.

Also, REST also does not explicitly state the meanings of the links nor how to extract the appropriate links. Fielding states in his blog "REST APIs must be hypertext-driven" at http://roy.gbiv.com/untangled/2008/rest-apis-must-be-hypertext-driven:

> A REST API should be entered with no prior knowledge beyond the initial URI (bookmark) and set of standardized media types that are appropriate for the intended audience (i.e., expected to be understood by any client that might use the API). From that point on, all application state transitions must be driven by client selection of server-provided choices that are present in the received representations or implied by the user's manipulation of those representations.

IANA maintains a registry of relation types (IANA: Link Relations at http://www.iana.org/assignments/link-relations/link-relations.xhtml) that can be used. The Web Linking RFC 5988 describes the web linking registry (https://datatracker.ietf.org/doc/html/rfc5988). The HTML5

specification has a small number of defined relations and points to Microformats rel values at http://
microformats.org/wiki/existing-rel-values#HTML5_link_type_extensions for a larger list. These
documents, while helpful, are not immediately actionable. We will look at an example in a moment.

Mechanisms such as cookies, or external API specifications such as WSDL for SOAP, are effectively
excluded by REST. They are not hyperlinks contained in the representation of a resource. HATEOAS will
decouple the client from the server by allowing dynamic discovery beyond a well-known URI; allowing us to
independently evolve the API. This is unlike RPCs where the IDL drives the interface.

Representing Links

Links are standardized in HTML documents. The Link tag defines an HTML element that can only appear in
an HTML header section. For example, a book with chapters, etc., might look like this if the links were given
as HTML link elements:

```
<html>
  <head>
    <link rel= "author" title="Jan Newmarch" href="https://jan.newmarch.name">
    <link rel="chapter" title="Introduction" href="Introduction/">
    ...
```

Link relations in HTML are of two types: those that are needed for the current document such as CSS
files and those that point to related resources, as before. The first type is generally downloaded invisibly to
the user. The second type is generally not shown by browsers, but user agents following HATEOAS principles
will use them.

XML has a variety of link specifications. These include XLink and Atom . Atom seems to be more
popular.

Links based on XLink would appear as follows:

```
<People xmlns:xlink="http://www.w3.org/1999/xlink">
 <Person xlink:type="simple" xlink:href="http://...">
   ...
 </Person>
   ...
</People>
```

Links based on Atom would appear as follows:

```
<People xmlns:atom="http://www.w3.org/2005/Atom">
 <Person>
   <link  atom:href="http://..."/>
   ...
 </Person>
 ...
</People>
```

For JSON, the format is not normalized. The REST cookbook (http://restcookbook.com/Mediatypes/
json/) notes the lack of standardization and points to the W3C specification JSON-LD 1.0: "A JSON-based
Serialization for Linked Data" and to the HAL (Hypertext Application Language). Bodies such as the Open
Connectivity Foundation seem to use their own home-grown format, but that is for CoAP, another REST-
based system.

JSON-LD uses the term @id to signal a URL, as in

```
{
  "name": Jan Newmarch:,
  "homepage": {"@id": "https://jan.newmarch.name/"}
}
```

It is worth noting in this regard that the W3C also has a specification of an HTTP Link header at `https://www.w3.org/wiki/LinkHeader`, which may be returned by a server to a client. This is used by JSON-LD, for example, to point to a specification of the JSON document contained in the body of an HTTP response. Also of interest, some implementations treat the HTML Link or HTTP Header in the same way.

This can affect the serialization method in passing link information from servers to user agents. The user agent and server must agree on the format to be used. For HTML (or XHTML), this is standardized. For XML, a reference can be made in the document to the linking system. For JSON-LD, this can be signaled in the Accept HTTP header as `application/ld+json`.

Transactions with REST

How does REST handle transactions and indeed any other types of processes? They were not discussed in the original thesis by Fielding.

The Wikipedia entry for HATEOAS gives a poor example of managing transactions. It starts from an HTTP request like this.

```
GET /accounts/12345 HTTP/1.1
Host: bank.example.org
Accept: application/json
 ...
```

Which returns a JSON document as a representation of the account as follows.

```
HTTP/1.1 200 OK

{
    "account": {
        "account_number": 12345,
        "balance": {
            "currency": "usd",
            "value": 100.00
        },
        "links": {
            "deposits": "/accounts/12345/deposits",
            "withdrawals": "/accounts/12345/withdrawals",
            "transfers": "/accounts/12345/transfers",
            "close-requests": "/accounts/12345/close-requests"
        }
    }
}
```

If we asked for xml, we would see the following.

```
Content-Type: application/xml
Content-Length: ...
<?xml version="1.0"?>
<account>
    <account_number>12345</account_number>
    <balance currency="usd">100.00</balance>
    <link rel="deposit" href="http://bank.example.org/account/12345/deposit" />
    <link rel="withdraw" href="http://bank.example.org/account/12345/withdraw" />
    <link rel="transfer" href="http://somebank.org/account/12345/transfer" />
    <link rel="close" href="http://bank.example.org/account/12345/close" />
</account>
```

This gives the URIs of the related resources deposit, withdraw, transfer, and close. However, the resources are *verbs,* not *nouns,* and that is not good at all. How do they interact with the HTTP verbs? Do you GET a withdraw? POST it? PUT it? What happens if you DELETE a withdraw – is that supposed to roll back a transaction or what? In REST, we try to avoid using verbs as a resource; however, in RPC, it is not disallowed to have verbs as an endpoint/procedure call.

The better way, as discussed in, for example, the Stack Overflow post "Transactions in REST?" (see http://stackoverflow.com/questions/147207/transactions-in-rest) is to POST to the account asking for a new transaction to be created:

```
POST /account/12345/transaction HTTP/1.1
```

This will return the URL of a new transaction:

```
http://bank.example.org/account/12345/txn123
```

Interactions are now carried out with this transaction URL, such as by PUTing a new value that performs and commits the transaction. Here, we use XML.

```
PUT /account/12345/txn123
<transaction>
  <from>/account/56789</from>
  <amount>100</amount>
</transaction>
```

A more detailed discussion of transactions and REST is given by Mihindukulasooriya et al. in "Seven Challenges for RESTful Transaction Models" (see http://ws-rest.org/2014/sites/default/files/wsrest2014_submission_4.pdf). Similar models are proposed for managing processes that aren't just single step. From the preceding PDF, we can get an idea of the types of things to consider when designing our RESTful APIs to provide transaction abilities.

Table 14-1. *RESTful transaction models*

Key	Year	Transaction Model
1	~2000	Batched transactions with overloaded POST
2	2007	Transaction as resources
3	2009	Optimistic technique for transactions using REST
4	2009	A consistent and recoverable RESTful transaction model
5	2010	Timestamp-based two-phase commit protocol for RESTful services
6	2011	Try-Cancel/Confirm Pattern
7	2012	Atomic REST batched transactions

Table 14-2. *Analysis of existing RESTful transaction models*

Property	Transaction models						
	1	2	3	4	5	6	7
Transaction properties							
Atomicity	T	T	T^1	T	T	T	T
Isolation	T	T^2	F	T	F	F	T
REST constraints							
Uniform interfaces	T	F	T	T	T	T	T
Statelessness	T	T^3	F	T^3	F	T	T
HATEOAS	F	F	F	T	F	T	F
HTTP-related properties							
Semantics not violated	T	T	T	T	F	T	T
Common verbs supported	T	T	F	F	T	T	T
Low overhead	T	T	T	F	F	T	T
Miscellaneous properties							
Optionality	T	?	?	T	?	?	F
Discoverable	?	?	?	T	?	?	T
Distributed transactions	X	X	T	?	T	T	?
Theoretical proofs	?	?	?	T	T	T	?
Implementation available	T	?	?	T	?	T	T
Performance evaluation	?	?	?	?	?	T	?

Legend - T True / F False / ? Unknown or not defined in the model

1 – Given the actions can be compensated
2 – Possible lost update problem
3 – See Section 3.3

The Richardson Maturity Model

Many systems claim to be RESTful. Most are not. We even came across one that claimed that SOAP was RESTful, a clear case of a warped mental state. Martin Fowler discusses the Richardson Maturity Model, which classifies systems according to their conformance to REST. (See https://martinfowler.com/articles/richardsonMaturityModel.html.)

Level 0

The starting point for the model is using HTTP as a transport system for remote interactions, but without using any of the mechanisms of the Web. Essentially what you are doing here is using HTTP as a tunneling mechanism for your own remote interaction mechanism, usually based on Remote Procedure Invocation.

Level 1: Resources

The first step toward the Glory of Rest in the RMM is to introduce resources. So now rather than making all our requests to a singular service endpoint, we now start talking to individual resources.

Level 2: HTTP Verbs

I've used HTTP POST verbs for all my interactions here in levels 0 and 1, but some people use GETs instead or in addition. At these levels, it doesn't make much difference, they are both being used as tunneling mechanisms allowing you to tunnel your interactions through HTTP. Level 2 moves away from this, using the HTTP verbs as closely as possible to how they are used in HTTP itself.

Level 3: Hypermedia Controls

The final level introduces something that you often hear referred to under the ugly acronym of HATEOAS (Hypertext As The Engine Of Application State). It addresses the question of how to get from a list of open slots to knowing what to do to book an appointment.

Flashcards Revisited

In Chapter 10, we considered a web system consisting of a server and HTML pages rendered in a browser, using JavaScript and CSS to control the browser-side interaction. There was no attempt to do anything particularly structured, rather just as a traditional web system.

■ **Recap** The web system of Chapter 10 was used to demonstrate language learning using so-called flashcards. The user is presented with a set of cards one at a time, showing a word in one language, and then hopes to remember the translation, which is shown by "turning over" the card. The system presented a list of different card sets and then showed the cards one at a time in the selected set.

We now approach the same situation as an HTTP client-server system built using the REST approach. We will make a number of changes:

- URLs will be given appropriate to the situation. These will include the "root" URL / as well as URLs for each flashcard set and, in addition, a URL for each flashcard.

- All user interaction code (HTML, JavaScript, and CSS) is omitted. The server will be talking to an arbitrary user agent, and many will not understand the UI code.

- The server will not maintain or manage any client state. In the web example, form data was sent from the browser to the server, which promptly returned it in a slightly different form. A client that wants to maintain state should do so itself.

- The server will be set up to manage a number of different serialization formats and will deliver as appropriate after client-server negotiation.

- Heavy use will be made of HTTP mechanisms, particularly for error handling and content negotiation.

URLs

The URLs for this system and the actions that can be performed are as follows:

URL	Action	Effect
/	GET	Gets a list of flashcard sets
	POST	Creates a new flashcard set
/flashcardSets/<set>	GET	Gets a list of cards in the set
	POST	Creates a new card for the set
	DELETE	Deletes the flashcard set if empty
/flashcardSets/<set>/<card>	GET	Gets the contents of the card
	DELETE	Deletes the card from the set

This differs a little from the system described in Chapter 10. The main structural difference is that each card is given its own URL as a member of a flashcard set.

Example URLs that will be handled by the server include these:

Root URL	URL for Flashcard Set	URL for One Flashcard
/	/flashcardSet/CommonWords	/flashcardSet/CommonWords/你好

ServeMux (The Demultiplexer)

REST is based on a small number of actions applied to URLs. A system that attempts to use REST principles must be URL based.

A server mux will examine URLs requested by clients and call handlers based on the URL pattern. The standard Go demuxer net/http.ServeMux uses a particular pattern-matching mechanism: if a URL ends in /, it denotes a subtree of URLs rooted at that URL. If it ends without a /, it represents that URL only. A URL is matched against the handler with the longest pattern match. A URL can even include a domain as a qualifier.

We need a handler for the root URL /. That will also match any URL such as /passwords unless another handler catches it. In this system, no other handler will, so in the handler for /, we need to return errors for such attempts.

A tricky part occurs because we used a hierarchical structure to our URLs. One particular flashcard set will be /flashcardSets/CommonWords. This will actually be a directory of the cards for that particular set. We have to register *two* handlers: one for the URL /flashcardSets/CommonWords, which is the flashcard set resource, and one for /flashcardSets/CommonWords/ (note the trailing /), which is the subtree containing the individual cards and their URLs.

The code in the main function to register these is as follows:

```
http.HandleFunc(`/`, handleFlashCardSets)
files, err := ioutil.ReadDir(`flashcardsets`)
checkError(err)
for _, file := range files {
        fmt.Println(file.Name())
        cardset_url := `/flashcardSets/` + url.QueryEscape(file.Name())
        http.HandleFunc(cardset_url, handleOneFlashCardSet)
        http.HandleFunc(cardset_url + `/`, handleOneFlashCard)
}
```

Note that we have the function QueryEscape. This is to escape any special characters that might occur in URLs. For example, a $ in a file name should be encoded as %44;. We *do* need to use such a function: our URLs will include Chinese characters, which need to be escape-encoded to be represented in URLs. This is done by QueryEscape, with one exception: a space in a path should be encoded as %20 but in form data should be encoded as +. The PathEscape function does this correctly. We will remove spaces from URLs to avoid this issue.

Content Negotiation

Any web user agent can try to talk to any web server. The typical case of a browser talking to an HTML server is what we are used to on the Web, but many will be familiar with using other user agents such as curl, wget, and even telnet! The browser and other tools will use the Content-Type in HTTP replies to work out what to do with content supplied.

With a Web application, the user agent must be able to understand what the server is delivering because it is trying to play a part in an interaction that probably doesn't have a user to help. RPC systems often use an external specification that the client and server conform to. That is not the case here.

The solution is that both parties must agree on a content format. This is done at the HTTP level. A client will state that it will accept a range of formats. If the server agrees, then they carry on. If not, the server will tell the client which formats it can accept, and the client can start afresh if possible.

The negotiation uses MIME types. There are hundreds of standard ones: text/html, application/pdf, application/xml, etc. A browser can render any HTML document it receives. An HTTP-aware music player such as VLC can play any MP3 file it receives. But for the flashcard application, it can't handle any general format, only messages that conform to an expected structure. These aren't any standard MIME types that would be suitable for negotiating a specialized protocol for this flashcard application. So we make up our own. The client and the server have to know that they are dealing with a shared MIME type, or they can't talk properly.

There are rules from IANA for making up your own MIME types. I use the type application/x. flashcards. The server will be able to deliver JSON and XML, so the two acceptable MIME types are application/x.flashcards+xml and application/x.flashcards+json.

HTTP content negotiation says that the user agent can suggest a list of acceptable formats, weighted between zero and one, as follows:

```
Accept: application/x.flashcards+xml; q=0.8,
        application/x.flashcards+json; q=0.4
```

The server can examine the request and decide if it can handle the format. We use the following code in the server to determine for any type if the user agent has requested it and with what weighting (zero means not requested):

```go
const flashcard_xml string = "application/x.flashcards+xml"
const flashcard_json string = "application/x.flashcards+json"

type ValueQuality struct {
        Value   string
        Quality float64
}

/* Based on https://siongui.github.io/2015/02/22/go-parse-accept-language/ */
func parseValueQuality(s string) []ValueQuality {
        var vqs []ValueQuality
        strs := strings.Split(s, `,`)
        for _, str := range strs {
                trimmedStr := strings.Trim(str, ` `)
                valQ := strings.Split(trimmedStr, `;`)
                if len(valQ) == 1 {
                        vq := ValueQuality{valQ[0], 1}
                        vqs = append(vqs, vq)
                } else {
                        qp := strings.Split(valQ[1], `=`)
                        q, err := strconv.ParseFloat(qp[1], 64)
                        if err != nil {
                                q = 0
                        }

                        vq := ValueQuality{valQ[0], q}
                        vqs = append(vqs, vq)
                }
        }
        return vqs
}

func qualityOfValue(value string, vqs []ValueQuality) float64 {
        for _, vq := range vqs {
                if value == vq.Value {
                        return vq.Quality
                }
        }
        // not found
        return 0
}
```

If the server does not accept any of the types requested by the user agent, it returns an HTTP code of 406 "Not acceptable" and supplies a list of accepted formats. The code segment to do this in the server is as follows:

```
func handleFlashCardSets(rw http.ResponseWriter, req *http.Request) {
        ...
        if req.Method == "GET" {
                acceptTypes := parseValueQuality(req.Header.Get("Accept"))
                q_xml := qualityOfValue(flashcard_xml, acceptTypes)
                q_json := qualityOfValue(flashcard_json, acceptTypes)
                if q_xml == 0 && q_json == 0 {
                        // can't find XML or JSON in Accept header
                        rw.Header().Set("Content-Type", "flashcards+xml, flashcards+json")
                        rw.WriteHeader(http.StatusNotAcceptable)
                        return
                }
                ...
        }
```

This illustrates a common REST pattern for HTTP servers: given an HTTP request, examine it to see if the server can manage it. If not, return an HTTP error. If okay, attempt to handle it. If the attempt fails, return an HTTP error. On success, return an appropriate HTTP success code and the results.

GET /

The flashcard sets are all stored in the directory flashcardsets. The GET / request needs to list all those files and prepare them in a suitable format for the client. The format is a list of flashcard set names and *their URLs*. The URLs are required by HATEOAS: the list of names tells us what the sets are, but the client will need their URLs in order to move to the stage of interacting with one of them.

The struct type for each FlashcardSet in the server contains the name of the set and its URL (as a string):

```
type FlashcardSet struct {
        Name string
        Link string
}
```

The set of flashcard sets on the server can be built from the directory of flashcard sets. The ioutil. ReadDir() will create an array of os.FileInfo. This needs to be converted to a list of file names as follows:

```
files, err := ioutil.ReadDir(`flashcardsets`)
checkError(err)
numfiles := len(files)
cardSets := make([]FlashcardSet, numfiles, numfiles)
for n, file := range files {
        fmt.Println(file.Name())
        cardSets[n].Name = file.Name()
        // should be PathEscape, not in go 1.6
        cardSets[n].Link = `/flashcardSets/` + url.QueryEscape(file.Name())
}
```

This creates an array of file names and relative links to the resource on the server as /<name>. For the CommonWords set, the relative link URL would be /flashcardSets/CommonWords. The scheme (http or https) and the host (e.g., "localhost") are left up to the client to work out.

Unfortunately, the file name may contain characters not legal in URL path names. The function url.PathEscape escapes them all correctly. The function url.QueryEscape gets everything right except for spaces in the file name, which it replaces with + instead of %20;.

Finally, the server figures out if JSON or XML is preferred and runs it through a template to generate the right output to the client. For XML, the template code is as follows:

```
...
if q_xml >= q_json {
        // XML preferred
        t, err := template.ParseFiles("xml/ListFlashcardSets.xml")
        if err != nil {
                fmt.Println("Template error")
                http.Error(rw, err.Error(), http.StatusInternalServerError)
                return
        }
        rw.Header().Set("Content-Type", flashcard_xml)
        t.Execute(rw, cardSets)
} else {
// JSON preferred
...
```

The XML template is as follows:

```
ch14 % cat xml/ListFlashcardSets.xml

<?xml version="1.0" encoding="UTF-8"?>

<cardsets xmlns="http://www.w3.org/2005/Atom">
  {{range .}}
  <cardset href="{{.Link}}">
    <name>
      {{.Name}}
    </name>
  </cardset>
  {{end}}
</cardsets>
```

For a listing of only two sets, CommonWords and Lesson04, the content sent to the client is as follows:

```
<?xml version="1.0" encoding="UTF-8"?>
<cardsets xmlns="http://www.w3.org/2005/Atom">
  <cardset href="/CommonWords">
    <name>
      Common Words
    </name>
  </cardset>
```

```
  <cardset href="/Lesson04">
    <name>
      Lesson04
    </name>
  </cardset>
</cardsets>
```

POST /

Here, a client is asking for a new flashcard set to be created. The expectation is that the client will supply the name of the flashcard set. We make it look like form submission data:

```
name=<new flashcard set name>
```

This is much simpler than GET in this case. Get the value out of the request as form data. Then check that the requested name doesn't have nasties in it like calling the flashcard set /etc/passwd. If it does, return 403 "Forbidden". If it appears to be okay, create a directory with that name. Return a 403 again if it fails (the directory may already exist). Otherwise, return 201 "Created" and the new relative URL:

```
...
} else if req.Method == "POST" {
        name := req.FormValue(`name`)
        if hasIllegalChars(name) {
                rw.WriteHeader(http.StatusForbidden)
                return
        }
        // lose all spaces as they are a nuisance
        name = strings.Replace(name, ` `, ``, -1)
        err := os.Mkdir(`flashcardsets/`+name,
                (os.ModeDir | os.ModePerm))
        if err != nil {
                rw.WriteHeader(http.StatusForbidden)
                return
        }
        rw.WriteHeader(http.StatusCreated)
        base_url := req.URL.String()
        new_url := base_url + `flashcardSets/` + name + `/`
        rw.Write([]byte(new_url))
} else {
        rw.WriteHeader(http.StatusMethodNotAllowed)
}
...
```

Handling Other URLs

We discussed the code for the server handling the / URL with GET and POST requests. There are two other types of URL for this application – handling the cards in a set and handling each individual card. In terms of the coding, though, this presents no new ideas.

- Getting a list of cards in a set is another directory listing.

- Posting a new card to a set means creating a file in the appropriate directory with content from the client.

- Deleting a set means removing a directory. This is okay if the directory is empty; otherwise, it creates an error.

- Getting a card means reading the card file and sending its contents.

- Deleting a card means removing a file.

There is nothing particularly new about any of these. We have not completed the code for some operations such as DELETE: these return the HTTP code 501 'Not implemented'. We also return the contents of individual cards as text/plain: they have a complex JSON/Go structure as used in Chapter 10, but that is not needed for the discussion of the REST aspects of this system.

The Complete Server

The complete server to handle requests to / and from there to other URLs follows. It requires the flashcard sets and individual cards in order to run, and these are in the ch14 folder here https://github.com/Apress/network-prog-with-go-2e.

```
ch14$ vi server.go

/* Server
 */

package main

import (
        "fmt"
        "html/template"
        "log"
        "net/http"
        "net/url"
        "os"
        "regexp"
        "strconv"
        "strings"
)

type FlashcardSet struct {
        Name string
        Link string
}

type Flashcard struct {
        Name string
        Link string
}
```

```
const flashcard_xml string = "application/x.flashcards+xml"
const flashcard_json string = "application/x.flashcards+json"

type ValueQuality struct {
        Value   string
        Quality float64
}

/* Based on https://siongui.github.io/2015/02/22/go-parse-accept-language/ */
func parseValueQuality(s string) []ValueQuality {
        var vqs []ValueQuality

        strs := strings.Split(s, `,`)
        for _, str := range strs {
                trimmedStr := strings.Trim(str, ` `)
                valQ := strings.Split(trimmedStr, `;`)
                if len(valQ) == 1 {
                        vq := ValueQuality{valQ[0], 1}
                        vqs = append(vqs, vq)
                } else {
                        qp := strings.Split(valQ[1], `=`)
                        q, err := strconv.ParseFloat(qp[1], 64)
                        if err != nil {
                                q = 0
                        }
                        vq := ValueQuality{valQ[0], q}
                        vqs = append(vqs, vq)
                }
        }
        return vqs
}

func qualityOfValue(value string, vqs []ValueQuality) float64 {
        for _, vq := range vqs {
                if value == vq.Value {
                        return vq.Quality
                }
        }
        return 0
}

func main() {
        if len(os.Args) != 2 {
                log.Fatalln("Usage: ", os.Args[0], ":port\n")
        }
        port := os.Args[1]

        http.HandleFunc(`/`, handleFlashCardSets)
        files, err := os.ReadDir(`flashcardsets`)
        checkError(err)
```

```
        for _, file := range files {
                fmt.Println(file.Name())
                cardset_url := `/flashcardSets/` + url.QueryEscape(file.Name())
                fmt.Println("Adding handlers for ", cardset_url)
                http.HandleFunc(cardset_url, handleOneFlashCardSet)
                http.HandleFunc(cardset_url+`/`, handleOneFlashCard)
        }

        // deliver requests to the handlers
        err = http.ListenAndServe(port, nil)
        checkError(err)
}

func hasIllegalChars(s string) bool {
        // check against chars to break out of current dir
        b, err := regexp.Match("[/$~]", []byte(s))
        if err != nil {
                fmt.Println(err)
                return true
        }
        if b {
                return true
        }
        return false
}

func handleOneFlashCard(rw http.ResponseWriter, req *http.Request) {
        // should be PathUnescape
        path, _ := url.QueryUnescape(req.URL.String())
        // lose intial '/'
        path = path[1:]
        if req.Method == http.MethodGet {
                fmt.Println("Handling card: ", path)
                json_contents, err := os.ReadFile(path)
                if err != nil {
                        rw.WriteHeader(http.StatusNotFound)
                        rw.Write([]byte(`Resource not found`))
                        return
                }
                // Be lazy here, just return the content as text/plain
                rw.Write(json_contents)
                return
        } else if req.Method == http.MethodDelete {
                rw.WriteHeader(http.StatusNotImplemented)
        } else {
                rw.WriteHeader(http.StatusMethodNotAllowed)
        }
        return
}
```

```go
func handleFlashCardSets(rw http.ResponseWriter, req *http.Request) {
        if req.URL.String() != `/` {
                // this function only handles '/'
                rw.WriteHeader(http.StatusNotFound)
                rw.Write([]byte("Resource not found\n"))
                return
        }
        if req.Method == "GET" {
                acceptTypes := parseValueQuality(req.Header.Get("Accept"))
                fmt.Println(acceptTypes)

                q_xml := qualityOfValue(flashcard_xml, acceptTypes)
                q_json := qualityOfValue(flashcard_json, acceptTypes)
                if q_xml == 0 && q_json == 0 {
                        // can't find XML or JSON in Accept header
                        rw.Header().Set("Content-Type", "flashcards+xml, flashcards+json")
                        rw.WriteHeader(http.StatusNotAcceptable)
                        return
                }

                files, err := os.ReadDir(`flashcardsets`)
                checkError(err)
                numfiles := len(files)
                cardSets := make([]FlashcardSet, numfiles, numfiles)
                for n, file := range files {
                        fmt.Println(file.Name())
                        cardSets[n].Name = file.Name()
                        // should be PathEscape, not in go 1.6
                        cardSets[n].Link = `/flashcardSets/` + url.QueryEscape(file.Name())
                }
                parseFile := "xml/ListFlashcardSets.xml"
                flashcardType := flashcard_xml
                if q_xml < q_json {
                        parseFile = "json/ListFlashcardSets.json"
                        flashcardType = flashcard_json
                }
                t, err := template.ParseFiles(parseFile)
                if err != nil {
                        fmt.Println("Template error")
                        http.Error(rw, err.Error(), http.StatusInternalServerError)
                        return
                }
                rw.Header().Set("Content-Type", flashcardType)
                t.Execute(rw, cardSets)
        } else if req.Method == "POST" {
                name := req.FormValue(`name`)
                if hasIllegalChars(name) {
                        rw.WriteHeader(http.StatusForbidden)
                        return
                }
```

```
            // lose all spaces as they are a nuisance
            name = strings.Replace(name, ` `, ``, -1)
            err := os.Mkdir(`flashcardsets/`+name,
                    (os.ModeDir | os.ModePerm))
            if err != nil {
                    rw.WriteHeader(http.StatusForbidden)
                    return
            }
            rw.WriteHeader(http.StatusCreated)
            base_url := req.URL.String()
            new_url := base_url + `flashcardSets/` + name + `/`
            rw.Write([]byte(new_url))
    } else {
            rw.WriteHeader(http.StatusMethodNotAllowed)
    }
    return
}

func handleOneFlashCardSet(rw http.ResponseWriter, req *http.Request) {
    cooked_url, _ := url.QueryUnescape(req.URL.String())
    fmt.Println("Handling one set for: ", cooked_url)

    if req.Method == http.MethodGet {
            acceptTypes := parseValueQuality(req.Header.Get("Accept"))
            fmt.Println(acceptTypes)

            q_xml := qualityOfValue(flashcard_xml, acceptTypes)
            q_json := qualityOfValue(flashcard_json, acceptTypes)
            if q_xml == 0 && q_json == 0 {
                    // can't find XML or JSON in Accept header
                    rw.Header().Set("Content-Type", "flashcards+xml, flashcards+json")
                    rw.WriteHeader(http.StatusNotAcceptable)
                    return
            }

            path := req.URL.String()
            // lose leading /
            relative_path := path[1:]
            files, err := os.ReadDir(relative_path)
            checkError(err)
            numfiles := len(files)
            cards := make([]Flashcard, numfiles, numfiles)
            for n, file := range files {
                    fmt.Println(file.Name())
                    cards[n].Name = file.Name()
                    // should be PathEscape, not in go 1.6
                    cards[n].Link = path + `/` + url.QueryEscape(file.Name())
            }
```

```go
                if q_xml >= q_json {
                        // XML preferred
                        t, err := template.ParseFiles("xml/ListOneFlashcardSet.xml")
                        if err != nil {
                                fmt.Println("Template error")
                                http.Error(rw, err.Error(), http.StatusInternalServerError)
                                return
                        }
                        rw.Header().Set("Content-Type", flashcard_xml)
                        t.Execute(os.Stdout, cards)
                        t.Execute(rw, cards)
                } else {
                        // JSON preferred
                        t, err := template.ParseFiles("json/ListOneFlashcardSet.json")
                        if err != nil {
                                fmt.Println("Template error", err)
                                http.Error(rw, err.Error(), http.StatusInternalServerError)
                                return
                        }
                        rw.Header().Set("Content-Type", flashcard_json)
                        t.Execute(rw, cards)

                }
        } else if req.Method == http.MethodPost {
                name := req.FormValue(`name`)
                if hasIllegalChars(name) {
                        rw.WriteHeader(http.StatusForbidden)
                        return
                }
                err := os.Mkdir(`flashcardsets/`+name,
                        (os.ModeDir | os.ModePerm))
                if err != nil {
                        rw.WriteHeader(http.StatusForbidden)
                        return
                }
                rw.WriteHeader(http.StatusCreated)
                base_url := req.URL.String()
                new_url := base_url + `flashcardSets/` + name
                _, _ = rw.Write([]byte(new_url))
        } else if req.Method == http.MethodDelete {
                rw.WriteHeader(http.StatusNotImplemented)
        } else {
                rw.WriteHeader(http.StatusMethodNotAllowed)
        }
        return
}

func checkError(err error) {
        if err != nil {
                log.Fatalln("Fatal error ", err.Error())
        }
}
```

It is run as follows:

```
ch14$ go run server.go :8000
```

Client

The client is relatively straightforward, offering nothing really new. This client asks for the content only in XML format. A new part is that the content for the flashcard sets includes links as hypertext attributes within a cardset tag. This may be turned into a field of a struct by the tag label xml:"href,attr" in the Card struct.

This client gets the list of flashcard sets and their URLs in the getFlashcardSets() function (step 1). This returns a FlashcardSets struct. This can be used to present a list to a user, say, for selection of a particular set. Once selected, the URL of that set can be used to interact with the resource.

This client then creates a new flashcard set with name NewSet in the createFlashcardSet() function (step 2). The first time the client runs, it will create the set, and the URL for that set will be returned. The second time it is run, it will get an error from the server as a prohibited operation, since the set already exists.

This client then takes the first set of flashcards from the URLs given by the server and asks for the set of cards it holds (step 3). It then picks the first card from the set and gets its content (step 4).

The client is client.go:

```
ch14$ vi client.go

/* Client
 */

package main

import (
        "encoding/xml"
        "fmt"
        "io"
        "log"
        "net/http"
        "net/http/httputil"
        "net/url"
        "os"
        "strings"
)

const flashcard_xml string = "application/x.flashcards+xml"
const flashcard_json string = "application/x.flashcards+json"

type FlashcardSets struct {
        XMLName string     `xml:"cardsets"`
        CardSet []CardSet `xml:"cardset"`
}
```

285

```
type CardSet struct {
        XMLName string `xml:"cardset"`
        Name    string `xml:"name"`
        Link    string `xml:"href,attr"`
        Cards   []Card `xml:"card"`
}

type Card struct {
        Name string `xml:"name"`
        Link string `xml:"href,attr"`
}

func getter(url *url.URL, client *http.Client, acceptType string) *http.Response {
        request, err := http.NewRequest("GET", url.String(), nil)
        checkError(err)

        if acceptType != "" {
                request.Header.Add("Accept", flashcard_xml)
        }
        response, err := client.Do(request)
        checkError(err)
        if response.StatusCode != http.StatusOK {
                log.Fatalln(err, response)
        }

        fmt.Println("The response header is")
        b, _ := httputil.DumpResponse(response, false)
        fmt.Print(string(b))
        return response
}

func getOneFlashcard(url *url.URL, client *http.Client) string {
        // Get the card as a string, don't do anything with it
        response := getter(url, client, "")

        body, err := io.ReadAll(response.Body)
        checkError(err)
        content := string(body[:])
        //fmt.Printf("Body is %s", content)

        return content
}

func getOneFlashcardSet(url *url.URL, client *http.Client) CardSet {
        // Get one set of cards
        response := getter(url, client, flashcard_xml)

        body, err := io.ReadAll(response.Body)
        content := string(body[:])
        fmt.Printf("Body is %s", content)
```

```go
            var sets CardSet
            contentType := getContentType(response)
            if contentType == "XML" {

                    err = xml.Unmarshal(body, &sets)
                    checkError(err)
                    fmt.Println("XML: ", sets)
                    return sets
            }
            /* else if contentType == "JSON" {
                    var sets FlashcardSetsJson
                    err = json.Unmarshal(body, &sets)
                    checkError(err)
                    fmt.Println("JSON: ", sets)
            }
            */
            return sets
    }

    func getFlashcardSets(url *url.URL, client *http.Client) FlashcardSets {
            // Get the toplevel /
            response := getter(url, client, flashcard_xml)

            body, err := io.ReadAll(response.Body)
            content := string(body[:])
            fmt.Printf("Body is %s", content)

            var sets FlashcardSets
            contentType := getContentType(response)
            if contentType == "XML" {
                    err = xml.Unmarshal(body, &sets)
                    checkError(err)
                    fmt.Println("XML: ", sets)
                    return sets
            }
            return sets
    }

    func createFlashcardSet(url1 *url.URL, client *http.Client, name string) string {
            data := make(url.Values)
            data[`name`] = []string{name}
            response, err := client.PostForm(url1.String(), data)
            checkError(err)
            if response.StatusCode != http.StatusCreated {
                    fmt.Println(`Error: `, response.Status)
                    return ``
            }
            body, err := io.ReadAll(response.Body)
            content := string(body[:])
            return content
    }
```

```go
func main() {
        if len(os.Args) != 2 {
                log.Fatalln("Usage: ", os.Args[0], "http://host:port/page")
        }
        url, err := url.Parse(os.Args[1])
        checkError(err)

        client := &http.Client{}

        // Step 1: get a list of flashcard sets
        flashcardSets := getFlashcardSets(url, client)
        fmt.Println("Step 1: ", flashcardSets)

        // Step 2: try to create a new flashcard set
        new_url := createFlashcardSet(url, client, `NewSet`)
        fmt.Println("Step 2: New flashcard set has URL: ", new_url)

        // Step 3: using the first flashcard set,
        //         get the list of cards in it
        set_url, _ := url.Parse(os.Args[1] + flashcardSets.CardSet[0].Link)

        fmt.Println("Asking for flashcard set URL: ", set_url.String())
        oneFlashcardSet := getOneFlashcardSet(set_url, client)
        fmt.Println("Step 3:", oneFlashcardSet)

        // Step 4: get the contents of one flashcard
        //         be lazy, just get as text/plain and
        //         don't do anything with it
        card_url, _ := url.Parse(os.Args[1] + oneFlashcardSet.Cards[0].Link)
        fmt.Println("Asking for URL: ", card_url.String())
        oneFlashcard := getOneFlashcard(card_url, client)
        fmt.Println("Step 4", oneFlashcard)
}

func getContentType(response *http.Response) string {
        contentType := response.Header.Get("Content-Type")
        if strings.Contains(contentType, flashcard_xml) {
                return "XML"
        }
        if strings.Contains(contentType, flashcard_json) {
                return "JSON"
        }
        return ""
}

func checkError(err error) {
        if err != nil {
                log.Fatalln("Fatal error ", err.Error())
        }
}
```

It is run as follows:

```
ch14$ go run client.go http://localhost:8000/

... (all about flashcards) ...
```

Using REST or RPC

The primary difference between REST and RPC is the interaction style. In RPC, you are calling functions, passing objects or primitive types as arguments, and getting objects or primitive types in return. The functions are *verbs*: do *this* to *that*. REST, on the other hand, is about interacting with objects, asking them to show their state or to change it in some way.

The difference is shown by the Go RPC mechanism discussed in the last chapter and the REST mechanism of this chapter. In Go RPC over HTTP, the server registers *functions*, while in REST, the server registers handlers for *URLs*.

Which is better? Neither. Which is faster? Neither. Which is better for a controlled environment? Possibly RPC. Which is better for an open environment? Possibly REST.

You will see arguments based on speed and resource allocation. RPC based on binary systems will probably be faster than text-based HTTP systems. But SOAP is a text-based RPC system using HTTP and is probably slower than REST. HTTP2 uses a binary format and, when conveying binary data such as BSON, will probably be equivalent in speed to other binary systems. Just to confuse things further, the Apache Thrift RPC allows a choice of data formats (binary, compact binary, JSON, and text) and transports (sockets, files, and shared memory). One system demonstrates all options!

A more important factor might be how tightly controlled the operational environment is. RPC systems are tightly coupled, and a failure in one component could bring an entire system down. When there are a single administrative authority, a limited set of hardware and software configurations, and a clear channel for fixing problems, then an RPC system can work well.

On the other side, the Web is uncontrolled. There is no single authority – even such "universal" services such as DNS are highly distributed. There is a huge variety of hardware, operating systems, and software; there will be little prospect of enforcing any policies; and if something breaks, then there is often no one who can be pointed at to fix it. In such a case, a loosely coupled system may be better.

REST over HTTP is a good match for this. HATEOAS allows servers to be reconfigured on the fly, changing URLs as needed (even pointing to different servers!). HTTP is designed to cache results when it can. Firewalls are usually configured to allow HTTP traffic and block most other. REST is a good choice here.

It should be noted that REST is not the only HTTP-based system possible. SOAP has already been mentioned. There are many commercial and highly successful systems that are "almost" REST – Richardson levels 1 and 2. They do not enjoy the full benefits of the REST/HTTP match but still work.

No doubt in the future, other models will arise. In the IoT space, CoAP is popular for low-power wireless systems. It is also REST based, but in a slightly different way than HTTP-REST.

Conclusion

REST is the architectural model of the Web. It can be applied in many different ways, particularly as HTTP and CoAP (e.g., low power, lossy network protocol). This chapter illustrated REST as applied to HTTP.

CHAPTER 15

WebSockets

The standard model of interaction between a web user agent such as a browser and a web server such as Apache is that the user agent makes HTTP requests and the server makes a single reply to each one. In the case of a browser, the request is made by clicking on a link, entering a URL into the address bar, clicking on the forward or back buttons, etc. The response is treated as a new page and is loaded into a browser window.

This traditional model has many drawbacks. The first is that each request opens and closes a new TCP connection. HTTP 1.1 solved this by allowing persistent connections so that a connection could be held open for a short period to allow for multiple requests (e.g., for images) to be made on the same server.

While HTTP 1.1 persistent connections alleviate the problem of slow loading of a page with many graphics, it does not improve the interaction model. Even with forms, the model is still that of submitting the form and displaying the response as a new page. JavaScript helps in allowing error checking to be performed on form data before submission but does not change the model.

AJAX (Asynchronous JavaScript and XML) made a significant advance to the user interaction model. This allows a browser to make a request and just use the response to update the display in place using the HTML Document Object Model (DOM). But again, the interaction model is the same. AJAX just affects how the browser manages the returned pages. There is no explicit extra support in Go for AJAX, as none is needed: the HTTP server just sees an ordinary HTTP POST request with possibly some XML or JSON data, and this can be dealt with using techniques already discussed.

All of these are still browser (or user agent)-to-server communication. What is missing is server-to-browser communications where a browser has set up a TCP connection to a server and reads messages from the server. This can be filled by WebSockets: the browser (or any user agent) keeps open a long-lived TCP connection to a WebSockets server. The TCP connection allows either side to send arbitrary packets, so any application protocol can be used on a WebSocket.

How a WebSocket is started is by the user agent sending a special HTTP request that says "switch to WebSockets." The TCP connection underlying the HTTP request is kept open, but both user agent and server switch to using the WebSockets protocol instead of getting an HTTP response and closing the socket.

Note that it is still the browser or user agent that initiates the WebSockets connection. The browser does not run a TCP server of its own. While the specification as IETF RFC 6455 is complex (see `https://tools.ietf.org/html/rfc6455`), the protocol is designed to be fairly easy to use. The client opens an HTTP connection and then replaces the HTTP protocol with its own WS protocol, reusing the same TCP or a new connection.

Go has some support for WebSockets in a subrepository but actually recommends a third-party package. This chapter considers both packages.

© Jan Newmarch and Ronald Petty 2022
J. Newmarch and R. Petty, *Network Programming with Go Language*,
https://doi.org/10.1007/978-1-4842-8095-9_15

WebSockets Server

A WebSockets server starts off by being an HTTP server, accepting TCP connections and handling the HTTP requests on the TCP connection. When a request comes in that switches that connection to being a WebSockets connection, the protocol handler is changed from an HTTP handler to a WebSocket handler. So it is only that TCP connection that gets its role changed; the server continues to be an HTTP server for other requests, while the TCP socket underlying that one connection is used as a WebSocket.

One of the simple servers discussed in Chapter 8, HTTP, registered various handlers such as a file handler or a function handler. To handle WebSockets requests, we simply register a different type of handler – a WebSockets handler. Which handler the server uses is based on the URL pattern. For example, a file handler might be registered for /, a function handler for /cgi-bin/..., and a WebSockets handler for /ws.

An HTTP server that is only expecting to be used for WebSockets might run as follows:

```
func main() {
        http.Handle("/", websocket.Handler(WSHandler))
        err := http.ListenAndServe(":12345", nil)
        checkError(err)
}
```

A more complex server might handle both HTTP and WebSockets requests simply by adding more handlers.

We have a variety of options when it comes to implementation, including manually managing the original HTTP connection (TCP hijacking) and the use of the x package WebSocket implementation or even well-known third-party packages.

The golang.org/x/net/websocket Package

Go has the subrepository package called golang.org/x/net/websocket.

The package documentation states the following:

> This package currently lacks some features found in an alternative and more actively maintained WebSockets package: https://pkg.go.dev/github.com/ gorilla/websocket. Unfortunately, even the Gorilla WebSocket package is looking for an active lead maintainer. Still, it remains a leading implementation.

This suggests that you might be better off using the alternative package. Nevertheless, we consider this package here in keeping with the rest of this book of using the packages from the Go team. A later section looks at the alternative package.

The Message Object

HTTP is a stream protocol. WebSockets are frame based. You prepare a block of data (of any size) and send it as a set of frames. Frames can contain strings in UTF-8 encoding or a sequence of bytes.

The simplest way of using WebSockets is just to prepare a block of data and ask the Go WebSockets library to package it as a set of frame data, send it across the wire, and receive it as the same block. The websocket package contains a convenience object called Message to do just that. The Message object has two methods – Send and Receive – that take a WebSocket as the first parameter. The second parameter is either the address of a variable to store data in or the data to be sent. Code to send string data looks like this:

```
msgToSend := "Hello"
err := websocket.Message.Send(ws, msgToSend)
var msgToReceive string
err := websocket.Message.Receive(conn, &msgToReceive)
```

Code to send byte data looks like this:

```
dataToSend := []byte{0, 1, 2}
err := websocket.Message.Send(ws, dataToSend)
var dataToReceive []byte
err := websocket.Message.Receive(conn, &dataToReceive)
```

An echo server to send and receive string data is given next. Note that in WebSockets, either side can initiate sending of messages, and in this server, we send messages from the server to a client when it connects (send/receive) instead of the more normal receive/send server. The server is echoserver.go:

```
$ mkdir ch15
$ cd ch15
$ vi echoserver.go

/* EchoServer
 */
package main

import (
        "fmt"
        "golang.org/x/net/websocket"
        "log"
        "net/http"
)

func Echo(ws *websocket.Conn) {
        fmt.Println("Echoing")
        for n := 0; n < 10; n++ {
                msg := "Hello  " + string(n+48)
                fmt.Println("Sending to client: " + msg)
                err := websocket.Message.Send(ws, msg)
                if err != nil {
                        fmt.Println("Can't send")
                        break
                }
                var reply string
                err = websocket.Message.Receive(ws, &reply)
                if err != nil {
                        fmt.Println("Can't receive")
                        break
                }
```

```
                fmt.Println("Received back from client: " + reply)
        }
}
func main() {
        http.Handle("/", websocket.Handler(Echo))
        err := http.ListenAndServe(":12345", nil)
        checkError(err)
}
func checkError(err error) {
        if err != nil {
                log.Fatalln("Fatal error ", err.Error())
        }
}
```

It is run as follows:

```
ch15$ go mod init example.com/user/echoserver
ch15$ go mod tidy

ch15$ go run echoserver.go
```

A client that talks to this server is echoclient.go:

```
ch15$ vi echoclient.go

/* EchoClient
 */
package main

import (
        "fmt"
        "golang.org/x/net/websocket"
        "io"
        "os"
        "log"
)

func main() {
        if len(os.Args) != 2 {
                log.Fatalln("Usage: ", os.Args[0], "ws://host:port")
        }
        service := os.Args[1]
        conn, err := websocket.Dial(service, "",
                "http://localhost:12345")
        checkError(err)
        var msg string
        for {
                err := websocket.Message.Receive(conn, &msg)
                if err != nil {
                        if err == io.EOF {
                                // graceful shutdown by server
```

```
                                    break
                        }
                        fmt.Println("Couldn't receive msg " +
                                err.Error())
                        break
                }
                fmt.Println("Received from server: " + msg)
                // return the msg
                err = websocket.Message.Send(conn, msg)
                if err != nil {
                        fmt.Println("Couldn't return msg")
                        break
                }
        }
}
func checkError(err error) {
        if err != nil {
                log.Fatalln("Fatal error ", err.Error())
        }
}
```

It is run as follows:

```
ch15$ go run echoclient.go ws://localhost:12345
```

The output on the *client* side is what is sent by the *server*:

```
Received from server: Hello  0
...
Received from server: Hello  9
```

Back on the server, we see the following:

```
Echoing
Sending to client: Hello  0
Received back from client: Hello  0
...
Sending to client: Hello  9
Received back from client: Hello  9
```

The preceding session provides evidence we are able to send data to and from via a WebSocket. Take note of the Message object and its usage in the preceding server and client code. Per the documentation:

```
ch15$ go doc golang.org/x/net/websocket.Message

package websocket // import "golang.org/x/net/websocket"

var Message = Codec{marshal, unmarshal}
    Message is a codec to send/receive text/binary data in a frame on WebSocket
    connection. To send/receive text frame, use string type. To send/receive
    binary frame, use []byte type.
```

Trivial usage:

```
import "websocket"

// receive text frame
var message string
websocket.Message.Receive(ws, &message)

// send text frame
message = "hello"
websocket.Message.Send(ws, message)

// receive binary frame
var data []byte
websocket.Message.Receive(ws, &data)

// send binary frame
data = []byte{0, 1, 2}
websocket.Message.Send(ws, data)
```

The JSON Object

It is expected that many WebSockets clients and servers will exchange data in JSON format. For Go programs, this means that a Go object will be marshalled into the JSON format, as described in Chapter 4, and then sent as UTF-8 strings, while the receiver will read this string and unmarshal it back into a Go object.

The websocket convenience object called JSON will do this for you. It has Send and Receive methods for sending and receiving data, just like the Message object.

We consider a case where a client sends a Person object to a server using WebSockets (which can send messages both ways). A server that reads the message from the client and prints it to the server's standard output is personserverjson.go:

```
ch15$ vi personserverjson.go

/* PersonServerJSON
 */
package main

import (
        "fmt"
        "golang.org/x/net/websocket"
        "log"
        "net/http"
)

type Person struct {
        Name    string
        Emails []string
}
```

```go
func ReceivePerson(ws *websocket.Conn) {
        var person Person
        err := websocket.JSON.Receive(ws, &person)
        if err != nil {
                fmt.Println("Can't receive")
        } else {
                fmt.Println("Name: " + person.Name)
                for _, e := range person.Emails {
                        fmt.Println("An email: " + e)
                }
        }
}
func main() {
        http.Handle("/", websocket.Handler(ReceivePerson))
        err := http.ListenAndServe(":12345", nil)
        checkError(err)
}
func checkError(err error) {
        if err != nil {
                log.Fatalln("Fatal error ", err.Error())
        }
}
```

A client that sends a Person object in JSON format is personclientjson.go:

```
ch15$ vi personclientjson.go
```

```go
/* PersonClientJSON
 */
package main

import (
        "fmt"
        "golang.org/x/net/websocket"
        "log"
        "os"
)

type Person struct {
        Name    string
        Emails  []string
}

func main() {
        if len(os.Args) != 2 {
                log.Fatalln("Usage: ", os.Args[0], "ws://host:port")
        }
        service := os.Args[1]
        conn, err := websocket.Dial(service, "",
                "http://localhost")
        checkError(err)
```

```go
        person := Person{Name: "Jan",
                Emails: []string{"ja@newmarch.name",
                        "jan.newmarch@gmail.com"},
        }
        err = websocket.JSON.Send(conn, person)
        if err != nil {
                fmt.Println("Couldn't send msg " + err.Error())
        }
}
func checkError(err error) {
        if err != nil {
                log.Fatalln("Fatal error ", err.Error())
        }
}
```

The server is run as follows:

```
ch15$ go run personserverjson.go
```

The client is run as follows:

```
ch15$ go run personclientjson.go ws://localhost:12345
```

The output on the *server* side is what is sent by the *client*:

```
Name: Jan
An email: ja@newmarch.name
An email: jan.newmarch@gmail.com
```

As before, review the related JSON object documentation.

```
ch15$ go doc golang.org/x/net/websocket.JSON

package websocket // import "golang.org/x/net/websocket"

var JSON = Codec{jsonMarshal, jsonUnmarshal}
    JSON is a codec to send/receive JSON data in a frame from a WebSocket
    connection.

    Trivial usage:

        import "websocket"

        type T struct {
                Msg string
                Count int
        }

        // receive JSON type T
        var data T
        websocket.JSON.Receive(ws, &data)
```

```
    // send JSON type T
    websocket.JSON.Send(ws, data)
```

The Codec Type

The Message and JSON objects are both instances of the type Codec. This type is defined as follows:

```
type Codec struct {
    Marshal   func(v interface{}) (data []byte, payloadType byte, err error)
    Unmarshal func(data []byte, payloadType byte, v interface{}) (err error)
}
```

The Codec type implements the Send and Receive methods used earlier. See more on this type with

```
ch15$ go doc golang.org/x/net/websocket.Codec
```

It is likely that WebSockets will also be used to exchange XML data. We can build an XML Codec object by wrapping the XML marshal and unmarshal methods discussed in Chapter 12 to give a suitable Codec object.

We can create an XMLCodec package in this way, called xmlcodec.go:

```
ch15$ vi xmlcodec.go
```

```
/* XMLCodec
 */
package main

import (
        "encoding/xml"
        "golang.org/x/net/websocket"
)

func xmlMarshal(v interface{}) (msg []byte, payloadType byte, err error) {
        msg, err = xml.Marshal(v)
        return msg, websocket.TextFrame, nil
}
func xmlUnmarshal(msg []byte, payloadType byte, v interface{}) (err error) {
        err = xml.Unmarshal(msg, v)
        return err
}

var XMLCodec = websocket.Codec{xmlMarshal, xmlUnmarshal}
```

We can then serialize Go objects such as a Person into an XML document and send them from a client to a server. The server to receive the document and print it to standard output is as follows, personserverxml.go:

```
ch15$ vi personserverxml.go

/* PersonServerXML
 */
package main

import (
        "fmt"
        "golang.org/x/net/websocket"
        "log"
        "net/http"
)

type Person struct {
        Name    string
        Emails []string
}

func ReceivePerson(ws *websocket.Conn) {
        var person Person
        err := XMLCodec.Receive(ws, &person)
        if err != nil {
                fmt.Println("Can't receive")
        } else {
                fmt.Println("Name: " + person.Name)
                for _, e := range person.Emails {
                        fmt.Println("An email: " + e)
                }
        }
}
func main() {
        http.Handle("/", websocket.Handler(ReceivePerson))
        err := http.ListenAndServe(":12345", nil)
        checkError(err)
}
func checkError(err error) {
        if err != nil {
                log.Fatalln("Fatal error ", err.Error())
        }
}
```

The client sending the Person object in XML form is personclientxml.go:

```
ch15$ vi personclientxml.go

/* PersonClientXML
 */
package main
```

```go
import (
        "fmt"
        "golang.org/x/net/websocket"
        "log"
        "os"
)

type Person struct {
        Name    string
        Emails  []string
}

func main() {
        if len(os.Args) != 2 {
                log.Fatalln("Usage: ", os.Args[0], "ws://host:port")
        }
        service := os.Args[1]
        conn, err := websocket.Dial(service, "", "http://localhost")
        checkError(err)
        person := Person{Name: "Jan",
                Emails: []string{"ja@newmarch.name",
                        "jan.newmarch@gmail.com"},
        }
        err = XMLCodec.Send(conn, person)
        if err != nil {
                fmt.Println("Couldn't send msg " + err.Error())
        }
        os.Exit(0)
}
func checkError(err error) {
        if err != nil {
                log.Fatalln("Fatal error ", err.Error())
        }
}
```

The server is run as follows:

```
ch15$ go run personserverxml.go xmlcodec.go
```

The client is run as follows:

```
ch15$ go run personclientxml.go xmlcodec.go ws://localhost:12345
```

The output on the *server* side is what is sent by the *client*:

```
Name: Jan
An email: ja@newmarch.name
An email: jan.newmarch@gmail.com
```

As before, review the related codec object documentation (go doc encoding/xml).
A reasonable next step is improve our security; we next upgrade our WebSocket to use TLS.

WebSockets over TLS

A WebSocket can be built above a secure TLS socket. We discussed in Chapter 8 how to use a TLS socket using the certificates from Chapter 7. That is used unchanged for WebSockets. That is, we use http. ListenAndServeTLS instead of http.ListenAndServe.

Here is the echo server using TLS, echoservertls.go.

```
ch15$ vi echoservertls.go

/* EchoServerTLS
 */
package main

import (
        "log"
        "fmt"
        "golang.org/x/net/websocket"
        "net/http"
)

func Echo(ws *websocket.Conn) {
        fmt.Println("Echoing")
        for n := 0; n < 10; n++ {
                msg := "Hello   " + string(n+48)
                fmt.Println("Sending to client: " + msg)
                err := websocket.Message.Send(ws, msg)
                if err != nil {
                        fmt.Println("Can't send")
                        break
                }
                var reply string
                err = websocket.Message.Receive(ws, &reply)
                if err != nil {
                        fmt.Println("Can't receive")
                        break
                }
                fmt.Println("Received back from client: " + reply)
        }
}
func main() {
        http.Handle("/", websocket.Handler(Echo))
        err := http.ListenAndServeTLS(":12345",
                "jan.newmarch.name.pem",
                "private.pem", nil)
        checkError(err)
}
func checkError(err error) {
        if err != nil {
                log.Fatalln("Fatal error ", err.Error())
        }
}
```

Before running the server, we need our certificate and key, created and used from Chapter 7/8.

```
ch15$ cp ../ch7/jan.newmarch.name.pem . ; cp ../ch7/private.pem .
ch15$ go run echoservertls.go
```

The client is the same echo client as before. All that changes is the URL, which uses the wss scheme instead of the ws scheme:

```
ch15$ go run echoclient wss://localhost:12345/
```

```
Fatal error  websocket.Dial wss://localhost:12345: x509: certificate signed by unknown
authority
exit status 1
```

That will work fine if the TLS certificate offered by the server is valid. The certificate I am using is not: it is self-signed, and that is often a signal that you are entering a danger zone. If you want to keep going anyway, you need to employ the same "remove the safety check" that we did in Chapter 8 by turning on the TLS InsecureSkipVerify flag. That is done by the program echoclienttls.go, which sets up a configuration using this flag and then calls DialConfig in place of Dial.

```
ch15$ vi echoclienttls.go
```

```
/* EchoClientTLS
 */
package main

import (
        "crypto/tls"
        "fmt"
        "golang.org/x/net/websocket"
        "io"
        "log"
        "os"
)

func main() {
        if len(os.Args) != 2 {
                log.Fatalln("Usage: ", os.Args[0], "wss://host:port")
        }
        config, err := websocket.NewConfig(os.Args[1],
                "http://localhost")
        checkError(err)
        tlsConfig := &tls.Config{InsecureSkipVerify: true}
        config.TlsConfig = tlsConfig
        conn, err := websocket.DialConfig(config)
        checkError(err)
        var msg string
        for {
                err := websocket.Message.Receive(conn, &msg)
                if err != nil {
                        if err == io.EOF {
```

303

```
                                    // graceful shutdown by server
                                    break
                            }
                            fmt.Println("Couldn't receive msg " +
                                    err.Error())
                            break
                    }
                    fmt.Println("Received from server: " + msg)
                    // return the msg
                    err = websocket.Message.Send(conn, msg)
                    if err != nil {
                            fmt.Println("Couldn't return msg")
                            break
                    }
            }
    }
}
func checkError(err error) {
        if err != nil {
                log.Fatalln("Fatal error ", err.Error())
        }
}
```

Run the client as follows (assuming echoservertls.go is running):

```
ch15$ go run echoclienttls.go wss://localhost:12345

Received from server: Hello  0
...
Received from server: Hello  9
```

Back on the server, we see the following:

```
Echoing
Sending to client: Hello  0
Received back from client: Hello  0
...
Sending to client: Hello  9
Received back from client: Hello  9
```

WebSockets in an HTML Page

The original driver for WebSockets was to allow full duplex interaction between an HTTP user agent such as a browser and a server. The typical use case is expected to involve a JavaScript program in a browser interacting with a server. In this section, we build a web/WebSockets server that delivers an HTML page that sets up a WebSocket and displays information from that server using WebSockets. We are looking at the situation illustrated in Figure 15-1.

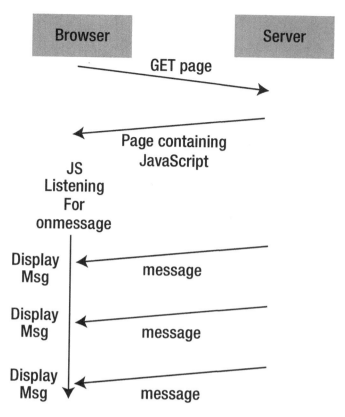

Figure 15-1. *Full duplex interaction situation*

The age of the Internet of Things (IoT) is upon us. Consequently, we can expect data from sensors and sensor networks to be used to drive actuators and to display information about an IoT network in browsers. There are innumerable books about using Raspberry Pis and Arduinos for building sensor networks, but we will drastically simplify the situation by showing the CPU temperatures on a "sensor," updating in a web page every few seconds.

The Linux sensors command from the Debian package lm-sensors writes to standard output the values of sensors it knows about. The command sensors on my desktop machine produces output such as the following:

```
acpitz-virtual-0
Adapter: Virtual device
temp1:        +27.8°C  (crit = +105.0°C)
temp2:        +29.8°C  (crit = +105.0°C)

coretemp-isa-0000
Adapter: ISA adapter
Physical id 0:  +58.0°C  (high = +105.0°C, crit = +105.0°C)
Core 0:         +57.0°C  (high = +105.0°C, crit = +105.0°C)
Core 1:         +58.0°C  (high = +105.0°C, crit = +105.0°C)
```

On refresh, typically, the temperature on Core 0 and Core 1 may change.

On Windows, a command to do the same is this:

```
wmic /namespace:\\root\wmi PATH MSAcpi_ThermalZoneTemperature get CurrentTemperature
```

When this runs, it has output such as

```
42.4° C
```

On the Mac, use the command osx-cpu-temp from https://github.com/lavoiesl/osx-cpu-temp.

If you don't want to go through these steps, just substitute a more mundane program such as the date.

We provide a Go program to deliver HTML documents from the ROOT_DIR directory and to then set up a WebSocket from the URL GetTemp. The WebSocket on the server side gets the output from sensors every two seconds and sends it to the client end of the socket. The web/WebSockets server runs on port 12345 for no particular reason. Substitute any other interesting system call for the exec.Command call. Here, we use the simple "sensors.sh" as our temperature program (random number between 1 and 100).

```
ch15$ vi sensors.sh
```

```
#!/bin/sh
echo $(( ( RANDOM % 100 )  + 1 ))
```

Be sure to make it executable: chmod 700 sensors.sh.

The server is temperatureserver.go:

```
ch15$ vi temperatureserver.go
```

```go
/* TemperatureServer
 */
package main

import (
        "fmt"
        "golang.org/x/net/websocket"
        "log"
        "net/http"
        "os/exec"
        "time"
)

var ROOT_DIR = "."

func GetTemp(ws *websocket.Conn) {
        for {
                msg, err := exec.Command(ROOT_DIR + "/sensors.sh").CombinedOutput()
                checkError(err)
                fmt.Println("Sending to client: " + string(msg[:]))
                err = websocket.Message.Send(ws, string(msg[:]))
                if err != nil {
                        fmt.Println("Can't send")
                        break
                }
```

```
                time.Sleep(time.Duration(2) * time.Second)
                var reply string
                err = websocket.Message.Receive(ws, &reply)
                if err != nil {
                        fmt.Println("Can't receive")
                        break
                }
                fmt.Println("Received back from client: " + reply)
        }
}
func main() {
        fileServer := http.FileServer(http.Dir(ROOT_DIR))
        http.Handle("/GetTemp", websocket.Handler(GetTemp))
        http.Handle("/", fileServer)
        err := http.ListenAndServe(":12345", nil)
        checkError(err)
}
func checkError(err error) {
        if err != nil {
                log.Fatalln("Fatal error ", err.Error())
        }
}
```

It is run as follows:

```
ch15$ go run temperatureserver.go
```

The top-level HTML file to kick this off is websocket.html; be sure to copy this to the ROOT_DIR.

```
<!DOCTYPE HTML>
<html>
  <head>
    <script type="text/javascript">
      function WebSocketTest()
      {
        if ("WebSocket" in window)
        {
          alert("WebSocket is supported by your Browser!");
          // Let us open a web socket
          var ws = new WebSocket("ws://localhost:12345/GetTemp");
          ws.onopen = function()
          {
            alert("WS is opened...");
          };
          ws.onmessage = function (evt)
          {
            var received_msg = evt.data;
            // uncomment next line if you want to get alerts on each message
            //alert("Message is received..." + received_msg);
            document.getElementById("temp").innerHTML = "<pre>" + received_msg + "</pre>"
            ws.send("Message received")
          };
```

```
          ws.onclose = function()
          {
            // websocket is closed.
            alert("Connection is closed...");
          };
        }
        else
        {
          // The browser doesn't support WebSocket
          alert("WebSocket NOT supported by your Browser!");
        }
      }
    </script>
  </head>
  <body>
    <div id="temp">
      <a href="javascript:WebSocketTest()">Run temperature sensor</a>
    </div>
  </body>
</html>
```

In a browser, visit `http://localhost:12345/websocket.html`; click "Run temperature sensor" to see the temperature relayed.

The program uses JavaScript to open a WebSockets connection and to handle the onopen, onmessage, and onclose events. It reads and writes using evt.data and the send function. It presents the data in a preformatted element, exactly as the data before. It is refreshed every two seconds. The structure of the HTML document is based on HTML5 - WebSockets: `https://www.tutorialspoint.com/html5/html5_websocket.htm`.

The github.com/gorilla/websocket Package

The alternative package for WebSockets functionality is the `github.com/gorilla/websocket` package.

Echo Server

The echo server using this package is echoservergorilla.go. It makes the HTTP-to-WebSockets transition more explicit by introducing a call to a websocket.Upgrader object. It also more clearly distinguishes between sending text and binary messages.

```
ch15$ vi echoservergorilla.go

/* EchoServerGorilla
 */
package main

import (
        "fmt"
        "github.com/gorilla/websocket"
        "log"
        "net/http"
```

```
)

var upgrader = websocket.Upgrader{
        ReadBufferSize:  1024,
        WriteBufferSize: 1024,
}

func Handler(w http.ResponseWriter, r *http.Request) {
        fmt.Println("Handling /")
        conn, err := upgrader.Upgrade(w, r, nil)
        if err != nil {
                fmt.Println(err)
                return
        }
        for n := 0; n < 10; n++ {
                msg := "Hello  " + string(n+48)
                fmt.Println("Sending to client: " + msg)
                err = conn.WriteMessage(websocket.TextMessage,
                        []byte(msg))
                _, reply, err := conn.ReadMessage()
                if err != nil {
                        fmt.Println("Can't receive")
                        break
                }
                fmt.Println("Received back from client: " +
                        string(reply[:]))
        }
        conn.Close()
}
func main() {
        http.HandleFunc("/", Handler)
        err := http.ListenAndServe("localhost:12345", nil)
        checkError(err)
}
func checkError(err error) {
        if err != nil {
                log.Fatalln("Fatal error ", err.Error())
        }
}
```

The server is run as follows:

```
ch15$ go mod init example.com/user/echoservergorilla # or skip and use existing module name
ch15$ go mod tidy
ch15$ go run echoservergorilla.go
```

Echo Client

The echo client using this package is echoclientgorilla.go:

```
ch15% vi echoclientgorilla.go

/* EchoClientGorilla
 */
package main

import (
        "fmt"
        "github.com/gorilla/websocket"
        "io"
        "log"
        "net/http"
        "os"
)

func main() {
        if len(os.Args) != 2 {
                log.Fatalln("Usage: ", os.Args[0], "ws://host:port")
        }
        service := os.Args[1]
        header := make(http.Header)
        header.Add("Origin", "http://localhost:12345")
        conn, _, err := websocket.DefaultDialer.Dial(service, header)
        checkError(err)
        for {
                _, reply, err := conn.ReadMessage()
                if err != nil {
                        if err == io.EOF {
                                // graceful shutdown by server
                                fmt.Println(`EOF from server`)
                                break
                        }
                        if websocket.IsCloseError(err,
                                websocket.CloseAbnormalClosure) {
                                fmt.Println(`Close from server`)
                                break
                        }
                        fmt.Println("Couldn't receive msg " +
                                err.Error())
                        break
                }
                fmt.Println("Received from server: " +
                        string(reply[:]))
                // return the msg
                err = conn.WriteMessage(websocket.TextMessage, reply)
                if err != nil {
```

```
                        fmt.Println("Couldn't return msg")
                        break
                }
        }
}
func checkError(err error) {
        if err != nil {
                log.Fatalln("Fatal error ", err.Error())
        }
}
```

The client is run as follows:

```
ch15$ go run echoclientgorilla.go ws://localhost:12345

Received from server: Hello  0
...
Received from server: Hello  9
Close from server
```

Back on the server, we see

```
Handling /
Sending to client: Hello  0
Received back from client: Hello  0
Sending to client: Hello  1
...
Sending to client: Hello  9
Received back from client: Hello  9
```

Conclusion

The WebSockets standard is an IETF RFC, so no major changes are anticipated. This will allow HTTP user agents and servers to set up bidirectional socket connections and should make certain interaction styles much easier. Go has support from these and additional WebSocket packages, such as https://pkg.go.dev/nhooyr.io/websocket.

## CHAPTER 16

Gorilla

The Go standard library and related "x" packages offer a lot of functionality that we can leverage to build a website. Go trends toward simpler coding styles if possible; simple doesn't always mean easy though. Until you have enough experience in the domain (web development) and the implementation stack (Go/Web), it might be easier and/or better to use a toolkit that provides additional ease-of-use features. Gorilla is one such toolkit. We have already touched upon Gorilla with WebSockets; now we take a more focused look at its major offerings and in the end see what it did for us vs. a pure Go implementation.

Per the Gorilla website (https://www.gorillatoolkit.org/), these are the current packages. We will learn how to use some of them and explore how they integrate and extend the standard library.

- mux: Is a powerful URL router and dispatcher that is fully compatible with the default http.ServeMux

- reverse: Produces reversible regular expressions for regexp-based muxes

- rpc: Implements RPC over HTTP with codec for JSON-RPC

- schema: Converts form values to a struct

- securecookie: Encodes and decodes authenticated and optionally encrypted cookie values

- sessions: Saves cookie and filesystem sessions and allows custom session back ends

- websocket: Implements the WebSocket protocol defined in RFC 6455

- csrf: Provides Cross-Site Request Forgery (CSRF) prevention middleware

- handlers: Is a collection of useful handlers for Go's net/http package

You may notice this is a top tool choice due to its well-thought-out architecture. Next, we discuss around the middleware pattern, which will guide how we integrate Gorilla.

Middleware Pattern

Middleware is described as "software glue" per https://en.wikipedia.org/wiki/Middleware. Middleware for a web service allows us to wrap functionality around our application-specific code. These wrappers, in turn, can be chained. We do this to add functionality like logging and/or authentication instead of polluting our business logic. For example, there is no need to "log" an HTTP request in our client handling logic; it can (and should) be done outside of it (in another wrapper).

```
The basic middleware pattern looks like this:router -> middleware -> application
```

We begin with a brief example and review of some of the built-in web functionality of Go. This will help us to understand how Gorilla integrates with our code (and Go stdlib) and what it offers beyond the standard library.

Go provides an HTTP client and server implementation via the net/http package. The package provides a "type Server" that works with a lower-level connection object and deserializes an HTTP request or serializes an HTTP response. That request is then handed to a type ServeMux. A ServeMux in turn does the routing for us (i.e., multiplexing). A default ServeMux is provided called DefaultServeMux. An interface called net.Handler is provided, this handler provides the methods used in dealing with the HTTP requests. As mentioned before, we can have more than one handler and chain these handlers together. It turns out that the ServeMux is also a Handler, meaning we can chain them as well.

We can now imagine a little deeper how Go itself is using the middleware pattern.

```
connection <-> Server <-> ServeMux <-> handler(s) <-> application functions
```

Let's review the primary documentation going backward from Handler.

```
$ go doc http.Handler
package http // import "net/http"

type Handler interface {
    ServeHTTP(ResponseWriter, *Request)
}
    A Handler responds to an HTTP request.

    ServeHTTP should write reply headers and data to the ResponseWriter and then
    return. Returning signals that the request is finished; it is not valid to
    use the ResponseWriter or read from the Request.Body after or concurrently
    with the completion of the ServeHTTP call.

    Depending on the HTTP client software, HTTP protocol version, and any
    intermediaries between the client and the Go server, it may not be possible
    to read from the Request.Body after writing to the ResponseWriter. Cautious
    handlers should read the Request.Body first, and then reply.

    Except for reading the body, handlers should not modify the provided
    Request.

    If ServeHTTP panics, the server (the caller of ServeHTTP) assumes that the
    effect of the panic was isolated to the active request. It recovers the
    panic, logs a stack trace to the server error log, and either closes the
    network connection or sends an HTTP/2 RST_STREAM, depending on the HTTP
    protocol. To abort a handler so the client sees an interrupted response but
    the server doesn't log an error, panic with the value ErrAbortHandler.

func AllowQuerySemicolons(h Handler) Handler
func FileServer(root FileSystem) Handler
func MaxBytesHandler(h Handler, n int64) Handler
func NotFoundHandler() Handler
func RedirectHandler(url string, code int) Handler
func StripPrefix(prefix string, h Handler) Handler
func TimeoutHandler(h Handler, dt time.Duration, msg string) Handler
```

For now, the critical parts revolve around Handler.ServeHTTP. This is where the request is passed into and ultimately responded to. Next, review the details of ServeMux and the relation to Handler.

```
$ go doc net/http ServeMux
package http // import "net/http"

type ServeMux struct {
    // Has unexported fields.
}
    ServeMux is an HTTP request multiplexer. It matches the URL of each incoming
    request against a list of registered patterns and calls the handler for the
    pattern that most closely matches the URL.

    Patterns name fixed, rooted paths, like "/favicon.ico", or rooted subtrees,
    like "/images/" (note the trailing slash). Longer patterns take precedence
    over shorter ones, so that if there are handlers registered for both
    "/images/" and "/images/thumbnails/", the latter handler will be called for
    paths beginning "/images/thumbnails/" and the former will receive requests
    for any other paths in the "/images/" subtree.

    Note that since a pattern ending in a slash names a rooted subtree, the
    pattern "/" matches all paths not matched by other registered patterns, not
    just the URL with Path == "/".

    If a subtree has been registered and a request is received naming the
    subtree root without its trailing slash, ServeMux redirects that request to
    the subtree root (adding the trailing slash). This behavior can be
    overridden with a separate registration for the path without the trailing
    slash. For example, registering "/images/" causes ServeMux to redirect a
    request for "/images" to "/images/", unless "/images" has been registered
    separately.

    Patterns may optionally begin with a host name, restricting matches to URLs
    on that host only. Host-specific patterns take precedence over general
    patterns, so that a handler might register for the two patterns
    "/codesearch" and "codesearch.google.com/" without also taking over requests
    for "http://www.google.com/".

    ServeMux also takes care of sanitizing the URL request path and the Host
    header, stripping the port number and redirecting any request containing .
    or .. elements or repeated slashes to an equivalent, cleaner URL.

func NewServeMux() *ServeMux
func (mux *ServeMux) Handle(pattern string, handler Handler)
func (mux *ServeMux) HandleFunc(pattern string, handler func(ResponseWriter, *Request))
func (mux *ServeMux) Handler(r *Request) (h Handler, pattern string)
func (mux *ServeMux) ServeHTTP(w ResponseWriter, r *Request)
```

As you can see, ServeMux matches a given pattern and passes to the configured Handler, which in turn calls our business logic. Continuing to the left, let's look at the abbreviated Server documentation.

```
$ go doc net/http.Server
package http // import "net/http"

type Server struct {
    // Addr optionally specifies the TCP address for the server to listen on,
    // in the form "host:port". If empty, ":http" (port 80) is used.
    // The service names are defined in RFC 6335 and assigned by IANA.
    // See net.Dial for details of the address format.
    Addr string

    Handler Handler // handler to invoke, http.DefaultServeMux if nil
...
```

While truncated, we can see right at the start, a Server holds a Handler, and based on the comment, it seems we have an instance of ServeMux called DefaultServeMux.

With the wiring in mind, we now look at some examples.

Standard Library ServeMux Examples

Here, we demo potentially the simplest web service Go provides (at least in net/http package) and one that demonstrates the middleware pattern a little more clearly.

```
$ mkdir ch16
$ ch16
ch16$ vi simple.go

package main

import (
    "net/http"
    "fmt"
)

func main() {
    err := http.ListenAndServe(":8080",nil)
    fmt.Println(err)
}
```

Running the server "go run simple.go", access via any method/path to localhost:8080 returns a 404.

```
ch16$ curl -v --head localhost:8080

*   Trying ::1:8080...
* Connected to localhost (::1) port 8080 (#0)
> HEAD / HTTP/1.1
> Host: localhost:8080
> User-Agent: curl/7.77.0
> Accept: */*
>
* Mark bundle as not supporting multiuse
```

```
< HTTP/1.1 404 Not Found
HTTP/1.1 404 Not Found
< Content-Type: text/plain; charset=utf-8
Content-Type: text/plain; charset=utf-8
< X-Content-Type-Options: nosniff
X-Content-Type-Options: nosniff
< Date: Mon, 31 Jan 2022 00:43:57 GMT
Date: Mon, 31 Jan 2022 00:43:57 GMT
< Content-Length: 19
Content-Length: 19
<
* Connection #0 to host localhost left intact
```

What this implies is there is a default handler, returning a 404. Next, we try a GET request.

```
ch16$ curl -X GET localhost:8080/didthiswork
```

```
404 page not found
```

It turns out, under the hood, we already have a chain of handlers. The Server is calling the ServeMux ServeHTTP, which then calls NotFoundHandler. ServeMux supports the Handler interface via the ServeHTTP method. As an eagle eye observer, you may have noticed that in the preceding Handler documentation, NotFoundHandler is listed.

```
ch16$ go doc net/http NotFoundHandler
```

```
package http // import "net/http"
```

```
func NotFoundHandler() Handler
    NotFoundHandler returns a simple request handler that replies to each
    request with a "404 page not found" reply.
```

If you are adventurous, you can peek at the code to start to see how these are wired up.

```
ch16$ vi /usr/local/go/src/net/http/server.go
```

```
...
// NotFound replies to the request with an HTTP 404 not found error.
func NotFound(w ResponseWriter, r *Request) { Error(w, "404 page not found",
StatusNotFound) }

// NotFoundHandler returns a simple request handler
// that replies to each request with a ``404 page not found'' reply.
func NotFoundHandler() Handler { return HandlerFunc(NotFound) }
...
```

As you can see, the "NotFound" function is casted to a HandlerFunc (which proxies the ServeHTTP call to NotFound in our case). HandlerFunc is known as a function adapter in Go.

Customizing Muxes

Our last example focusing on the standard library will show us how to manage multiple ServeMux instances. The goal in this example is to show how "registering" a new ServeMux can handle a subset of routes. Here, we have the "default" (DefaultServeMux) handling the route "/outermux", while our new "inner" ServeMux will handle the deeper nested routes (e.g., "/outermux/innermux").

```
ch16$ vi complex.go

package main

import (
    "net/http"
)

func main() {
    http.Handle("/outermux", http.HandlerFunc(func(w http.ResponseWriter, r *http.Request) {
        w.Write([]byte("/outermux"))
    }))

    inner := http.NewServeMux()

    inner.Handle("/innermux/", http.HandlerFunc(func(w http.ResponseWriter, r *http.
    Request) {
        w.Write([]byte("../innermux"))
    }))

    http.Handle("/outermux/innermux/", http.StripPrefix("/outermux", inner))

    http.ListenAndServe(":8080", nil)
}
```

As we exercise our tests in the following, take note of the requested path and the log generated. Per the preceding ServeMux documentation, take extra note on how you end the paths, with a trailing slash "/" or not.

```
ch16$ curl localhost:8080/outermux

/outermux

ch16$ curl localhost:8080/outermux/

404 page not found

ch16$ curl localhost:8080/outermux/innermux

<a href="/outermux/innermux/">Moved Permanently</a>.

ch16$ curl -iL localhost:8080/outermux/innermux

HTTP/1.1 301 Moved Permanently
```

```
Content-Type: text/html; charset=utf-8
Location: /outermux/innermux/
Date: Mon, 31 Jan 2022 01:16:24 GMT
Content-Length: 54

HTTP/1.1 200 OK
Date: Mon, 31 Jan 2022 01:16:24 GMT
Content-Length: 11
Content-Type: text/plain; charset=utf-8

../innermux

ch16$ curl -iL localhost:8080/outermux/innermux/

HTTP/1.1 200 OK
Date: Mon, 31 Jan 2022 01:16:28 GMT
Content-Length: 11
Content-Type: text/plain; charset=utf-8

../innermux
```

You may wonder what the final line is doing (http.ListenAndServe(":8080", nil)).

Specifically, what is "nil" doing? This is where we can override the default ServeMux. When you pass in nil, the "first" mux remains the precreated instance called DefaultServeMux used by type Serve. You can confirm these relations by reviewing the code here "GOROOT/src/net/http/server.go".

gorilla/mux

We begin our learning of Gorilla by looking at the mux package. The "mux" package is designed to work with the existing type Serve of the standard library.

```
ch16$ vi gmux.go

package main

import (
    "net/http"
    "github.com/gorilla/mux"
)

func buildHandler(message string) func(http.ResponseWriter, *http.Request) {
    return http.HandlerFunc(func(w http.ResponseWriter, r *http.Request) {
        w.Write([]byte(message))
    })
}

func main() {
    r := mux.NewRouter()
    r.HandleFunc("/", buildHandler("HomeHandler"))
    r.HandleFunc("/products", buildHandler("ProductsHandler"))
```

```
    r.HandleFunc("/articles", buildHandler("ArticlesHandler"))
    http.ListenAndServe(":8080", r)
}
```

Based on what we know, by overwriting the last parameter of ListenAndServe, we are setting overwriting the default ServeMux with our own (call Router in mux speak).

```
ch16$ go mod init ch16.example.com
ch16$ go mod tidy
ch16$ go run gmux.go
```

The tests that follow hopefully show not much has changed.

```
ch16$ curl localhost:8080/articles

ArticlesHandler

ch16$ curl localhost:8080/

HomeHandler
```

If we review the Router code, specifically its ServerHTTP method, we can confirm our route mapping is now handled by Gorilla mux.

```
~/ch16$ go doc --src mux Router.ServeHTTP

package mux // import "github.com/gorilla/mux"

// ServeHTTP dispatches the handler registered in the matched route.
//
// When there is a match, the route variables can be retrieved calling
// mux.Vars(request).
func (r *Router) ServeHTTP(w http.ResponseWriter, req *http.Request) {
    if !r.skipClean {
        path := req.URL.Path
        if r.useEncodedPath {
            path = req.URL.EscapedPath()
        }
        // Clean path to canonical form and redirect.
        if p := cleanPath(path); p != path {

            // Added 3 lines (Philip Schlump) - It was dropping the query string and
            #whatever from query.
            // This matches with fix in go 1.2 r.c. 4 for same problem.  Go Issue:
            // http://code.google.com/p/go/issues/detail?id=5252
            url := *req.URL
            url.Path = p
            p = url.String()

            w.Header().Set("Location", p)
            w.WriteHeader(http.StatusMovedPermanently)
```

```
            return
        }
    }
    var match RouteMatch
    var handler http.Handler
    if r.Match(req, &match) {
        handler = match.Handler
        req = requestWithVars(req, match.Vars)
        req = requestWithRoute(req, match.Route)
    }

    if handler == nil && match.MatchErr == ErrMethodMismatch {
        handler = methodNotAllowedHandler()
    }

    if handler == nil {
        handler = http.NotFoundHandler()
    }

    handler.ServeHTTP(w, req)
}
```

Why Should We Care

So far, it doesn't seem we have added any value to the already-provided DefaultServeMux. Looks are deceiving though. Based on ServeMux documentation, we only seem to be provided with ways to easily parse the "path" to make a routing decision. Can we match a request based on other criteria (aside path), such as query parameters or HTTP headers? We have access to such things without Gorilla; what we don't have is a structured way of using them

Requests can be matched based on the following criteria:

- URL host (example.com)
- Path (/about)
- Path prefix (/animals/cats)
- Schema (posted form values)
- HTTP headers (Content-Type: text/html; charset=UTF-8)
- Query values (?key=value&dog=cat)
- HTTP methods (GET /search?q=test HTTP/2)
- Custom matchers (a custom function)

One nice feature of Gorilla is the use of chaining to have several matching elements related. Here is an example of that, modifying our prior example using various matchers.

```
~/ch16$ vi gmux.go

package main

import (
        "github.com/gorilla/mux"
        "net/http"
)

func buildHandler(message string) func(http.ResponseWriter, *http.Request) {
        return http.HandlerFunc(func(w http.ResponseWriter, r *http.Request) {
                w.Write([]byte(message))
        })
}

func main() {
        r := mux.NewRouter()
        r.HandleFunc("/", buildHandler("HomeHandler"))
        r.HandleFunc("/products", buildHandler("ProductsHandler"))
        r.HandleFunc("/articles", buildHandler("ArticlesHandler")).Host("example.com").
Methods("GET").Schemes("http")
        http.ListenAndServe(":8080", r)
}
```

Run the server.`~/ch16$ go run gmux.go`

Now we exercise our new and existing routes; notice "/articles" is not limited to a particular domain, method, and scheme.

```
~/ch16$ curl --resolve example.com:8080:127.0.0.1 -IX GET http://example.com:8080/articles

HTTP/1.1 200 OK
Date: Mon, 07 Mar 2022 18:40:46 GMT
Content-Length: 15
Content-Type: text/plain; charset=utf-8

~/ch16$ curl --resolve example.com:8080:127.0.0.1 -IX POST http://example.com:8080/articles

HTTP/1.1 405 Method Not Allowed
Date: Mon, 07 Mar 2022 18:40:54 GMT
Content-Length: 0

~/ch16$ curl 127.0.0.1:8080/articles

404 page not found

~/ch16$
```

Here are examples from the official documentation:

- r.PathPrefix("/products/")

- r.Methods("GET", "POST")

- r.Schemes("https")

- r.Headers("X-Requested-With", "XMLHttpRequest")

- r.Queries("key", "value")

- r.MatcherFunc(func(r *http.Request, rm *RouteMatch) bool { return r.ProtoMajor == 0 })

Again, we can accomplish all of this with the standard library (which many developers think you should), yet having a toolkit at the ready makes it an easy choice. There is much more to Gorilla mux. Our goal is to highlight the relation to the standard library and how it extends (additional functionality). You can learn more here: https://github.com/gorilla/mux.

Gorilla Handlers

Gorilla provides a set of handlers in the "handlers" package. Sticking with the theme, ease of use, it includes the following handlers for us to use in our middleware chain.
Here are the official descriptions:

- LoggingHandler: For logging HTTP requests in the Apache Common Log Format

- CombinedLoggingHandler: For logging HTTP requests in the Apache Combined Log Format commonly used by both Apache and Nginx

- CompressHandler: For gzipping responses

- ContentTypeHandler: For validating requests against a list of accepted content types

- MethodHandler: For matching HTTP methods against handlers in a map[string]http.Handler

- ProxyHeaders: For populating r.RemoteAddr and r.URL.Scheme based on the X-Forwarded-For, X-Real-IP, X-Forwarded-Proto, and RFC7239 Forwarded headers when running a Go server behind an HTTP reverse proxy

- CanonicalHost: For redirecting to the preferred host when handling multiple domains (i.e., multiple CNAME aliases)

- RecoveryHandler: For recovering from unexpected panics

Let's take a look at a couple of these, starting with the LoggingHandlers.

```
~/ch16$ go get github.com/gorilla/handlers

~/ch16$ go doc handlers.LoggingHandler

package handlers // import "github.com/gorilla/handlers"

func LoggingHandler(out io.Writer, h http.Handler) http.Handler
    LoggingHandler return a http.Handler that wraps h and logs requests to out
    in Apache Common Log Format (CLF).
```

See http://httpd.apache.org/docs/2.2/logs.html#common for a description of this format.

LoggingHandler always sets the ident field of the log to -

Example:

```
r := mux.NewRouter()
r.HandleFunc("/", func(w http.ResponseWriter, r *http.Request) {
    w.Write([]byte("This is a catch-all route"))
})
loggedRouter := handlers.LoggingHandler(os.Stdout, r)
http.ListenAndServe(":1123", loggedRouter)
```

Let's copy our original example adding this middleware.

~/ch16$ cat logging.go

```
package main

import (
        "github.com/gorilla/mux"
        "github.com/gorilla/handlers"
        "os"
        "net/http"
)

func buildHandler(message string) func(http.ResponseWriter, *http.Request) {
        return http.HandlerFunc(func(w http.ResponseWriter, r *http.Request) {
                w.Write([]byte(message))
        })
}

func main() {
        r := mux.NewRouter()
        r.HandleFunc("/", buildHandler("HomeHandler"))
        r.HandleFunc("/products", buildHandler("ProductsHandler"))
        r.HandleFunc("/articles", buildHandler("ArticlesHandler")).Host("example.com").
        Methods("GET").Schemes("http")
        loggedRouter := handlers.LoggingHandler(os.Stdout, r)
        http.ListenAndServe(":8080", loggedRouter)
}
```

Notice the chaining in the preceding code. Instead of passing the router object to ListenAndServe, we pass it to LoggingHandler, which chains it. We then use its result, a ServeMux satisfying object to ListenAndServe.

If you run the server and access from another terminal, you will see a request and response information logged.

```
~/ch16$ go run logging.go
```

```
~/ch16$ curl --resolve example.com:8080:127.0.0.1 -IX GET http://example.com:8080/articles
```

```
HTTP/1.1 200 OK
Date: Sun, 03 Apr 2022 04:38:07 GMT
Content-Length: 15
Content-Type: text/plain; charset=utf-8
```

```
Back on the server, we see127.0.0.1 - - [07/Mar/2022:19:04:20 +0000] "GET /articles
HTTP/1.1" 200 15
```

This format is defined here: http://httpd.apache.org/docs/2.2/logs.html#common. You will notice we have another handler called CombinedLoggingHandler; this format is defined here: http://httpd.apache.org/docs/2.2/logs.html#combined. Here is a brief comparison of the formats.

- Common – "%h %l %u %t \"%r\" %>s %b"

- Combined – "%h %l %u %t \"%r\" %>s %b \"%{Referer}i\" \"%{User-agent}i\""

We now try an example of the ContentTypeHandler handler.

```
~/ch16$ go doc handlers.ContentTypeHandler
```

```
package handlers // import "github.com/gorilla/handlers"
```

```
func ContentTypeHandler(h http.Handler, contentTypes ...string) http.Handler
    ContentTypeHandler wraps and returns a http.Handler, validating the request
    content type is compatible with the contentTypes list. It writes a HTTP 415
    error if that fails.
```

```
    Only PUT, POST, and PATCH requests are considered.
```

Take note, it only works for a subset of HTTP methods (ones that create/update); others are passed through silently.`~/ch16$ cat contenttype.go`

```
package main
```

```
import (
        "github.com/gorilla/handlers"
        "github.com/gorilla/mux"
        "net/http"
)
```

```
func buildHandler(message string) func(http.ResponseWriter, *http.Request) {
        return http.HandlerFunc(func(w http.ResponseWriter, r *http.Request) {
                w.Write([]byte(message))
        })
}
```

```
func main() {
        r := mux.NewRouter()
        r.HandleFunc("/", buildHandler("HomeHandler"))
        r.HandleFunc("/products", buildHandler("ProductsHandler"))
        l := handlers.ContentTypeHandler(http.HandlerFunc(func(w http.ResponseWriter,
        r *http.Request) {
                w.Write([]byte("json articles only"))
        }), "application/json")
        r.Handle("/articles", l)
        http.ListenAndServe(":8080", r)
}
```

We can see for the "/articles" route, we want to make sure any data being uploaded has a json content type.

```
~/ch16$ go run contenttype.go
```

Here, we exercise the expected catching (validate "application/json" on POST) and where we ignore it.

```
~/ch16$ curl -IX POST -H 'Content-Type: application/json' 127.0.0.1:8080/articles

HTTP/1.1 200 OK
Date: Mon, 07 Mar 2022 19:28:04 GMT
Content-Length: 18
Content-Type: text/plain; charset=utf-8

~/ch16$ curl -IX POST -H 'Content-Type: application/xml' 127.0.0.1:8080/articles

HTTP/1.1 415 Unsupported Media Type
Content-Type: text/plain; charset=utf-8
X-Content-Type-Options: nosniff
Date: Mon, 07 Mar 2022 19:28:11 GMT
Content-Length: 81

~/ch16$ curl -IX GET -H 'Content-Type: application/xml' 127.0.0.1:8080/articles

HTTP/1.1 200 OK
Date: Mon, 07 Mar 2022 19:28:20 GMT
Content-Length: 18
Content-Type: text/plain; charset=utf-8
```

The handlers can be used per route, or all routes. Other handlers are available; review the documentation to see them: "go doc gorilla/handlers | grep ^func".

Additional Gorilla Examples

What remains is a sampling of Gorilla packages demoing their primary mechanics. For our purpose, we try to focus on how it compares or contrasts to the standard library offerings.

gorilla/rpc

The json package of Gorilla provides us similar capabilites as what we learned in Chapter 13 about rpc leveraging JSON. We register our service, which in turn receives the HTTP request.

```
ch16$ vi rpc.go

package main

import (
    "github.com/gorilla/rpc"
    "github.com/gorilla/rpc/json"
    "net/http"
)

type HelloArgs struct {
    Who string
}

type HelloReply struct {
    Message string
}

type HelloService struct{}

func (h *HelloService) Say(r *http.Request, args *HelloArgs, reply *HelloReply) error {
    reply.Message = "Hello, " + args.Who + "!"
    return nil
}

func main() {
    s := rpc.NewServer()
    s.RegisterCodec(json.NewCodec(), "application/json")
    s.RegisterService(new(HelloService), "")
    http.Handle("/rpc", s)
    http.ListenAndServe(":8080", nil)
}
```

```
We launch the server.~/ch16$ go mod tidy
~/ch16$ go run rpc.go
```

From the client, we send our json-based payload to the proper endpoint.

```
~/ch16$ curl -X POST -H "Content-Type: application/json" \
-d '{"method":"HelloService.Say","params":[{"Who":"Test"}], "id":"1"}' \
http://localhost:8080/rpc

{"result":{"Message":"Hello, Test!"},"error":null,"id":"1"}
```

The Gorilla rpc package derives from the net/rpc package, with the noted differences.

```
~/ch16$ go doc gorilla/rpc

package rpc // import "github.com/gorilla/rpc"

Package gorilla/rpc is a foundation for RPC over HTTP services, providing
access to the exported methods of an object through HTTP requests.

This package derives from the standard net/rpc package but uses a single
HTTP request per call instead of persistent connections. Other differences
compared to net/rpc:

    - Multiple codecs can be registered in the same server.
    - A codec is chosen based on the "Content-Type" header from the request.
    - Service methods also receive http.Request as parameter.
    - This package can be used on Google App Engine.
...
```

While not in the documentation example, "other" codecs for XML, for example, have been created by third parties that leverage the Gorilla rpc package interface.

gorilla/schema

The Gorilla schema package makes it easy to unmarshal fields from form into our struct. Here, we create a Person struct with two fields. Ultimately, we "submit" a form that contains those and fills them.

```
~/ch16$ cat schema.go

package main

import (
    "fmt"
    "github.com/gorilla/schema"
    "net/http"
)

var decoder = schema.NewDecoder()

type Person struct {
    Name  string
    Phone string
}

func main() {
    http.HandleFunc("/schema", func(res http.ResponseWriter, req *http.Request) {
        req.ParseMultipartForm(0)
        var person Person
        decoder.Decode(&person, req.PostForm)
        message := fmt.Sprintf("Hello %v from area %v", person.Name, person.Phone)
```

```
        res.Write([]byte(message))
    })

    http.ListenAndServe(":8080", nil)
}
```

Launch the server.~/ch16$ go mod tidy
~/ch16$ go run schema.go

Notice how curl fills in the Content-Type for us, "multipart/form-data" (HTML forms in a browser will fill the Content-Type as well).

~/ch16$ curl -sF "Name=Ron" -F "Phone=312" -v localhost:8080/schema && echo

```
*   Trying 127.0.0.1:8080...
* TCP_NODELAY set
* Connected to localhost (127.0.0.1) port 8080 (#0)
> POST /schema HTTP/1.1
> Host: localhost:8080
> User-Agent: curl/7.68.0
> Accept: */*
> Content-Length: 239
> Content-Type: multipart/form-data; boundary=------------------------0458a5d725c3c300
>
* We are completely uploaded and fine
* Mark bundle as not supporting multiuse
< HTTP/1.1 200 OK
< Date: Mon, 07 Mar 2022 21:57:45 GMT
< Content-Length: 23
< Content-Type: text/plain; charset=utf-8
<
* Connection #0 to host localhost left intact
Hello Ron from area 312
```

gorilla/securecookie

The securecookie documentation starts as follows:

~/ch16$ go doc securecookie

```
package securecookie // import "github.com/gorilla/securecookie"

Package securecookie encodes and decodes authenticated and optionally
encrypted cookie values.

Secure cookies can't be forged, because their values are validated using
HMAC. When encrypted, the content is also inaccessible to malicious eyes.
...
```

While debate rages on about the use of cookies, we simply show the creation and round trip back to the server. We do not concern ourselves about local storage (client side).

AES encryption is used under the hood; standard length block keys are supported (16, 24, 32 bytes). In our example, we set to nil; thus, we are not using encryption.

```
~/ch16$ cat securecookie.go

package main

import (
    "fmt"
    "github.com/gorilla/securecookie"
    "net/http"
)

var hashKey = []byte("very-secret")
var s = securecookie.New(hashKey, nil)

func SetCookieHandler(w http.ResponseWriter, r *http.Request) {
    value := map[string]string{
        "foo": "bar",
    }
    if encoded, err := s.Encode("cookie-name", value); err == nil {
        cookie := &http.Cookie{
            Name:  "cookie-name",
            Value: encoded,
            Path:  "/",
        }
        http.SetCookie(w, cookie)

        fmt.Println(cookie)
    }
}

func ReadCookieHandler(w http.ResponseWriter, r *http.Request) {
    if cookie, err := r.Cookie("cookie-name"); err == nil {
        value := make(map[string]string)
        fmt.Println(cookie.Value)
        if err = s.Decode("cookie-name", cookie.Value, &value); err == nil {
            fmt.Fprintf(w, "The value of foo is %q", value["foo"])
        }

        fmt.Println(cookie, err)
    }

}

func main() {
    http.HandleFunc("/set", SetCookieHandler)
    http.HandleFunc("/read", ReadCookieHandler)
    http.ListenAndServe(":8080", nil)
}
```

Launch the server.~/ch16$ go mod tidy
~/ch16$ go run securecookie.go

The "/set" endpoint will simply create our cookie.~/ch16$ curl -I localhost:8080/set

```
HTTP/1.1 200 OK
Set-Cookie: cookie-name=MTY0NjY5MDU3MXxEdi1CQkFFQ18OSUFBUXdCREFFBQURQLUNBQUVEWmO5dkEySmhjZzO9
fMds29irowo8h_9MByVigjT1qhOt7hnvAHprwtX9nc1h; Path=/
Date: Mon, 07 Mar 2022 22:02:51 GMT
```

To confirm it was received, we send back our encoded cookie (be sure to use yours previously).

```
~/ch16$ curl -b "cookie-name=MTY0NjY5MDU3MXxEdi1CQkFFQ18OSUFBUXdCREFFBQURQLUNBQUVEWmO5dkEyS
mhjZzO9fMds29irowo8h_9MByVigjT1qhOt7hnvAHprwtX9nc1h" localhost:8080/read && echo
The value of foo is "bar"
```

Conclusion

The name "Gorilla" starts with Go and brings attention to endangered primates. As time goes on, Gorilla is not the only toolkit in the jungle, yet it remains in the conversation. We did not cover all the packages here, but hopefully this gives you some insight into how the standard library is extended.

## CHAPTER 17

Testing

In this chapter, we will look at ways and examples of testing network-related code. Using unit and integration testing techniques, we strive to capture the known and expected behavior. A unit test should ideally avoid all external factors. For example, a test that leverages the network is most accurately described as an integration test. The network (being external) to our code may exert undo influence such as delays or limiting payload size. It is not always easy to know how to design a test, much less how to separate and reduce outside influences. Having many unknown or controlled internal mechanisms can lead to flaky tests, ones that randomly seem to fail.

This chapter is not about learning the basics of Go test tooling. Excellent resources for the basics exist, for example:

- `https://pkg.go.dev/testing`

- `https://quii.gitbook.io/learn-go-with-tests/`

- go doc testing

Our goal is to learn some techniques that help us design and manage network-related tests.

Simple and Broken

We begin with a simple set of tests, where both tests are sending a request and then confirming we get a response. The only difference is one test has a client that times out and the other does not. In both tests, the server fakes work by sleeping for five seconds in both tests. We will run each test individually, then as a suite, reviewing the results.

```
$ mkdir ch17
$ cd ch17

ch17$ vi basic_http_test.go

package ch17

import (
    "net/http"
    "testing"
    "time"
)
```

```go
func TestHTTPRoundTrip(t *testing.T) {
    path := "/"
    c := make(chan struct{})
    //server
    go func() {
        http.HandleFunc(path, func(w http.ResponseWriter, req *http.Request) {
            time.Sleep(5 * time.Second) // holding connection
        })
        http.ListenAndServe(":8080", nil)
    }()

    //client
    go func() {
        resp, err := http.Get("http://localhost:8080" + path)
        if err != nil {
            t.Error(err)
        } else {
            if resp == nil || resp.StatusCode != http.StatusOK {
                t.Error(resp)
            }
        }

        defer func() {
            c <- struct{}{}
        }()
    }()
    <-c
}

func TestHTTPRoundTripTimeout(t *testing.T) {
    path := "/"
    c := make(chan struct{})
    //server
    go func() {
        http.HandleFunc(path, func(w http.ResponseWriter, req *http.Request) {
            time.Sleep(5 * time.Second) // holding connection
        })
        http.ListenAndServe(":8080", nil)
    }()

    //client
    go func() {
        var client = &http.Client{
            Timeout: time.Second * 2,
        }
        resp, err := client.Get("http://localhost:8080" + path)
        if err != nil {
            t.Error(err)
        } else {
            if resp == nil || resp.StatusCode != http.StatusOK {
```

```
                t.Error(resp)
            }
        }

        defer func() {
            c <- struct{}{}
        }()
    }()
    <-c
}
```

We begin by running the first test:

```
ch17$ go test -test.run "TestHTTPRoundTrip$" basic_http_test.go

=== RUN    TestHTTPRoundTrip
--- PASS: TestHTTPRoundTrip (5.00s)
PASS
ok      command-line-arguments  5.132s
```

and now the second test:

```
ch17$ go test -test.run "TestHTTPRoundTripTimeout$" basic_http_test.go

--- FAIL: TestHTTPRoundTripTimeout (2.00s)
    basic_http_test.go:56: Get "http://localhost:8080/": context deadline exceeded (Client.
Timeout exceeded while awaiting headers)
FAIL
FAIL    command-line-arguments  2.131s
FAIL
```

Upon reading the tests, it may seem obvious that the second test was going to fail. The client is set to expire after two seconds where the server is taking five seconds to process. An untrained eye might miss the reason for these related tests. The default HTTP client has an unlimited timeout. In our case, the server in the first test could take double the time and the test would still pass. This is not specific to Go, but it is specific to this implementation of the Go HTTP client. What happens if we simply run both tests.

```
ch17$ go test basic_http_test.go

panic: http: multiple registrations for /

goroutine 31 [running]:
net/http.(*ServeMux).Handle(0x1529fa0, {0x137fe80, 0x1}, {0x1381c00?, 0x132fee0})
    /usr/local/go/src/net/http/server.go:2478 +0x226
net/http.(*ServeMux).HandleFunc(...)
    /usr/local/go/src/net/http/server.go:2515
net/http.HandleFunc(...)
    /usr/local/go/src/net/http/server.go:2527
command-line-arguments.TestHTTPRoundTripTimeout.func1()
    /Users/ronaldpetty/github.com/apress/network-prog-with-go-2e/ch17/basic_http_test.
go:43 +0x37
```

```
created by command-line-arguments.TestHTTPRoundTripTimeout
    /Users/ronaldpetty/github.com/apress/network-prog-with-go-2e/ch17/basic_http_test.
go:42 +0x5e
FAIL    command-line-arguments  5.225s
FAIL
```

This error is exposing a test antipattern, where the tests are not independent of each other. Like the prior run, this also exposes some of the implementation details. The default ServeMux has a default handler; per code at server.go:2478, we are not allowed to remap the path.

We can see there a few things to consider including the following:

- What are we actually trying to test?

- Are we adhering to good testing practices (i.e., test independence)?

- Are we correct and performant?

How can we solve the preceding issue? As we saw in an earlier chapter, we could make a new "mux" per test. Another approach could be to set up all the test routes before the running of the tests. More fundamentally though, we should consider what exactly are we testing. For example, are we testing that the server listens? Or are we testing that our Handler provides the correct response based on a provided request? After all, if we consider the OSI model of thinking, HTTP is where our request/response protocol lives (L7), where TCP/IP maintains our connection (L4 and below). Since the layers can be decoupled, we should be able to decouple our tests. Even with this separation in mind, it's not immediately clear where the pieces will be tested (i.e., unit or integration). Thinking about the handler mappings, are those something you unit test, or is that something worthy of an integration test? After all, the handler isn't even triggered unless the given path was used.

As you can see, how we think about the network components can lead to potentially different testing arrangements. We should also remember that tests run out of order. While it seems tests run top to bottom, that is an implementation side effect and not a specified behavior in the testing package.

As we refactor, we will first look at what Go provides regarding testing helpers.

httptest Package

The httptest package provides functions and types to assist with HTTP focused testing.

```
ch17$ go doc httptest

package httptest // import "net/http/httptest"

Package httptest provides utilities for HTTP testing.

const DefaultRemoteAddr = "1.2.3.4"
func NewRequest(method, target string, body io.Reader) *http.Request
type ResponseRecorder struct{ ... }
    func NewRecorder() *ResponseRecorder
type Server struct{ ... }
    func NewServer(handler http.Handler) *Server
    func NewTLSServer(handler http.Handler) *Server
    func NewUnstartedServer(handler http.Handler) *Server
```

Let's create a new test, one that is similar to our prior ones yet does not actually connect to a server. To save room, we will not list the existing tests.

```
ch17$ vi basic_http_test.go
package ch17

import (
        "net/http"
        "net/http/httptest"
        "testing"
        "time"
)

func TestHTTPRoundTripNoConnection(t *testing.T) {
        path := "/"
        req := httptest.NewRequest("GET", path, nil)
        res := httptest.NewRecorder()

        f := func(w http.ResponseWriter, req *http.Request) {
                time.Sleep(5 * time.Second) // holding connection
        }

        f(res, req)

        if res == nil || res.Result().StatusCode != http.StatusOK {
                t.Error(res)
        }
}

func TestHTTPRoundTrip(t *testing.T) {
    ...

func TestHTTPRoundTripTimeout(t *testing.T) {
    ...
```

We have made a few changes but capture our request, response, and the related assertion. Things to notice: we have removed the server (i.e., http.ListenAndServe); the path to handler mapping remains, but it is explicit inside httptest.NewRequest vs. http.HandleFunc. Since we are using a new package (i.e., httptest), we had to modify the result check in order to more closely match an actual response.

Our call to httptest.NewRecorder returns a new httptest.ResponseRecorder type, which in turn implements the http.ResponseWriter interface. This allows an http.Response to be indirectly populated. The result though is not fit for a deep comparison (i.e., reflect.DeepEqual).

Beyond a handler, how can we test the client and a mocked back end? The httptest package provides the ability to also create a test server endpoint.

```
ch17$ vi basic_http_test.go

... other tests and imports

func TestHTTPTestRoundTripTimeout(t *testing.T) {
        ts := httptest.NewServer(http.HandlerFunc(func(w http.ResponseWriter, req *http.
Request) {
```

```
                time.Sleep(5 * time.Second) // holding connection
        }))
        defer ts.Close()

        var c = &http.Client{
                Timeout: time.Second * 2,
        }
        req, _ := http.NewRequest("GET", ts.URL, nil)
        res, err := c.Do(req)
        if err != nil {
                t.Fatal(err)
        }

        err = res.Body.Close()
        if err != nil {
                t.Fatal(err)
        }
}
```

We can run this test as follows:

```
ch17$ go test -test.run "TestHTTPTestRoundTripTimeout$" -v basic_http_test.go

=== RUN    TestHTTPTestRoundTripTimeout
    basic_http_test.go:68: Get "http://127.0.0.1:50866": context deadline exceeded (Client.
Timeout exceeded while awaiting headers)
--- FAIL: TestHTTPTestRoundTripTimeout (5.00s)
FAIL
FAIL    command-line-arguments  5.155s
FAIL
```

In these particular examples, you would not want the actual tests to fail. You would want to fix the pathing (to be unique) and the timeouts to only trigger an error if it was unexpected.

Below HTTP

The preceding tooling focused on HTTP. Is there a more general technique? Included in the net package is type Pipe.

```
ch17$ go doc net.Pipe

package net // import "net"

func Pipe() (Conn, Conn)
    Pipe creates a synchronous, in-memory, full duplex network connection; both
    ends implement the Conn interface. Reads on one end are matched with writes
    on the other, copying data directly between the two; there is no internal
    buffering.
```

As is mentioned, we are provided connection objects that act like a more general client and server.
```
... prior tests and imports

func TestPipe(t *testing.T) {
        c := make(chan struct{})
        server, client := net.Pipe()
        go func() {
                time.Sleep(2 * time.Second)
                req := make([]byte, 15)
                server.SetDeadline(time.Now().Add(1 * time.Second))
                _, err := server.Read(req)
                t.Log(string(req))
                if err != nil {
                        t.Error(err)
                }
                defer func() {
                        server.Close()
                        c <- struct{}{}
                }()
        }()
        client.SetDeadline(time.Now().Add(1 * time.Second))
        _, err := client.Write([]byte("my http request"))
        if err != nil {
                t.Error(err)
        }
        defer func() {
                client.Close()
        }()
        <-c
}
```

In the preceding example, we are trying to emulate some of the failure behavior we saw with HTTP-related timeouts.ch17$ go test -test.run "TestPipe$" -v basic_http_test.go

```
=== RUN    TestPipe
    basic_http_test.go:131: write pipe: i/o timeout
    basic_http_test.go:119:
    basic_http_test.go:121: read pipe: i/o timeout
--- FAIL: TestPipe (3.00s)
FAIL
FAIL    command-line-arguments    3.137s
FAIL
```

Take note, we are operating at a lower layer than HTTP (i.e., L7). For the most part, this implies we will need to take care of our request and responses vs. leveraging existing higher-level types like http.Request or http.Response.

Leveraging the Standard Library

The Internet is full of examples, and so is the Go standard library. In this section, we will look at a couple of existing tests, with the intent to focus on the style and (required) complexity.

```
ch17$ go test -test.count=1 -v -test.list ".*" $(go env GOROOT)/src/net/...  | head

TestSortByRFC6724
TestRFC6724PolicyTableClassify
TestRFC6724ClassifyScope
TestRFC6724CommonPrefixLength
TestCgoLookupIP
TestCgoLookupIPWithCancel
TestCgoLookupPort
TestCgoLookupPortWithCancel
TestCgoLookupPTR
TestCgoLookupPTRWithCancel
```

There are several thousand tests, most with no documentation. We first take a look at

```
$(go env GOROOT)/src/net/http/requestwrite_test.go
```

Let's attempt to run the related tests (start with TestRequestWrite).

```
ch17$ cd $(go env GOROOT)/src/net/http
http$ go test -test.count=1 -v -test.run "TestRequestWrite*"

=== RUN    TestRequestWrite
--- PASS: TestRequestWrite (0.00s)
=== RUN    TestRequestWriteTransport
=== PAUSE TestRequestWriteTransport
=== RUN    TestRequestWriteClosesBody
--- PASS: TestRequestWriteClosesBody (0.00s)
=== RUN    TestRequestWriteError
--- PASS: TestRequestWriteError (0.00s)
=== RUN    TestRequestWriteBufferedWriter
--- PASS: TestRequestWriteBufferedWriter (0.00s)
=== CONT   TestRequestWriteTransport
--- PASS: TestRequestWriteTransport (0.20s)
PASS
ok      net/http      0.363s
```

It's nice that we can run the provided tests and even modify them to test things out (but be careful, make backups).

If you open requestwrite_test.go (e.g., sudo vi $(go env GOROOT)/src/net/http/requestwrite_test.go), notice the structure of the test table; here, we list the first entry.

```
// from requestwrite_test.go
...
type reqWriteTest struct {
        Req  Request
```

```
        Body any // optional []byte or func() io.ReadCloser to populate Req.Body

        // Any of these three may be empty to skip that test.
        WantWrite string // Request.Write
        WantProxy string // Request.WriteProxy

        WantError error // wanted error from Request.Write
}

var reqWriteTests = []reqWriteTest{
        // HTTP/1.1 => chunked coding; no body; no trailer
        0: {
                Req: Request{
                        Method: "GET",
                        URL: &url.URL{
                                Scheme: "http",
                                Host:   "www.techcrunch.com",
                                Path:   "/",
                        },
                        Proto:      "HTTP/1.1",
                        ProtoMajor: 1,
                        ProtoMinor: 1,
                        Header: Header{
                                "Accept":           {"text/html,application/
                                xhtml+xml,application/xml;q=0.9,*/*;q=0.8"},
                                "Accept-Charset":   {"ISO-8859-1,utf-8;q=0.7,*;q=0.7"},
                                "Accept-Encoding":  {"gzip,deflate"},
                                "Accept-Language":  {"en-us,en;q=0.5"},
                                "Keep-Alive":       {"300"},
                                "Proxy-Connection": {"keep-alive"},
                                "User-Agent":       {"Fake"},
                        },
                        Body:  nil,
                        Close: false,
                        Host:  "www.techcrunch.com",
                        Form:  map[string][]string{},
                },

                WantWrite: "GET / HTTP/1.1\r\n" +
                        "Host: www.techcrunch.com\r\n" +
                        "User-Agent: Fake\r\n" +
                        "Accept: text/html,application/xhtml+xml,application/
                        xml;q=0.9,*/*;q=0.8\r\n" +
                        "Accept-Charset: ISO-8859-1,utf-8;q=0.7,*;q=0.7\r\n" +
                        "Accept-Encoding: gzip,deflate\r\n" +
                        "Accept-Language: en-us,en;q=0.5\r\n" +
                        "Keep-Alive: 300\r\n" +
                        "Proxy-Connection: keep-alive\r\n\r\n",

                WantProxy: "GET http://www.techcrunch.com/ HTTP/1.1\r\n" +
                        "Host: www.techcrunch.com\r\n" +
```

341

```
                                    "User-Agent: Fake\r\n" +
                                    "Accept: text/html,application/xhtml+xml,application/
                                    xml;q=0.9,*/*;q=0.8\r\n" +
                                    "Accept-Charset: ISO-8859-1,utf-8;q=0.7,*;q=0.7\r\n" +
                                    "Accept-Encoding: gzip,deflate\r\n" +
                                    "Accept-Language: en-us,en;q=0.5\r\n" +
                                    "Keep-Alive: 300\r\n" +
                                    "Proxy-Connection: keep-alive\r\n\r\n",
                },
                // HTTP/1.1 => chunked coding; body; empty trailer
                1: {
...
```

As with many tests in Go, we see a very long testing table. We have a Request instance (Req) along with a very similar stringified result (WantWrite and WantProxy). Before we dive in, let's review one of the tests.

```
// from requestwrite_test.go
...
func TestRequestWrite(t *testing.T) {
        for i := range reqWriteTests {
                tt := &reqWriteTests[i]

                setBody := func() {
                        if tt.Body == nil {
                                return
                        }
                        switch b := tt.Body.(type) {
                        case []byte:
                                tt.Req.Body = io.NopCloser(bytes.NewReader(b))
                        case func() io.ReadCloser:
                                tt.Req.Body = b()
                        }
                }
                setBody()
                if tt.Req.Header == nil {
                        tt.Req.Header = make(Header)
                }

                var braw bytes.Buffer
                err := tt.Req.Write(&braw)
                if g, e := fmt.Sprintf("%v", err), fmt.Sprintf("%v", tt.WantError); g != e {
                        t.Errorf("writing #%d, err = %q, want %q", i, g, e)
                        continue
                }
                if err != nil {
                        continue
                }

                if tt.WantWrite != "" {
                        sraw := braw.String()
                        if sraw != tt.WantWrite {
```

```
                            t.Errorf("Test %d, expecting:\n%s\nGot:\n%s\n", i,
                            tt.WantWrite, sraw)
                            continue
                    }
            }

            if tt.WantProxy != "" {
                    setBody()
                    var praw bytes.Buffer
                    err = tt.Req.WriteProxy(&praw)
                    if err != nil {
                            t.Errorf("WriteProxy #%d: %s", i, err)
                            continue
                    }
                    sraw := praw.String()
                    if sraw != tt.WantProxy {
                            t.Errorf("Test Proxy %d, expecting:\n%s\nGot:\n%s\n", i,
                            tt.WantProxy, sraw)
                            continue
                    }
            }
        }
    }
}
...
```

That is a fair bit of code. What is it doing? Here is a list of activities:

- Enumerate the test table (reqWriteTests).

- Set up a real Request object with headers and body.

- Serialize the Request object (sraw) and compare with WantWrite or WantProxy.

Some additional items to note are

- io.NopCloser

The NopCloser is an example of a function that reduces functionality, in this case, prevent the closing of a resource.

```
http$ go doc -u -all io.nopCloser

package io // import "io"

func NopCloser(r Reader) ReadCloser
    NopCloser returns a ReadCloser with a no-op Close method wrapping the
    provided Reader r.

type nopCloser struct {
    Reader
}

func (nopCloser) Close() error
```

- tt.Req.Write and tt.Req.WriteProxy

If we review the related documentation for these methods:

```
http$ go doc net/http.Request.Write

package http // import "net/http"

func (r *Request) Write(w io.Writer) error
    Write writes an HTTP/1.1 request, which is the header and body, in wire
    format. This method consults the following fields of the request:

        Host
        URL
        Method (defaults to "GET")
        Header
        ContentLength
        TransferEncoding
        Body

    If Body is present, Content-Length is <= 0 and TransferEncoding hasn't been
    set to "identity", Write adds "Transfer-Encoding: chunked" to the header.
    Body is closed after it is sent.

http$ go doc net/http.Request.WriteProxy

package http // import "net/http"

func (r *Request) WriteProxy(w io.Writer) error
    WriteProxy is like Write but writes the request in the form expected by an
    HTTP proxy. In particular, WriteProxy writes the initial Request-URI line of
    the request with an absolute URI, per section 5.3 of RFC 7230, including the
    scheme and host. In either case, WriteProxy also writes a Host header, using
    either r.Host or r.URL.Host.
```

We see both methods take a Writer, and both serialize the Request object in slightly different ways based on their utility. We won't inspect the differences here, but it gives us an idea on how to approach our own testing.

We next review the test in the net package: TestTCPConnSpecificMethods.

```
// from protoconn_test.go
...
func TestTCPConnSpecificMethods(t *testing.T) {
        la, err := ResolveTCPAddr("tcp4", "127.0.0.1:0")
        if err != nil {
                t.Fatal(err)
        }
        ln, err := ListenTCP("tcp4", la)
        if err != nil {
                t.Fatal(err)
        }
        ch := make(chan error, 1)
```

```
handler := func(ls *localServer, ln Listener) { ls.transponder(ls.Listener, ch) }
ls := (&streamListener{Listener: ln}).newLocalServer()
defer ls.teardown()
if err := ls.buildup(handler); err != nil {
        t.Fatal(err)
}

ra, err := ResolveTCPAddr("tcp4", ls.Listener.Addr().String())
if err != nil {
        t.Fatal(err)
}
c, err := DialTCP("tcp4", nil, ra)
if err != nil {
        t.Fatal(err)
}
defer c.Close()
c.SetKeepAlive(false)
c.SetKeepAlivePeriod(3 * time.Second)
c.SetLinger(0)
c.SetNoDelay(false)
c.LocalAddr()
c.RemoteAddr()
c.SetDeadline(time.Now().Add(someTimeout))
c.SetReadDeadline(time.Now().Add(someTimeout))
c.SetWriteDeadline(time.Now().Add(someTimeout))
if _, err := c.Write([]byte("TCPCONN TEST")); err != nil {
        t.Fatal(err)
}
rb := make([]byte, 128)
if _, err := c.Read(rb); err != nil {
        t.Fatal(err)
}

for err := range ch {
        t.Error(err)
}
}
...
```

The test itself is focused on setting a variety of client connection-related options, then uses the client, and in turn hopes nothing goes wrong. From our point of view, we are interested in how they wrote the test itself. We are down in the L3/L4 layers of the stack. At a high level, here is what is happening:

- Preparing and validating a known IP Address (i.e., 127.0.0.1) and port (:0)

- Create a TCP-based Listener.

- Launch the server (more to follow).

- Retrieve the IP and assigned port of the server.

- Create a client using the remote address.

- Configure client.

- Write data from client to server and then read the result.

Running the TestTCPConnSpecificMethods test, we see the following:

```
net$ go test -test.count=1 -v -test.run "TestTCPConnSpecificMethods$"

=== RUN    TestTCPConnSpecificMethods
--- PASS: TestTCPConnSpecificMethods (0.00s)
PASS
Socket statistical information:
(inet4, stream, default): opened=2 connected=1 listened=1 accepted=1 closed=3 openfailed=0
connectfailed=1 listenfailed=0 acceptfailed=1 closefailed=0

ok      net 0.210s
```

The middle of the test looks more complicated than what we have seen before.

```
ch := make(chan error, 1)
handler := func(ls *localServer, ln Listener) { ls.transponder(ls.Listener, ch) }
ls := (&streamListener{Listener: ln}).newLocalServer()
defer ls.teardown()
if err := ls.buildup(handler); err != nil {
        t.Fatal(err)
}
```

The preceding code is defined elsewhere: mockserver_test.go. The call to buildup runs the handler code in a Go routine. At a high level, Accept is run in the transponder, so why not just a "nonmock" setup? Upon further review, you see "someTimeout" being applied to most timeout-related settings (i.e., SetDeadline). Interesting enough, since the code lives in a file ending with "_test.go", we cannot review it via "go doc".

Review $(go env GOROOT)/src/net/mockserver_test.go for more details.

Conclusion

This chapter was intended to get you thinking about the techniques and layers involved when testing network related code. Additional concepts and tooling are needed to become expert network test developers. For example, how can fuzzing or generics help secure and streamline our code. What should we consider when integration tests get more complicated, for example where we chain several network services together, even when the protocol changes along the way.

Fuzzing

Fuzzing is a technique where one automatically generates inputs, which in turn causes the receiving program to respond in some unexpected way. How a fuzzing program manipulates inputs is often classified from simple to complex. For example, the inputs could simply be randomly generated, or you can provide an initial set of values, or even more complex fuzzing systems can be rule driven (including deriving new rules that generate potential values). Due to time constraints, sometimes lack of creativity, it's hard to know how our code will fail; letting the computer (fuzzer) drive this testing process allows us to find new ways to break our code (bugs, vulnerabilities).

Wikipedia offers a nice introduction on the topic (`https://en.wikipedia.org/wiki/Fuzzing`).

Fuzzing in Go

Third-party fuzzing software has been around for a long time (even for Go), but in Go 1.18, the technique was integrated into the testing package. You can read the original (draft) proposal here:

- `https://go.googlesource.com/proposal/+/master/design/draft-fuzzing.md`

and more in-depth conversation here:

- `https://github.com/golang/go/issues/44551`

The goal for us is to learn the basic mechanics of using Go's fuzzing functionality and tie it back to a networking test example.

Before we look at code, take some time to review the initial documentation via "go doc testing.F". Our first example leverages the documentation example. As you read through the example:

- Note how testing.F is used along with testing.T.

- Note the use of seed data (more on this later).

- Think about the actual test, is it a regular looking unit test (yes!).

Before creating the first example, consider what fuzzing in Go requires us to do.

- A fuzz test must be named like FuzzXxx and only accepts *testing.F, no return value.

- Fuzz tests must be in files named *_test.go, like any test in Go.

- A fuzz target must be a method call to (*testing.F).Fuzz, which accepts a *testing.T as the first parameter, followed by the fuzzing arguments. There is no return value.

- There must be exactly one fuzz target per fuzz test.

© Jan Newmarch and Ronald Petty 2022

J. Newmarch and R. Petty, *Network Programming with Go Language*,

https://doi.org/10.1007/978-1-4842-8095-9

- All seed corpus entries must have types that are identical to the arguments being fuzzed, in the same order. This is true for calls to (*testing.F).Add and any corpus files in the testdata/fuzz directory of the fuzz test.

- The fuzzing arguments can only be the following types:

  - string, []byte

  - int, int8, int16, int32/rune, int64

  - uint, uint8/byte, uint16, uint32, uint64

  - float32, float64

  - bool

```
$ mkdir appx-fuzzing
$ cd appx-fuzzing

appx-fuzzing$ vi fuzzing_test.go

package main

import (
    "bytes"
    "encoding/hex"
    "testing"
)

func FuzzMe(f *testing.F) {
    for _, seed := range [][]byte{{}, {0}, {9}, {0xa}, {0xf}, {1, 2, 3, 4}} {
        f.Add(seed)
    }

    // the fuzz runner f leverages the test runner t,
    // this is so the fuzzer can manage the tests, it generates (or uses seed) inputs
    // calling the passed in test
    f.Fuzz(func(t *testing.T, in []byte) {
        enc := hex.EncodeToString(in)
        out, err := hex.DecodeString(enc)
        if err != nil {
            t.Fatalf("%v: decode: %v", in, err)
        }
        if !bytes.Equal(in, out) {
            t.Fatalf("%v: not equal after round trip: %v", in, out)
        }
    })
}
```

To run the embedded seed corpus we simply use the regular test runner.

```
appx-fuzzing$ go test fuzzing_test.go

ok      command-line-arguments      0.103s
```

To see more details, use -v.

```
appx-fuzzing$ go test -v fuzzing_test.go

=== RUN    FuzzMe
=== RUN    FuzzMe/seed#0
=== RUN    FuzzMe/seed#1
=== RUN    FuzzMe/seed#2
=== RUN    FuzzMe/seed#3
=== RUN    FuzzMe/seed#4
=== RUN    FuzzMe/seed#5
--- PASS: FuzzMe (0.00s)
    --- PASS: FuzzMe/seed#0 (0.00s)
    --- PASS: FuzzMe/seed#1 (0.00s)
    --- PASS: FuzzMe/seed#2 (0.00s)
    --- PASS: FuzzMe/seed#3 (0.00s)
    --- PASS: FuzzMe/seed#4 (0.00s)
    --- PASS: FuzzMe/seed#5 (0.00s)
PASS
ok      command-line-arguments  0.105s
```

As you can see, we have six runs executed; this maps to the number of seeds included via "f.Add(seed)". By including seeds, we are afforded the opportunity to have regression protection, just like a typical unit test. The mode of execution happened because it did not specify the test to fuzz. An alternative way to execute the same thing (using seeded vs. generated data) is "go test -v --test.run "FuzzMe" fuzzing_test.go".

While regression protection is important, we haven't actually fuzzed anything, simply ran our basic comparisons. To Fuzz, we need to specify our test. To generate new results (a.k.a. bad inputs caught by fuzzing), specify the test (grab a drink; it's going to be a long time – if ever – to complete). When you are tired of waiting, hit control c.

```
appx-fuzzing$ go test -fuzz=FuzzMe fuzzing_test.go

=== FUZZ   FuzzMe
fuzz: elapsed: 0s, gathering baseline coverage: 0/29 completed
fuzz: elapsed: 0s, gathering baseline coverage: 29/29 completed, now fuzzing with 12 workers
fuzz: elapsed: 3s, execs: 780426 (260128/sec), new interesting: 0 (total: 29)
fuzz: elapsed: 6s, execs: 1577625 (265663/sec), new interesting: 0 (total: 29)
fuzz: elapsed: 9s, execs: 2369952 (264185/sec), new interesting: 0 (total: 29)
fuzz: elapsed: 12s, execs: 3024147 (218055/sec), new interesting: 0 (total: 29)
fuzz: elapsed: 15s, execs: 3759791 (245166/sec), new interesting: 0 (total: 29)
fuzz: elapsed: 18s, execs: 4470924 (237062/sec), new interesting: 0 (total: 29)
fuzz: elapsed: 21s, execs: 5178109 (235752/sec), new interesting: 0 (total: 29)
fuzz: elapsed: 24s, execs: 5898784 (240167/sec), new interesting: 0 (total: 29)
^C
```

```
fuzz: elapsed: 25s, execs: 6211453 (222820/sec), new interesting: 0 (total: 29)
--- PASS: FuzzMe (25.41s)
PASS
ok      command-line-arguments   25.545s
```

The immediate change is we specify a test to fuzz via --test.fuzz "FuzzMe". Instead of just running the embedded seeds, we are now generating new inputs and testing them. This process will continue for a very long time, hence the need to stop it. The reason it takes (hours, days, more!) is because the range of inputs can be huge (just a single integer has billions of potential values). We do have some additional controls though, vs. waiting forever.

- Fuzzing stops when a test fails.

- Limit time to fuzz via -fuzztime (e.g., -fuzztime 30s).

- Hit control^c or send SIGINT (e.g., using a signal in your CI pipeline).

Fuzzing Failures

In our prior example, we did not see a failure; however, we only ran for under a minute; it could take days to maybe find invalid input. Let's create a bad test to highlight the process and what we can do with fuzzing generated test inputs.

The following test will error if the value is greater than 100 or less than 1000.

```
func FuzzBad(f *testing.F) {
    f.Fuzz(func(t *testing.T, i int) {
        if i > 100 && i < 1000 {
            t.Fatalf("want: 101-999, got: %v", i)
        }
    })
}
```

Running the fuzzing directly against this test produces the following:

```
appx-fuzzing$ go test -fuzz=FuzzBad fuzzing_test.go

=== RUN    FuzzMe
=== RUN    FuzzMe/seed#0
=== RUN    FuzzMe/seed#1
=== RUN    FuzzMe/seed#2
=== RUN    FuzzMe/seed#3
=== RUN    FuzzMe/seed#4
=== RUN    FuzzMe/seed#5
--- PASS: FuzzMe (0.00s)
    --- PASS: FuzzMe/seed#0 (0.00s)
    --- PASS: FuzzMe/seed#1 (0.00s)
    --- PASS: FuzzMe/seed#2 (0.00s)
    --- PASS: FuzzMe/seed#3 (0.00s)
    --- PASS: FuzzMe/seed#4 (0.00s)
    --- PASS: FuzzMe/seed#5 (0.00s)
=== FUZZ   FuzzBad
fuzz: elapsed: 0s, gathering baseline coverage: 0/1 completed
fuzz: elapsed: 0s, gathering baseline coverage: 1/1 completed, now fuzzing with 12 workers
```

```
fuzz: elapsed: 0s, execs: 9 (530/sec), new interesting: 0 (total: 1)
--- FAIL: FuzzBad (0.02s)
    --- FAIL: FuzzBad (0.00s)
        fuzzing_test.go:28: want: 101-999, got: 174

    Failing input written to testdata/fuzz/FuzzBad/
daef2fa4fc63690477c788772f4488eb55a67946e4bed16916b63688c2c99935
    To re-run:
    go test -run=FuzzBad/daef2fa4fc63690477c788772f4488eb55a67946e4bed16916b63688c2c99935
FAIL
exit status 1
FAIL    command-line-arguments  0.151s
```

We see the original test still runs over the provided seeds. This is by design meant to run the seeds as a regression protective measure. If no seeds were available, the test would not run without using direct invocation via --test.fuzz.

More importantly, we see a failing set of input(s) was identified. In the example, the value 174 was attempted and failed. The result is stored in a directory called testdata. This directory will in turn be used as the "seed" for future regression runs.

We see the directory structure as follows.

```
appx-fuzzing$ tree testdata

testdata
└── fuzz
    └── FuzzBad
        └── daef2fa4fc63690477c788772f4488eb55a67946e4bed16916b63688c2c99935

2 directories, 1 file
```

Reviewing the auto-generated file, we see the encoded bad input.

```
appx-fuzzing$ cat testdata/fuzz/FuzzBad/
daef2fa4fc63690477c788772f4488eb55a67946e4bed16916b63688c2c99935

go test fuzz v1
int(174)
```

In our result, it is simply an int, but for more complex results, we will see more complex encodings. If you run the test again, it simply fails again, treating the testdata now as a seed.

```
appx-fuzzing$ go test -fuzz=FuzzBad fuzzing_test.go

fuzz: elapsed: 0s, gathering baseline coverage: 0/2 completed
failure while testing seed corpus entry: FuzzBad/
daef2fa4fc63690477c788772f4488eb55a67946e4bed16916b63688c2c99935
fuzz: elapsed: 0s, gathering baseline coverage: 0/2 completed
--- FAIL: FuzzBad (0.02s)
    --- FAIL: FuzzBad (0.00s)
        fuzzing_test.go:28: want: 101-999, got: 174
```

```
FAIL
exit status 1
FAIL    command-line-arguments  0.126s
```

Let's almost fix this; let's simply reduce from 1000 to 150, shrinking our error range.

```
func FuzzBad(f *testing.F) {
        f.Fuzz(func(t *testing.T, i int) {
                if i > 100 && i < 150 {
                        t.Fatalf("want: 101-150, got: %v", i)
                }
        })
}
```

Running once more:

```
appx-fuzzing$ go test --test.fuzz "FuzzBad" fuzzing_test.go

fuzz: elapsed: 0s, gathering baseline coverage: 0/2 completed
fuzz: elapsed: 0s, gathering baseline coverage: 2/2 completed, now fuzzing with 12 workers
fuzz: elapsed: 0s, execs: 4 (205/sec), new interesting: 0 (total: 2)
--- FAIL: FuzzBad (0.02s)
    --- FAIL: FuzzBad (0.00s)
        fuzzing_test.go:28: want: 101-150, got: 117

    Failing input written to testdata/fuzz/FuzzBad/7bd545fe2a8997effdf791253ba576f785189c9
2f46c205024dc835aa7f63b27
    To re-run:
    go test -run=FuzzBad/7bd545fe2a8997effdf791253ba576f785189c92f46c205024dc835aa7f63b27
FAIL
exit status 1
FAIL    command-line-arguments  0.234s
```

Reviewing the new failure:

```
appx-fuzzing$ tree testdata

testdata
└── fuzz
    └── FuzzBad
        ├── 7bd545fe2a8997effdf791253ba576f785189c92f46c205024dc835aa7f63b27
        └── daef2fa4fc63690477c788772f4488eb55a67946e4bed16916b63688c2c99935

2 directories, 2 files

appx-fuzzing$ cat testdata/fuzz/FuzzBad/7bd545fe2a8997effdf791253ba576f785189c92f46c205024
dc835aa7f63b27

go test fuzz v1
int(117)
```

As expected, a new failing case was identified and stored. If we removed the failing logic, can we fuzz?

```
appx-fuzzing$ vi fuzzing_test.go

...

func FuzzBad(f *testing.F) {
        f.Fuzz(func(t *testing.T, i int) {
                # hope this never fails
                if i != i {
                        t.Fatalf("want: %v, got: %v", i, i)
                }
        })
}
```

Running with a ten-second fuzzing time:

```
appx-fuzzing$ go test -fuzz=FuzzBad fuzzing_test.go --test.fuzztime 10s

fuzz: elapsed: 0s, gathering baseline coverage: 0/3 completed
fuzz: elapsed: 0s, gathering baseline coverage: 3/3 completed, now fuzzing with 12 workers
fuzz: elapsed: 3s, execs: 794663 (264831/sec), new interesting: 0 (total: 3)
fuzz: elapsed: 6s, execs: 1608866 (271422/sec), new interesting: 0 (total: 3)
fuzz: elapsed: 9s, execs: 2400547 (263916/sec), new interesting: 0 (total: 3)
fuzz: elapsed: 10s, execs: 2642809 (217213/sec), new interesting: 0 (total: 3)
PASS
ok      command-line-arguments  10.273s
```

We still see the seeds (from previous failures) are executed, and we fuzz for an additional ten seconds.

Fuzzing Network-Related Artifacts

Now that we have some of the basics of fuzzing, how might this help us with networking? Fuzzing is often associated with security. The original fuzzing project found security issues in dozens of programs including standard tools that are included with modern operating systems.

For simplicity, we will keep our example as part of our test file.

```
appx-fuzzing$ vi fuzzing_test.go

package main

import (
    "bytes"
    "encoding/base64"
    "encoding/hex"
    "net/http"
    "net/http/httptest"
    "testing"
)
```

```
... prior tests ...

func FuzzHandler(f *testing.F) {
    f.Fuzz(func(t *testing.T, data string) {
        v := base64.StdEncoding.EncodeToString([]byte(data))
        req := httptest.NewRequest("GET", "/?q="+v, nil)
        res := httptest.NewRecorder()

        f := func(w http.ResponseWriter, req *http.Request) {
            keys, ok := req.URL.Query()["q"]

            if !ok || len(keys) != 1 {
                t.Log(keys)
                t.Fatal("q param missing or more than one instance")
            }

            val := keys[0]

            if len(val) > 16384 {
                w.WriteHeader(http.StatusNotAcceptable)
            } else {
                w.WriteHeader(http.StatusOK)
            }
        }

        f(res, req)

        if res == nil || res.Result().StatusCode != http.StatusOK {
            t.Fatal(res)
        }
    })
}
```

This time, we explicitly fuzz the FuzzHandler test, with no runtime limit. Depending on your computer and luck, this will take a few minutes to execute (hopefully).

```
appx-fuzzing$ go test -v -fuzz=FuzzHandler fuzzing_test.go

...
=== FUZZ  FuzzHandler
fuzz: elapsed: 0s, gathering baseline coverage: 0/1 completed
fuzz: elapsed: 0s, gathering baseline coverage: 1/1 completed, now fuzzing with 12 workers
fuzz: elapsed: 3s, execs: 63259 (21080/sec), new interesting: 21 (total: 22)
fuzz: elapsed: 6s, execs: 161593 (32777/sec), new interesting: 23 (total: 24)
fuzz: elapsed: 9s, execs: 458132 (98870/sec), new interesting: 26 (total: 27)
fuzz: elapsed: 12s, execs: 1136629 (226110/sec), new interesting: 31 (total: 32)
fuzz: elapsed: 15s, execs: 1199874 (21082/sec), new interesting: 32 (total: 33)
fuzz: elapsed: 18s, execs: 1199874 (0/sec), new interesting: 32 (total: 33)
fuzz: elapsed: 21s, execs: 1352204 (50777/sec), new interesting: 32 (total: 33)
...
fuzz: elapsed: 3m3s, execs: 6601424 (50515/sec), new interesting: 35 (total: 36)
```

```
fuzz: minimizing 29399-byte failing input file
fuzz: elapsed: 3m6s, minimizing
...
fuzz: elapsed: 4m3s, minimizing
--- FAIL: FuzzHandler (243.19s)
    --- FAIL: FuzzHandler (0.00s)
        fuzzing_test.go:63: &{406 map[]  false 0xc0094c46c0 map[] true}

    Failing input written to testdata/fuzz/FuzzHandler/54a3e656e9424c2d80e33168b673d2688831f
8b0dc685dc545594a76752dcc85
    To re-run:
    go test -run=FuzzHandler/54a3e656e9424c2d80e33168b673d2688831f8b0dc685dc545594
a76752dcc85
FAIL
exit status 1
FAIL    command-line-arguments  243.458s
```

As you can see, it took just over four minutes to find an error. What caused the error?

```
appx-fuzzing$ ls -lh \
testdata/fuzz/FuzzHandler/54a3e656e9424c2d80e33168b673d2688831f8b0dc685dc545594a76752dcc85

-rw-r--r--  1 ronaldpetty  staff    29K Mar 23 12:19 testdata/fuzz/FuzzHandler/54a3e656e942
4c2d80e33168b673d2688831f8b0dc685dc545594a76752dcc85
```

Take note of the size of the result, 29 kilobytes. Our code errored at anything over 16KB. In this straightforward test, we are limiting the query search (q) params to be under a set length. Your own tests can have much more involved checks.

As the fuzzing ran, we see things such as

- "fuzz: elapsed: 3s, execs: 63259 (21080/sec), new interesting: 21 (total: 22)"

- "fuzz: elapsed: 3m6s, minimizing"

An "interesting" input is one that expands the test corpus to cover code it couldn't before with existing examples. Per the documentation, many interesting inputs are generated early and taper off as all the code is being covered (fuzzing instruments our code upon running; hence, we know what is covered or not). Ultimately, we don't want to store just any input; we want the input that fails, which we stopped when we got our input that was over 16KB.

Conclusion

While the fuzzing technique is not new, its arrival in Go 1.18 means it will be some time before we see more intersting examples. More about fuzzing in Go can be learned from here: https://go.dev/doc/tutorial/fuzz. Fuzzing is not enough to prove program correctness; for that, formal methods must be used. Features of Go itself are derived from work relating to formal methods. Channels (a key feature of Go) are derived from communicating sequential processes (CSP). CSP is a formal language describing concurrent systems (e.g., using channels between Go routines).

APPENDIX B

Generics

Generics are a programming mechanism where data types are abstracted from algorithms. In a programming language where generics are not available, you often have to duplicate code when using the same code with differing types.

Some languages, including Go, do not allow function overloading. This very issue is addressed in the Go FAQ located here: https://go.dev/doc/faq#overloading.

Why does Go not support overloading of methods and operators?

Method dispatch is simplified if it doesn't need to do type matching as well. Experience with other languages told us that having a variety of methods with the same name but different signatures was occasionally useful but that it could also be confusing and fragile in practice. Matching only by name and requiring consistency in the types was a major simplifying decision in Go's type system.

Regarding operator overloading, it seems more a convenience than an absolute requirement. Again, things are simpler without it.

Go produces the following error if overloading is attempted:

```
# sample Go code
func Identity(a int64) int64 { return a }
func Identity(a float64) float64 { return a}

# go run code.go
# command-line-arguments
./g.go:5:6: Identity redeclared in this block
    ./g.go:6:6: other declaration of Identity
```

A simple solution is to change the second function name to "IdentityFloat". A less simple solution would be to abstract the parameter (e.g., using any type as an example) and have one function (e.g., casting as needed from "any", or using reflection).

Generics have a long and interesting history; you can learn more here: https://en.wikipedia.org/wiki/Generic_programming.

© Jan Newmarch and Ronald Petty 2022
J. Newmarch and R. Petty, *Network Programming with Go Language*,
https://doi.org/10.1007/978-1-4842-8095-9

A Filtering Function Without Generics

Here, we show an example where we have two filter functions, each taking a particular type array. In Go prior to 1.18, we are required to have two functions unless we leverage the empty interface.

```
$ mkdir appx-generics
$ cd appx-generics

appx-generics$ vi no_generics.go

package main

import (
        "fmt"
)

func FilterInt(s []int, f func(int) bool) []int {
        var r []int
        for _, v := range s {
                if f(v) {
                        r = append(r, v)
                }
        }

        return r
}

func FilterString(s []string, f func(string) bool) []string {
        var r []string
        for _, v := range s {
                if f(v) {
                        r = append(r, v)
                }
        }

        return r
}

func main() {
        evens := FilterInt([]int{1, 2, 3, 4, 5}, func(i int) bool { return i%2 == 0 })
        fmt.Printf("%v\n", evens)

        shortStrings := FilterString([]string{"ok", "notok", "maybe", "maybe not"},
        func(s string) bool { return len(s) < 3 })
        fmt.Printf("%v\n", shortStrings)
}
```

The example simply creates two lists and in turn filters them by a function we provide.

```
appx-generics$ go run no_generics.go

[2 4]
[ok]
```

While not the end of the world, our code is duplicated. Code duplication is the source of many copy-paste bugs. Ideally, we would like to avoid those bugs. Bugs aside, we might start thinking about local optimizations based on types. While this may benefit some types, in our example, probably, no unique optimizations are needed.

Refactor Using Generics

With Go 1.18, initial support for generics arrived. We will not discuss the pros or cons any further, but if you are interested, take a look at the original proposal and related follow-up:

- https://github.com/golang/go/issues/43651

- https://go.dev/blog/generics-proposal

Next, we combine our two filter functions into a single function. Generics allow type parameters being used as constraints. Formerly, we could only use methods in an interface, but now types provide additional compile time checks.

In our generic filter function, we abstract the type information with the constraint "[T any]". T is an example type parameter; type parameter list looks like an ordinary function parameter list except they are in square brackets. "any" is the same as "interface{}" in prior editions of Go. This tells the compiler what types are allowed and in turn generates the required variant(s) of the code.

In the parameter list for Filter, we are limited to slice of type T; elements of type T are passed into a function we provide, ultimately yielding a slice with elements of type T.

```
appx-generics$ vi with_generics.go

package main

import (
        "fmt"
)

func Filter[T any](s []T, f func(T) bool) []T {
        var r []T
        for _, v := range s {
                if f(v) {
                        r = append(r, v)
                }
        }

        return r
}

func main() {
        evens := Filter([]int{1, 2, 3, 4, 5}, func(i int) bool { return i%2 == 0 })
        fmt.Printf("%v\n", evens)
```

```
        shortStrings := Filter([]string{"ok", "notok", "maybe", "maybe not"}, func(s string)
        bool { return len(s) < 3 })
        fmt.Printf("%v\n", shortStrings)
}
```

Running yields the same results as our prior version.

```
appx-generics$ go run with_generics.go

[2 4]
[ok]
```

While we are sticking to examples, its worth thinking about the impact of generics on our code.

- Line count: 35 vs. 24

- Binary size: Both around 1.8MB (using go build)

- Speed: Same (using time command)

Less code is typically considered a good thing. However, like any feature, even generics syntax can make code confusing.

There is more than one way to implement something like generics. One way is that the compiler could just make copies of the code and change the data types and function names; another way is a singular implementation with metadata holding various types of information to help guide the execution of a generic function. One generics proposal is to have multiple functions and a second proposal having a singular generic function with a dictionary containing the various types of information. Ultimately, these two competing proposals have merged into one:

```
    https://github.com/golang/proposal/blob/master/design/generics-implementation-
    dictionaries-go1.18.md
```

Further work on generics not covered by this proposal includes recursive functions.

Custom Constraints

In this example, we look at a function (SoundOff) where the parameter is limited to the custom constraint called Hybrid. The Hybrid constraint ultimately is limited to the interface Animal. Our function SoundOff not only accepts all Animals, it retrieves the value type in order to do something specific. This isn't unique to generics, we have to do this with interfaces if you want access to the value type. Take note that we cast our input parameter to the empty interface (any) in order to retrieve the concrete type. This casting is required as an interface is expected in the type switch, not a concrete type H.

```
appx-generics$ vi simple_generics.go

package main

import (
        "fmt"
)
```

```go
type Animal interface {
        Sound()
}

type Cat struct{}

func (c Cat) Sound() { fmt.Println("Meow") }

func (c Cat) SpecialToCat() { fmt.Println("Cat special") }

type Dog struct{}

func (d Dog) Sound() { fmt.Println("Woof") }

func (c Dog) UniqueToDog() { fmt.Println("Dog unique") }

type Domesticated interface {
        Cat | Dog // Not Owls
        Animal
}

// An Owl is an "wild" animal,
// Thus not in the above union of cats and dogs
type Owl struct{}

func (Owl) Sound() { fmt.Println("Owl hoo") }

// Here we limit ourselves to  domesticated animals
// If you passed in a 'wild' animal, it would not work
func SoundOff[H Domesticated](animal H) H {
        animal.Sound()

        switch a := any(animal).(type) {
        case Dog:
                a.UniqueToDog()
        case Cat:
                a.SpecialToCat()
        default:
                fmt.Println("Then hoo?")
        }
        return animal
}

func main() {
        var c Cat = SoundOff(Cat{})
        d := SoundOff(Dog{})

        c.Sound()
        c.SpecialToCat()
        d.Sound()
        d.UniqueToDog()
```

```
//          SoundOff(Owl{})
}
```

Sit back and listen to our zoo.

```
appx-generics$ go run simple_generics.go

Meow
Cat special
Woof
Dog unique
Meow
Cat special
Woof
Dog unique
```

If you uncomment the owl, it will not compile.

```
appx-generics$ go build simple_generics.go

# command-line-arguments
./simple_generics.go:59:10: Owl does not implement Domesticated
```

Per one of the lead developers, Ian Lance Taylor, here are guidelines when using generics. When to use generics:

- Functions that work on slices, maps, and channels of any element type and have no assumptions about a particular element type are used.

- General purpose data structures, that is, linked list, b-tree.

- Prefer functions vs. methods (allows the data structure to remain agnostic to the type).

- When elements have a common method with the same implementation (Read(network) and Read(file) have different implementations, so don't use generics).

When to not use generics:

- When just calling a method on the argument (use interfaces)

- When implementation of a common method differs

- When an operation differs per type (use reflection instead)

Using Generics on Collections

Collections such as arrays of "any" where we operate the same way on each item are prime targets for generics. In this example, we use a channel and our own linked list to show how we can generify our iteration code. Unlike prior examples, we have two constraints: "MustBe" (our input) and "Result" (our output). Notice they do not have to match.

In the following example, we create our own linked list and a channel instance, hydrating and iterating over each instance. Notice our Iterate function takes either type, channel or linked list as both satisfy the MustBe constraint.

```
appx-generics$ cat iterate.go

package main

import (
        "fmt"
        "sync"
        "time"
)

// Our LinkedList code
type LL struct {
        N    *LL
        data string
}

// Retreive the next node in the linkedlist
func (l LL) Next() *LL { return l.N }

// Here we use a union of types "|"
// Meaning our arguments must be of these types
// Either channel  or the above linkedlist type
type MustBe interface {
        chan string | LL
}

// We use the union technique once more on the return types
// Notice these can differ than the above "MustBe" types
type Result interface {
        string | LL
}

// This is the function we wish to make generic
// We are iterating over a instance of MustBe (either channel string or LL)
// Notice the return type must be a Result type (either string or LL)
func Iterate[M MustBe, R Result](o M, iter func(M) R) (r R) {
        return iter(o)
}

func main() {
        // Create channel for strings
        c := make(chan string, 5)
        c <- "ok"
        c <- "ok2"

        //This function is what we will pass into the above Iterate
        //Notice Iterate's first parameter is the same as the following
```

```go
        //lambdas parameter
        citer := func(c chan string) string {
                select {
                case msg1 := <-c:
                        return msg1
                case <-time.After(1 * time.Second):
                        return "nothing"
                }
        }

        // Here we "Iterate" through the channel
        var wg sync.WaitGroup
        wg.Add(2)
        go func(f func(chan string) string) {
                for {
                        fmt.Println(Iterate(c, f))
                        wg.Done()
                }
        }(citer)
        wg.Wait() // wait for iteration to finish

        // The remaining example shows passing a custom Linked List
        // iteration function

        // First we build a simple list
        n1 := LL{data: "n1"}
        n2 := LL{data: "n2"}
        n3 := LL{data: "n3"}
        n1.N = &n2
        n2.N = &n3

        // Like the above citer, the parameter type will match
        // the first parameter of Iterate above
        liter := func(l LL) LL {
                var zero LL

                if l.N != zero.N {
                        return *l.N
                } else {
                        return zero
                }
        }

        // We walk through the linked list
        n := n1
        for n.N != nil {
                fmt.Printf("node:%s\n",n.data)
                n = Iterate(n, liter)
        }
}
```

When we launch, the channel is consumed first; then we work through the linked list.

```
appx-generics$ go run iterate.go

ok
ok2
node:n1
node:n2
```

With generics, we are able to use a single function to handle multiple input types. The use of a function to retrieve the next element means we don't have to support a common interface with these types. This means in theory we can use other types as well.

How Not to Use Generics?

We show a counterexample, one where we see some issues using generics.

Here, we are going to convert an existing function and see if we can rewrite it leveraging generics. In this case, it's not about deduping a complete algorithm; its about potentially streamlining a switch statement (not recommended per the preceding text!).

The following code can be found in GOROOT/src/net/http/httptest/httptest.go. Take a moment to review, noting the use of a type switch in the middle of the function.

```
appx-generics$ go doc -src http/httptest.NewRequest

package httptest // import "net/http/httptest"

// NewRequest returns a new incoming server Request, suitable
// for passing to an http.Handler for testing.
//
// The target is the RFC 7230 "request-target": it may be either a
// path or an absolute URL. If target is an absolute URL, the host name
// from the URL is used. Otherwise, "example.com" is used.
//
// The TLS field is set to a non-nil dummy value if target has scheme
// "https".
//
// The Request.Proto is always HTTP/1.1.
//
// An empty method means "GET".
//
// The provided body may be nil. If the body is of type *bytes.Reader,
// *strings.Reader, or *bytes.Buffer, the Request.ContentLength is
// set.
//
// NewRequest panics on error for ease of use in testing, where a
// panic is acceptable.
//
// To generate a client HTTP request instead of a server request, see
// the NewRequest function in the net/http package.
func NewRequest(method, target string, body io.Reader) *http.Request {
```

```go
    if method == "" {
        method = "GET"
    }
    req, err := http.ReadRequest(bufio.NewReader(strings.NewReader(method + " " + target + "
HTTP/1.0\r\n\r\n")))
    if err != nil {
        panic("invalid NewRequest arguments; " + err.Error())
    }

    // HTTP/1.0 was used above to avoid needing a Host field. Change it to 1.1 here.
    req.Proto = "HTTP/1.1"
    req.ProtoMinor = 1
    req.Close = false

    if body != nil {
        switch v := body.(type) {
        case *bytes.Buffer:
            req.ContentLength = int64(v.Len())
        case *bytes.Reader:
            req.ContentLength = int64(v.Len())
        case *strings.Reader:
            req.ContentLength = int64(v.Len())
        default:
            req.ContentLength = -1
        }
        if rc, ok := body.(io.ReadCloser); ok {
            req.Body = rc
        } else {
            req.Body = io.NopCloser(body)
        }
    }

    // 192.0.2.0/24 is "TEST-NET" in RFC 5737 for use solely in
    // documentation and example source code and should not be
    // used publicly.
    req.RemoteAddr = "192.0.2.1:1234"

    if req.Host == "" {
        req.Host = "example.com"
    }

    if strings.HasPrefix(target, "https://") {
        req.TLS = &tls.ConnectionState{
            Version:           tls.VersionTLS12,
            HandshakeComplete: true,
            ServerName:        req.Host,
        }
    }

    return req
}
```

We can see that the same line of code is used in three cases and different in a fourth case. Can we dedup this code? A starter question could be the following: Why is it triplicated? Some potential reasoning includes the following:

- bytes.Buffer, bytes.Reader, and strings.Reader are the only types (and are io.Readers) where we care about the Len.

- Len() is not in a shared interface (not in io.Reader).

If you look at each types documentation, all of them have a Len method implemented. If you look deeper, you see a variety of interfaces are implemented, yet none of those include "Len() int". In fact, if you look around, we can almost be certain that is correct; hardly anyone implements an interface containing Len(). They do seem to implement the method Len though.

```
Here, we search for Len as part of an interface.appx-generics$ grep -nr "interface {" -A 10
$(go env GOROOT)/src | grep -E " Len\(\) int"

$GOROOT/src/net/http/h2_bundle.go-3549-func (s *http2sorter) Len() int { return len(s.v) }
$GOROOT/src/encoding/asn1/marshal.go-33-func (c byteEncoder) Len() int {

Here are the interfaces we found before; neither is used by our type switch value
types.GOROOT/src/net/http/h2_bundle.go
type http2pipeBuffer interface {
        Len() int
        io.Writer
        io.Reader
}

GOROOT/src/encoding/asn1/marshal.go
// encoder represents an ASN.1 element that is waiting to be marshaled.
type encoder interface {
        // Len returns the number of bytes needed to marshal this element.
        Len() int
        // Encode encodes this element by writing Len() bytes to dst.
        Encode(dst []byte)
}
```

Can we use generics to limit which types our function accepts? In turn, can we collapse the type switch to only our generic parameter type?

```
We can begin by trying to use generics to remove the triplicated check via the following
constraint:type MyType interface {
    bytes.Buffer | bytes.Reader | strings.Reader
}
```

We then change the signature to the following:

```
func NewRequest[M MyType](method, target string, body M) *http.Request {
```

This is a start, but we are missing the following:

- We are unable to simply check for nil (before the switch, we see "if body != nil") with generics.
- The compiler will tell us Len() is missing (since it's not part of our composition of types in our constraint).

We can address the first issue with checking a related zero value instead of nil. The original nil check becomes the following. Remember, generics will identify the arguments (and the actual types) to fill in what M should be.

```
...
    var zero M
    if body != zero {
...
```

This still leaves us with the case of the missing Len(). Originally, the parameter was an interface, "io. Reader", which doesn't have a Len() method. This drove the original need to use a switch statement to access the value types, which did each implement a Len() method. We could, for example, make a new interface, one that combines Reader and Len().

```
type LenReader interface {
        io.Reader
        Len() int
}
```

This, however, doesn't do the job; we are still exposed to any type that implements that interface (not limited at compiler time).

In the following code, we take the NewRequest function (borrowed from httptest.go) and refactor it.

```
appx-generics$ vi complex_generics.go

package main

import (
        "bufio"
        "bytes"
        "crypto/tls"
        "fmt"
        "io"
        "net/http"
        "strings"
)

type myStruct struct {
        s *strings.Reader
}

func (m myStruct) Len() int {
        return m.s.Len()
}
```

```go
func (m myStruct) Read(b []byte) (int, error) {
        return m.s.Read(b)
}

type MyType interface {
        *bytes.Buffer | *bytes.Reader | *strings.Reader | myStruct

        Len() int
        io.Reader
        comparable
}

type Lener interface {
        Len() int
}

// ./http/httptest/httptest.go
func NewRequest[M MyType](method, target string, body M) *http.Request {
        if method == "" {
                method = "GET"
        }
        req, err := http.ReadRequest(bufio.NewReader(strings.NewReader(method + " " + target
+ " HTTP/1.0\r\n\r\n")))
        if err != nil {
                panic("invalid NewRequest arguments; " + err.Error())
        }

        // HTTP/1.0 was used above to avoid needing a Host field. Change it to 1.1 here.
        req.Proto = "HTTP/1.1"
        req.ProtoMinor = 1
        req.Close = false

        var zero M
        if body != zero {
                switch i := any(body).(type) {
                case Lener, io.ReadCloser:
                        if b, ok := i.(Lener); ok {
                                req.ContentLength = int64(b.Len())
                        }
                        if rc, ok := i.(io.ReadCloser); ok {
                                req.Body = rc
                        }
                default:
                        req.Body = io.NopCloser(body)
                }
        } else {
                req.ContentLength = -1
        }

        // 192.0.2.0/24 is "TEST-NET" in RFC 5737 for use solely in
        // documentation and example source code and should not be
```

```
        // used publicly.
        req.RemoteAddr = "192.0.2.1:1234"

        if req.Host == "" {
                req.Host = "example.com"
        }

        if strings.HasPrefix(target, "https://") {
                req.TLS = &tls.ConnectionState{
                        Version:           tls.VersionTLS12,
                        HandshakeComplete: true,
                        ServerName:        req.Host,
                }
        }

        return req
}

func main() {
        fmt.Println(NewRequest("GET", "/", myStruct{strings.NewReader("")}).ContentLength)
        fmt.Println(NewRequest("GET", "/", myStruct{}).ContentLength)
        fmt.Println(NewRequest("GET", "/", strings.NewReader("")).ContentLength)
        fmt.Println(NewRequest("GET", "/", &bytes.Buffer{}).ContentLength)
        fmt.Println(NewRequest("GET", "/", bytes.NewReader([]byte("read me"))).
ContentLength)
}
```

Running the example works (output is not the important part here).

```
appx-generics$ go run complex_generics.go

0
-1
0
0
7
```

By moving our types and method requirements to our MyType constraint, we are now limited to a subset of types vs. all types that implement io.Reader.

I think most would argue this code is less readable than before. Should generics be used in this case? Based on other examples, it most likely should remain using io.Reader and a type switch. One could use the following alternative to manage Len calls:

```
...
    if body != nil {
        if b, ok := body.(interface{ Len() int }); ok {
            req.ContentLength = int64(b.Len())
        }
        if rc, ok := body.(io.ReadCloser); ok {
            req.Body = rc
        } else {
```

```
            req.Body = io.NopCloser(body)
        }
    } else {
        req.ContentLength = -1
    }
...
```

In the preceding code, the evil type is an example where MyType is not implemented. If you uncomment the call in main, you will see the following error:

```
# command-line-arguments
./complex_generics.go:101:24: evil does not implement MyType
```

Conclusion

Generics are here and will only improve future Go programs. What we have in Go 1.18 is not even the final take; new generic functions are to be included in the standard library along with potential other improvements. Until then, keep an eye on the official blog(s) such as this one: `https://go.dev/blog/why-generics`.

Index

© Jan Newmarch and Ronald Petty 2022
J. Newmarch and R. Petty, *Network Programming with Go Language*,
https://doi.org/10.1007/978-1-4842-8095-9

Printed in the United States
by Baker & Taylor Publisher Services